Praise for *Motherwell*

'Searching, truthful, shocking (and timely) . . . with a reporter's skill, she shows the interior life of her people. In the present climate, this book should be given out on the NHS . . . a masterpiece'   Andrew O'Hagan, *Guardian*

'Sharply intelligent and utterly unsentimental, *Motherwell* is a fitting legacy left by a blazing talent'   *Observer*

'An outstanding memoir . . . The writing is powerful and muscular; the bitterness raw and furious . . . as a legacy, this book will stand at least as long as Ravenscraig'   Jenny Colgan, *Spectator*

'Crammed with wit and intelligence . . . a clever, meticulous and intricate work. Although heart-rending at times, it is also surprising-ly funny . . . has a generosity of tone that means as you read it you experience sudden flashes from your own past: slights, plights, triumphs, mad asides'   Susie Boyt, *Financial Times*

'Filled with observational brilliance and wit . . . beautiful. Brilliant . . . not just an intelligent and honest personal memoir, not just an examination of narcissism, interdependence and repression, but a conjuring of a time, a moment in British history, that may otherwise be lost entirely. It is also funny. As funny, it would seem from the obituaries, as the woman herself'   Nell Frizzell, *Daily Telegraph*

'Complex and moving, this is an honest take on the close ties that can bind, hold us back and also set us free' *Stylist*, Best New Books of 2020

'[Orr's] masterpiece . . . the story of her family but also a social com-mentary of Britain . . . a fascinating look into the childhood of one of our most important journalists'   *Evening Standard*

'Intense and moving'   *Red*

'A remarkable memoir, the candour of it . . . Having grown up working-class in Scotland, there are a lot of resonances'   Val McDermid, *The i*

Deborah Orr was an award-winning journalist, whose work regularly appeared in the *Guardian*, the *Independent*, *The Sunday Times* and in many magazines including *Vogue*, *Grazia* and *Marie Claire*. She was a contributing editor to *AnOther Magazine* and was the first female editor of the *Guardian*'s *Weekend* Magazine at the age of thirty. Deborah was a co-creator of *Enquirer*, a play commissioned by the National Theatre of Scotland, performed in London, Glasgow and Belfast, broadcast by Radio 4 and shortlisted for new play of the year in the Critics' Awards for Theatre in Scotland.

MOTHERWELL

A GIRLHOOD

Deborah Orr

WEIDENFELD & NICOLSON

First published in Great Britain in 2020 by Weidenfeld & Nicolson
This paperback edition published in 2021 by Weidenfeld & Nicolson
an imprint of The Orion Publishing Group Ltd
Carmelite House, 50 Victoria Embankment
London EC4Y 0DZ

An Hachette UK Company

1 3 5 7 9 10 8 6 4 2

A CIP catalogue record for this book is
available from the British Library.

ISBN (Paperback) 978 1 4746 1146 6
ISBN (eBook) 978 1 4746 1147 3
ISBN (Audio) 978 1 4091 8720 2

Typeset by Input Data Services Ltd, Somerset

Printed and bound in Great Britain by Clays Ltd, Elcograf S.p.A.

MIX
Paper from
responsible sources
FSC
www.fsc.org   FSC® C104740

www.weidenfeldandnicolson.co.uk
www.orionbooks.co.uk

Contents

Prologue

That view. That stunning, dystopian panorama. A world unto itself, stretched out perfectly flat as far as the horizon, monochrome, like the telly. Except for the occasional blast of pale custard. Spikes of flame, so fast-moving that they seemed solid, roared implacably into the sky, day and night. Gas burn-off. A steelworks twice the size of Monaco.

At the time it was built, Ravenscraig was the largest, most technologically advanced strip mill in Europe: the black, thumping heart of our town and the lives of everyone in it. We Orrs lived pretty much on the edge of the complex. Everyone did. But you could only ever fully grasp the monolithic achievement of the place from one high point, as you came into town from the north. You were never, ever quite prepared for the Craig's dark, satanic majesty, no matter how many times you'd seen it. We lived in thrall to it.

Beyond all else, that denatured, slightly hell-like, hyper-mechanised landscape provoked awe. It seemed indestructible, irrevocable. But it survived, intact, for only thirty-three years, from 1959 until 1992. High industrial Gothic, one of the wonders of the post-war settlement. All gone now. The place turned out to be an elaborate folly.

Motherwell is the town I was born and bred in, a coal and steel town on the lip of the Clyde Valley. By the time I was thirty years old, it wasn't a coal and steel town any more. Motherwell lost its identity in the industrial restructuring of the 1980s, along with wave after wave of redundant workers. Personal identities were shattered. But group identity was shattered too. The people of Motherwell were used to being part of something much, much bigger than themselves. When it went, so quickly, Motherwell became a town without a purpose. I couldn't stand the place, even when it was still in its pomp. But I loved it too. Still do.

Motherwell is where my mum lived, because that's where my dad came from. Even at the start of the 1960s women did what their husbands wanted, in matters large and small. But Win was from rural Essex and found life in Lanarkshire challenging. She explained all this to me from when I was old enough to listen, or maybe even long before. Yet, despite all those confidences, over so many years, Motherwell is the place where I failed to get to know my mother very well at all. Until after she was dead. That was when I started to realise that there were respects in which she hadn't mothered well at all.

I

The Bureau

We were wary of the bureau, my brother and I, even though it was ours now and we could do what we liked with it. There was no one to stop us any more – no Mum, no Dad, no rules. Yet so much of the bureau had been a forbidden zone for such a long time, the administrative heart of our family home, at number 18 Clyde Terrace, Muirhouse, Motherwell ML1 2NG.

My parents had bought the bureau when they first got married and set up home, on Empress Avenue in Romford, Essex, at the start of the 1960s. It had made the journey with them up to Thistle Street, Motherwell, Lanarkshire less than a year later. That was where we lived when I was born. Four more years, and it had travelled another couple of miles, to Shields Drive, Muirhouse, Motherwell, and the birth of my younger brother David. Another six years, and another few hundred yards, and the bureau, along with its complete and perfect nuclear family, had reached Clyde Terrace, where it stayed for almost five decades before it headed back the way it had come and moved in with me in London.

At the time of their marriage, as the swinging sixties began, my parents had embraced the modern and the bureau is now quite the hipster accoutrement. For us, though, it was so much more than a stylish piece of furniture. It was

3

our *tabula rasa*, the place where the evidence of our family's transactions with officialdom was filed. It was made by Avalon, a furniture company based in Somerset that folded years ago. No build quality, the experts say. Not in quite the same league as G-Plan. You can still buy the same model, vintage, for around £120.

For ages it lurked at the top of the family home – as it was always called in the divorce proceedings. It sat in the corridor, outside the bedrooms of my two sons, its straitened circumstances forcing it to take in washing, or at least provide a flat surface to receive rumpled piles of the boys' laundered clothes.

How the mighty pieces of furniture have fallen.

The bureau, like all three of my childhood homes, was the unchallenged domain of my mother, scrupulously well organised and governed by a surprisingly complex web of boundaries. The upper of the two drawers on the right was accessible to everyone, full of Useful Things like scissors. The lower drawer was set aside for things that weren't important enough to go in the pigeonhole-lined section behind the flap on the left, but were still important. We kids would have little need to look in there, in theory at least, and we knew it. A display section underneath, with two sliding glass doors, had initially housed the best china. We both knew never to slide those glass doors open, like we knew never to pull down the flap, without specific permission.

But the possibility of hidden Useful Things, like Sellotape, Tippex, Quink or, as the white heat of technology seared through our lives, some Blu Tack, meant that we flouted the flap rule fairly often. Far more often than Dad, for sure. John never delved behind the flap in the bureau. Win handled all the household's paperwork, writing in her neat, cursive script or her neat block capitals. He would add his impressive signature where she told him to put it.

The rules were Win's – and the power – but John tended to be their enforcer. Mostly, he would use a couple of his many nicknames for us when he was guarding the bureau, which was a familiar signal of a ritual rather than a serious warning. Was he sending her up? Maybe. A bit.

'FANNY! What are you doing in that bureau?'

'OSWALD! What are you doing in that bureau?'

What, in 2014, were Fanny and Oswald doing in that bureau? We were taking up the mantle of family administration, because we were the only ones left to do it. At this point, the bureau had been in the house at Clyde Terrace for forty years, a wooden box inside a wooden box, on the scheme known locally as 'the Timbers'. We say 'housing scheme' in Scotland, not 'housing estate'. We don't know what a 'sink estate' even is. Or we didn't, until the 1980s rolled round.

The Timbers had been hastily assembled after the war, as prefabricated temporary homes. They squatted on plinths made of brick, to obviate the need for the time-consuming digging of foundations, I guess. They had tiled, gabled roofs and tongue-and-groove wooden walls. At the join where the brick met the wood, about two and a half feet up, the wood jutted proud of the brick by a bit more than an inch. That little overhanging space was always nice and dry. It was a good place for caterpillars to pupate, and I would crouch down and squint up to check for them. My hope was to see one at the moment of metamorphosis, when a butterfly emerged, its wings all damp and crumpled until they had dried in the sun and become gorgeous.

The pupae were of cabbage whites mainly, probably the least gorgeous among butterflies, the bane of the lives of growers of brassicas. Sometimes you'd be eating cabbage from Peter-Duncan-next-door's garden, kindly given, and you'd find a cabbage white caterpillar, all green, shiny, stretched and boiled. Or, as the joke goes, half of one. But a cabbage white pupa was still something, a lovely find. I still look for that pupa, the one I'll watch at the propitious moment when it emerges, fully formed, to begin another life in which it flies. Though I'm not searching quite so assiduously as I once did.

Each of the Timber houses had a porch at its front door, with a flat roof and graphic, diamond-patterned wooden railings, all painted kingfisher blue. The porches were held up by two fluted wooden pillars painted pale grey. There were little benches, also painted kingfisher blue, to sit on by each front door. They were great houses – still are. Instead of providing interim accommodation, as originally intended, they'd become creosoted jewels in Lanarkshire's council-housing crown. Back and front doors. Back and front gardens. The dream. We'd see other little groups of the same timber houses around Scotland when we were out for a run in the car. We'd always cheer at the sight of them. Those who lived in them were part of our tribe. The People of the Timbers.

Ours was the biggest scheme, though, the largest collection of Timbers that I've ever seen. It was still small, a quiet scheme, reserved even. It was arranged round a big green, for the kids to play on. We'd organise in the summer, for rounders, red rover or football, though the boys were always a bit snotty about playing football with the girls. Sometimes we'd make kites, which rarely flew.

There were three variations on the Timber theme: terraced, semi-detached and bungalow. The latter was the rarest and the most coveted. Ours was semi-detached. When we moved in, when I was ten, it was owned by the Scottish Special Housing Association, and rented and managed by the District Council of Motherwell and Wishaw. By 2014, when David and I prepared to start dismantling its contents, it was under private ownership. My parents had held out against right-to-buy for a long time. But when John was made redundant, that's what they spent the cash on. They'd been council tenants for almost four decades by that time, the discount was large, and they were only human. It was such a bargain, and it was so much a part of them. So they swallowed their principles and exercised the right they hadn't thought anyone should have. Houses like theirs, they'd predicted, would be bought, and council stock would become shrunken and vastly less diverse. They weren't wrong. Though even they, pessimistic by nature, didn't see the buy-to-let landlords coming.

The last street at the bottom of the scheme was right on the edge of the Clyde Valley, with a farm across the road and miles of field and wood, river, marsh and meadow all the way to the horizon, give or take a motorway or two. The last street at the top of the scheme backed on to a row of private houses, all different in design, that faced the main road and the Clyde Alloy, which had been there since 1937 and had become part of the Ravenscraig complex under nationalisation.

Iain Wallace, one of the cleverest boys from my class at primary school, lived in one of those private houses, which was a rare thing for kids at our school. When Iain had been given the job of assembling a team from the class for a general knowledge quiz, he'd picked me third. I remember the surprise of it. Could this mean that I – a girl – was considered one of the clever ones too? It had to. Good old Iain, with his fine, white-blond pudding-bowl haircut, his rosebud lips and the funny red mark below one eye. I still think of him fondly, not least because he casually lobbed me that delicious moment of self-revelation.

The Wallaces had been abroad. Iain's dad had ordered a

litre of beer in abroad, thinking it was equivalent to a pint. Iain had put his hand up and told the class this when we were learning about the metric system. I think the country in question had been Germany. Or France. Whatever. Abroad wasn't part of my ambit because my own parents were not in favour of abroad, all the more so now that we had 18 Clyde Terrace, Muirhouse, Motherwell ML1 2NG. Who could want for more? They died without passports.

We'd landed our corner of the Timbers in the summer of 1972. The big back garden had gone a bit feral, and it was full of self-seeded lupins, taller than me, in all sorts of wonderful colours – orange wings with yellow standards, crimson wings with purple standards, purple standards with blue wings, yellow wings with creamy standards. On hot days you could hear the furry charcoal seed pods popping from the kitchen. I still love lupins, would still feel thrilled every year when they bloomed in my London garden.

Clyde Terrace. Our chunk of paradise. We even acquired a phone in the move, heavy, classic, mustard yellow, with a finger dial. The in-thing, in 1972, was the Trimphone, with push buttons. If you yanked too hard on the receiver the phone itself would spring up on its short, aggressive spiral of a cord and whack you in the face. Too light. Rookie design error. Lots of those in 1970s Britain.

But ours was a great phone, with a really excellent phone number – Motherwell 61236. We had a party line that was hogged, my parents said, by Mrs Gold, our neighbour across the back on Merryton Road. But still. This new address, as my mother was wont to say, was 'a cut above'. We were virtually on a par with the Wallaces and their private house, though that was not something to be mentioned outside 18 Clyde Terrace, mainly because none of us actually believed it was true. We were a funny old family, heightened self-love in constant battle with exaggerated self-loathing. But my mother had been gone a few years before I saw that with any real clarity.

God, how Win had fought for that house. God, how she'd looked after that bureau. But by January 2014 the contents of the house, including the bureau, were coated in a delicate film of dust, hesitant dust that could barely believe it was getting away with this soft yet ruthless invasion. My mother had been a brilliant housewife, skilled, dedicated, unwavering. Or, to put it another way, the way that denigrates the work of women, obsessively house-proud. Win had lived her whole life as if failure to run the Hoover over the carpet for just one day would bring down a landslide of filth and decay. 'I've just got to run the Hoover over the carpet, John,' she'd say testily, as my dad waited for her to put her coat on, get out and get into the car. (Win never went anywhere unless John drove her.) Coming home, even from a very brief outing, to a crumb on the floor – that couldn't be allowed to happen.

It felt shaming, after all those years of vigilant toil, gazing at these signs of approaching entropy. I never thought I'd ever see this place so neglected.

Most shocking of all, our four pieces of silver were dark with tarnish. They'd always shone, and I'd been taught how to make them shine from when I was little. Win favoured liquid Brasso over linty Duraglit. I'm a Duraglit woman myself. Ever the rebel. Weirdly, it took me ages to work out the mystery of how the silver had got so blackened. It was simply inconceivable to me that my mother would have stopped cleaning it. I must have had some kind of mental block. Weeks after David and I had cleared the house, in the feverish confusion of a sleepless night, it hit me that – doh! Of course! – the silver hadn't been polished for the same reason as the dust had encroached. Win hadn't been there.

It had been fourteen months since my mother had given the family home its daily clean, sixty weeks since she'd sat at the kitchen table with her blackened cloth, her bottle of Brasso and her roll of kitchen paper, polishing the family silver – an eggcup, a christening cup, a teaspoon and a tablespoon, all but the last engraved in celebration of the birth of Orr males. The tablespoon had been my mother's father's. The handle was engraved with an ornate HA. Harold Avis. The females got bracelets.

It had been more than six months since any living soul had stepped over our threshold, more than six months since Win had died, inefficiently intestate. Despite plentiful evidence to the contrary, my mother had believed that she'd live for ever. 'I didn't think this would happen to me,' Win had said in her final weeks. This little white-headed woman, with ghostly hair that I'd never seen before that last illness, was not just perplexed but actually dumbfounded at the discovery of her own mortality, even though she was lying in a bed in the hospice where she'd watched her husband die six years before. I found it hard to stop myself from rolling my eyes. My poor mum. I'd found it hard to stop myself from rolling my eyes so often.

John had said something similar, not long after he'd been diagnosed with terminal secondary oesophageal cancer in the liver. They'd missed the primary cancer completely. Both of my parents were diagnosed with their terminal cancers after going to A&E, doubled over with pain, at Wishaw General Hospital. The conversation happened not long after the three of us had been told the devastating facts.

We were sitting in the living room at Clyde Terrace, me, Dad and Mum, trying to take in the news that John had been told he'd only got four months to live. 'You'll be here,' he'd said, nodding at Win. 'You'll be here,' he'd said, nodding at me. 'But I won't be here?' He'd shaken his head through a felty fog of incredulity, his head of still-blond hair. From my father's mouth, such a sentiment provoked only an enervating rush of painful love. He could do no wrong in my eyes, while my mother could, did and does irritate me from beyond the grave.

When he'd been told that death had marked his card, by a young consultant who prided himself on his bright, matter-of-fact delivery, John had howled in anguish, just for a second, then recovered himself completely. 'I'm sorry,' he'd quickly said to this man whose tone and demeanour I despised so much, 'I broke down there. I'm really sorry, so sorry.' And that was it for John on the breaking-down front, within the sight of another human being anyway. An instant of lost composure, and then an apology for it.

John died right on schedule, four months after the airy prediction, to the day. He refused morphine, said it made him feel weird. But they were clearly slipping him some anyway. He died painfully and apologetically, embarrassed at all the fuss and bother he was causing for others, and mostly concealing his anger, his vast, piercing unwillingness to go.

'Reserved,' my mother had said many times, and with great approval, of the Scottish family she'd married into. 'Very reserved.' They were diffident, in fact. Lacking in confidence. A bit dissociated.

All that made me, once I hit my very late puberty, want to run around the Timbers naked shouting, 'Fuck the fucking Pope!' Not that I did want the Pope fucked. I hated the sectarianism that pervaded the town, even though, when I was young, it had been a treat to go and watch the sheer oddness, feel the noise, of the Protestant processions of the Orange Walks, the feats of the young baton twirlers who led each little group, the bright, ornate sumptuousness of the tasselled banners that announced the singular identity of each Orange Lodge. The walks were a spectacle, providing a sense of belonging and a sense of superiority. For us Protestants anyway. I don't suppose it did much for the Catholics. I wanted that kind of excitement too, but not in celebration of King Billy and the Battle of the Boyne. I just wanted a little bit of meaningless anarchy. Was that too much to ask?

The nearest my parents had got to anarchy was the posthumous pile of post that, in 2014, my brother and I had found sprawling behind the door. Such a thing had never happened before. The couple of times we'd gone on caravan holidays, when David and I were still quite small, the post hadn't come in the junk mail torrents that started in the 1980s. The insurance man still visited in person to collect each week's money. The rent book kept you straight on the rent, which you went and paid at the council office, like you paid the telly at the Radio Rentals showroom and the electricity at the South of Scotland Electricity Board showroom. We never had gas. We were 'all-electric'. The fashion designers Christopher and Tammy Kane grew up in Newarthill, a village near Motherwell, and their scheme's fuelling system was so unusual that it was known simply as 'the gas scheme'.

A letter from the bank would have been the sign of some sort of financial cataclysm, unfathomable news about something that simply couldn't happen, because everyone was paid weekly wages, in cash, and 'checking accounts' were exotic things that only the upper classes had need of. Cheques were things that people grandly dashed out in the Agatha Christie novels that I adored, or were forged at university, which resulted in being 'sent down'. Whatever that may be. Mostly, the post contained actual letters from our English relatives, or Win's friend from her youth, Jean Regent. You could tell who the letter was from by the handwriting on the envelope.

I'd guess that Clyde Terrace had been empty overnight for maybe fifty nights of the four decades my parents had lived there, maybe six of those due to the grandparenting demands of their errant daughter. Mainly, the absences had been the result of 'decanting'. This was the word that was used when the council moved you into another, similar house while they updated their housing stock, in our case for the extremely welcome installation of central heating, and also new windows and doors. We preferred the old windows and doors. A few of the men, including John, made splendid greenhouses from the old windows.

My parents had not liked leaving the house empty, even for a couple of days, because they were compulsively security-conscious. When they'd been persuaded to do so, by some miracle of daughterly wheedling or a death in the Essex family, my mother, particularly, would fret about burglars. Once, the garage had been broken into, which made them all the more determined to defend their wooden castle.

'Look, Mum,' David and I wanted to say. 'Fourteen empty months, and no burglars. Think of all the holidays you missed.' Getting them to visit me, first in St Andrews, then in Edinburgh, then in London, was a Sisyphean feat.

'The train journey is so long. I'm too old for it,' my mother started saying at the age of forty-five.

'You could fly to London,' I'd sometimes suggest. 'I'd pay.'

'I think I'd need a passport for that,' my mother would reply icily, and that would be an end to it.

Among the circulars my brother and I picked up at the start of the weekend when we'd dismantle the psychological citadel my parents had created in 18 Clyde Terrace, Muirhouse, Motherwell ML1 2NG were letters from companies threatening legal action for non-payment of a couple of overlooked bills. My mother would have died of acute feelings of delinquency, if it hadn't been for the fact that her death was the only possible catalyst for something so remiss.

No bill remained unpaid when my mother was alive. Even the mortifying arrival of a red bill was not to be countenanced. The postman would know of our shame, and perhaps other neighbours. Never a borrower nor a lender be. My mother had many phrases and sayings, phrases and sayings for every occasion. An ugly mend is better than a pretty hole! A stitch in time saves nine! Pipped at the post again! Pride comes before a fall! Don't put off till tomorrow the things you can do today! Better the devil you know! Marry in haste, repent at leisure! You've made your bed and now you'll have to lie in it!

My parent's lives, like the bureau, like their cupboards and drawers, were ordered and disciplined. Some of the things in those cupboards had sat in the dark, lurking, for all of their married lives. The incomplete harlequin tea set, which had been my Essex grandmother's. How many times had my mother told me she wanted me to have it when she was gone? It's mine now. I use it. More of it has broken. All of the glass tumblers with the frogspawn design have had their fifty-year-long day. The last time I remember them being used, before I got my hands on them, was at my fifth birthday party, to which I wore a dress that my mother made for me from her wedding dress. Which she also made. I still have the frogspawn jug. It is used sparingly and with infinite care, like it always was before it was mine.

And secrets. Secrets lurked in my parents' lives, in drawers, in cupboards, in the bureau. Or, rather, they didn't lurk. Things that should have been there just weren't. John's nick-names for his children were part of his linguistic adeptness, so often expressed in jokes, wit and wordplay but never on paper. Apart from that lovely signature, no written word of my father's existed in that bureau. John was clever, really clever. But he could barely write. I knew this from early childhood, because my mother told me.

That was the reason why Win did all the paperwork and John patrolled her boundaries around it so assiduously. From that bureau my mother reigned over my father, over all of us. Skills that my mother had, and my father did not have, were part of their marriage contract, part of a constant, complex, instinctive exchange of strengths and vulnerabilities. When I started hearing about 'co-dependent relationships' in the 1980s they just sounded like 'relationships' to me.

John wasn't illiterate. He was a good reader and got better as he got older. When I was young he'd read cowboy books in his lunch break at work. I remember the *Edge* series by George G. Gilman. He moved on to Sven Hassel's books, Second World War novels by a Danish former soldier who'd won the Iron Cross. By the time John got ill, his favourite writer was Ken Follett and his favourite novel *The Pillars of the Earth*. I still have his copy. I've never read it.

But John never developed the confidence to write, even, to my knowledge, one sentence. The only letter I ever got from him – the only collection of written words of his I ever saw, apart from his name – said: 'HUSH, HUSH DAD' in capitals. The note had a tenner with it, so it meant 'Don't tell Mum or David.' It took ages to arrive because he got the name of my student accommodation wrong. View Park, not Fife Park. I couldn't have loved him more for that. I still have the note, in the envelope, forty years after I received it. Both my brother and I have kept lots of things that connect us to our parents.

We took some daft stuff from that house in 2014, David and I, like ancient school projects that were falling apart and a couple of sets of golf clubs – plus a golf trolley – that would never be used again. It seemed awful to bin things that had been saved so long and looked after so well. The garden shears, circa 1972, were in better nick than mine, circa 2007. They were still stored in the plastic case they'd been bought in. I barely have the discipline to put the lid back on a felt-tip. We took an element designed to heat a single cup, for tea. We took lots of K-Tel-style gadgets, still in their boxes. They're still in their boxes.

The box that was the bureau, though? That was emptied completely and its contents were thoroughly sorted, sieved and occasionally disposed of, until all that was left was everything. The story of my childhood. Which became the story of my life.

2

Baby's First Haircut

A lot of people, while carrying out the doleful business of sifting through a dead mother's personal mementoes, find an envelope with their own name written on it, plus a date from the early part of their life. I found one of those envelopes myself, as I tackled the sacred bureau. In a pigeonhole, behind the flap, was a lock of my own hair, snipped from my own head, long ago. Baby's first haircut.

Except that twist of hair came not from my head, but from the head of someone I used to be, a small child I could barely even remember ever having been. Even the hair itself was completely alien to me. That hair was finer than my hair. The hair on my fifty-one-year-old head was coarse. And that hair was much more blonde. My own hair, my after-cancer-treatment hair, was dark and grey.

The lock of hair had been saved to evoke memories of me – but my mother's memories of me, not mine. Those memories must have been evoked fairly often, because the flap of the envelope my mother kept my hair in was soft and cloth-like. Win must have opened it many times and wondered, probably baffled by the cruelty of it all, what had become of her baby. Beside my soft envelope, some of my brother's curls were in another soft envelope – though less soft. Win didn't lose David like she lost me, not as early, not as completely. But the girl who was me, half a century ago? She was long gone. Gone for ever.

That hank of my hair would have been put in the bureau in 1963, almost four years before David's. He never lived at Thistle Street. At Thistle Street it was just Mum, Dad and me. I was born in late September 1962, but in my memories the early 1960s feel more like I'd imagine the 1930s to be. There's a photograph, black and white, of me as a newborn, with an improbable shock of black hair which gently wisped away during the first weeks of my life. I'm wearing some kind of elaborate-looking baby meringue dress and being held up by my dad. He's wearing a white shirt with a home-knit cable jumper over it. Both are tucked into his belted trousers. There's 1930s-looking wallpaper behind him.

I think I remember it. I think it was the colour of Elastoplast, with terracotta tones. Or maybe it was blue. I can remember something similar that was blue. Or I think I can. I have lots of memories from Thistle Street, where I lived until I was well into my fourth year of life. Or I think I do. In one 'memory', my mother is in the bedroom. She has a white bath towel wrapped under her armpits, her shoulders are hunched under her hands because her arms are crossed over her breasts. She's crying. My father is in the room with her, also distressed.

'Oh, John, John,' Win is weeping, 'I just can't do it. It hurts. The milk keeps coming.'

'Right. That's enough of that,' says John. 'That wean's going on the bottle.'

I remember the NHS formula too. Big white tins with blue writing. Absurd. The memory of the tins must be from when my brother was a baby. I don't actually remember any-thing from that time, of course. I must have been a couple of weeks old. Win told me that she hadn't breast-fed, and how decisively her husband had decided for her that she should not, when I was breast-feeding my first son in 1997.

'You don't really understand how much your mother did for you,' I'd said to her, breast-feeding away, 'until you're doing it for your own baby.'

'Oh, I didn't do breast-feeding!' Win replied. And she told me that story. It's so vivid in my mind, the scene she recalled, that only logic tells me the difference between the memory my mother conjured and a memory of my own.

Once you're 'remembering' things from this early in your life, your mind can't be trusted at all. Yet old memories shape you, whether they're real, imagined, a dream, a photograph you've seen or someone else's memory, passed on through your own perfidious filter. After a certain age, only a fool trusts her recollections. I'm nothing if not a fool.

I am sure of this, though: Mum, Dad and I lived in a one-bed tenement flat on Thistle Street, in town, which my parents had bought, like they'd bought Empress Avenue. We shared a loo and bathroom with the other people on the landing, but we had our own sink, in the kitchen-cum-living room. Open-plan, as it's called today. I must have slept in the same room as my parents, but I have no memory of the sleeping arrangements, no memory of my parents' bedroom there apart from that one of my mum's. It's possible, even, that Win and John slept in the living room, on the smart blue sofa bed that transformed so easily and magically to reveal a space for blankets and pillows. Though my Essex grandparents slept on that when they visited, for a fortnight, biennially. Or did they? Did my parents sleep there and give Win's parents their bedroom? Maybe they did. I'm not sure and they're all dead now, so I can't ever know.

The building was definitely handsome, of red sandstone, as Victorian blocks tended to be in that part of the world.

Four blocks made a courtyard, which was used as a drying green. Monday was wash day, though there wasn't much washing, comparatively. Shirts and sheets mostly. And terry-cloth nappies. That was fine for babies. But you wouldn't hang any actual underwear out where everyone could see it. Shameful.

A lot more airing, steaming and sponging went on back then because otherwise it was the washboard and the mangle. Win had both. I guess people smelled more, but people smoked more too. Everyone smoked. No one knew how good smoking was at masking other unpleasant smells until it was banned in pubs and we all got a whiff of stale each other, rolling off the upholstery and the carpets. Though even then there were outliers – people who stank of neglect.

'Bugsy'. That's what the kids at school who smelled – the outcasts – were called. I remember the names of the smelly outcasts of our class like it was yesterday. That's a real memory. For sure. I can't say the names, not even the initials, for fear that someone from that time might see. One of them had drifted away from schooling altogether by the time he was nine or so. One of the girls was elegant and beautiful, fragrant, by the time she was fourteen. She blushed easily – a delicate whisper of pink would fleetingly tint her cheeks at the slightest attention. All right. Phoenix. Her surname was Phoenix.

Everyone had their place, pretty much. Community life was still lived in an ordered framework. Everything was closed on a Sunday. Fish could be purchased at the Co-op on a Friday. Half-day closing was on Wednesday afternoon. Time off work still ran to the local industry calendar. So, summer holidays in Lanarkshire were taken in the local summer-holiday slot, the Fair Fortnight. Blackpool was the favoured destination for a short autumn break called the

September Weekend. (I went to Blackpool for the September Weekend one year with my Aunt Betty, and it was *wonderful*.) Children stayed with their mothers until they went to school. Pubs were for men, as, on the whole, were trousers. An older woman was a wife, a widow or a spinster. Being a widow was immeasurably preferable to being a spinster. Being a spinster was so pathetic and sad. There was nothing more pitiful, really. If you seemed perfectly happy with your solitary life, you were Very Brave.

Post-war renewal was enacted far more slowly than it was legislated for. In Motherwell, in any case, the nationalisation of the steel industry came first and foremost. The homes fit for heroes came after the jobs fit for them, with the exception, of course, of the Timbers. In the meantime we lived in our cosy flat on Thistle Street, unaware that by the time I was three years old it would be designated 'a slum', taken over by the council and bulldozed.

Our home was no slum. A lot of post-war slum clearance was a myth and an insult. People resisted eviction, tried to save their homes. There would be newspaper pieces for years to come about people holding out in Glasgow. One old lady, featured in a newspaper splash, was sitting by a roaring fire in her living room, and you could see the sky beyond the flames. Good on her. She was right. The real problem was that converting building after building of one- or two-room flats, with shared bathrooms, was much more expensive than flattening them and putting up modern towers and maisonettes in their place. A lot of post-war renewal was done in a fake spirit of do-gooding modernism, on the cheap and with plenty of bungs. Not that any of it ever fooled John and Win. They knew what was going on. John, particularly, saw human self-interest like other people see a hand held in front of their face.

The two of them had no idea how intelligent they were. Sometimes Win would say: 'You get your brains from your dad. Your dad is so clever, he could have been a doctor. He could have been anything.' Win never, ever vouchsafed any ideas about what she could have been, even though she too had promise like cucumbers have water. Maybe, however, I took her at her own valuation, and took him at hers too. John seemed more precious to me, more valuable, more heroic. John was the one who had been robbed of his potential, denied the chance to develop his mind and his talents and be who he could have been. It didn't hurt that he was film-star handsome. He was as romantic a figure to me as he was to my mother. More romantic, probably.

John was the one I idolised. He was the one with whom I'd have had this fabulous father-daughter thing if it wasn't for my mum, who came between us. That idea changed, quite recently. I didn't want it to change. But when my parents were both dead, and I started reassessing my relationship with them, I had no answers. Sure, my mum had some funny ideas, which got funnier as I got older. But my dad had backed her all the way and even, at some highly disturbing points, gone further than she ever had. For Dad, though, I always had excuses. The last thing he would have wanted was a daughter who was unthinkingly adept at making excuses for controlling, psychosexually fucked-up, abusive male behaviour. Through his own unthinking, automatic efforts, however, that's what he got.

But in the flat on Thistle Street, when I was little, insight into psychosexually fucked-up co-dependent parental behaviour lay years ahead of me. It was just the three of us then. This was my time as an only child, before David came along and we divided into two factions – Mum and David; Dad and me. All the warmth and safety of being a beloved toddler is stuff I remember in a happy haze.

I recall being coaxed by my parents into singing 'Hit the Road, Jack' to my parents' friends, Jean and Ian Walker – her English, him Scots, like Win and John. The adults all clapped at the end, and I felt like I was the world's most special little girl. Years later I discovered that it had been a Ray Charles hit. It was so unlike my parents, who would become ardent fans of Andy Williams and Perry Como and were at the time, by and large, still obsessed with Russ Conway, still embarrassed and disgusted by the pelvic thrusts of Elvis and still a bit frightened by black men, even blind ones.

I remember watching *Dr Who*, literally from behind that smart blue sofa, deliciously frightened, on our black and white television with its two channels and its elegant splayed legs, like Bambi's. I remember going to see *Bambi* at the Odeon in Motherwell. My first trip to the pictures. Apparently I snivelled all the way through, from the horrific moment when Bambi's mother was shot. Other than that, my main memories of screen entertainment at Thistle Street are *Watch With Mother* – a beloved ritual – and the football results, with the telex machine typing the results as they came in, the clatter of its noise broadcast to Britain every week early on Saturday evening.

'Heart of Midlothian, One' (high and bright). 'Motherwell, Nil' (low and sombre). We all had to be quiet to listen to the results because they had the potential to change our lives. John loved football. John loved doing the pools. Viv Nicholson's name was so often cited in our house that I thought she was an English relative. In 1977, when I was fourteen, my mum and I would watch the *Play for Today* about Viv, Britain's flamboyant 1961 pools winner, *Spend Spend Spend*. John was on night shift. We were both transfixed. We watched lots of *Plays for Today*, unaware that they were something amazing, written and directed by great men. (But hardly ever women, even though a female producer worked on the series.) Jack Rosenthal wrote *Spend Spend Spend*. And *Yentl*, with Barbra Streisand.

I remember going to the Duchess Park with my mum and playing in the sandpit. Later, when Neil Reid had won *Opportunity Knocks* in 1971, Win told me that he'd been one of the kids I'd played with at that time. Back then, a local twelve-year-old winning *Opportunity Knocks* had been the biggest fame-and-celebrity thing ever to hit Motherwell. He's still the youngest person ever to have had a number one record in the UK album charts. His big hit was 'Mother of Mine'. His mother, according to my mother, had been very nice. Perhaps she'd deserved the accolade she got in the final verse:

> Mother of mine, now I am grown
> Now I can walk straight
> All on my own
> I'd like to give you what you gave to me
> Mother, sweet mother of mine.

'A good skelp,' the kids joked in Motherwell, which is Scottish for a hiding. Being hit by your parents was a normal punishment then.

John coming home from work in his brown-paper-coloured boiler suit and tapping me on the head with his newspaper, like a caress from a god. John coming home from work one night with a big box, which I opened in a state of wild excitement to find Monica, a doll who was taller than me, in a long, full-skirted dress of turquoise and gold. Monica said 'Mama' in a strangled squeak from a cylinder inserted into a smooth, round hole in her tummy, if you propelled her 360 degrees. As you do. She became the immediate favourite of all my dolls.

I loved my dolls. I'd line them all up on the couch, in order of size, and just revel in them. A new addition was as exciting as Christmas. Win knitted me a couple of dolls too – Sally, the big one, and Looby Loo, the little one. She did all the naming – Monica, Sally, Looby Loo, Belinda. I can't remember the others. Win was in charge of all the words.

The bad things that happened when we were at Thistle Street – I remember them more clearly and sharply. Or I think I do. A terrible winter, bitterly cold, that records tell me fell in the early months of 1963 and involved the sea freezing over for a mile out from Herne Bay, Kent. So, again, when I was still a baby. Do babies remember anything? Can a six-month-old file away the sensation of living in record-breaking cold? If a six-month-old can, then it appears that I did. Though it's not the cold I remember. It's the noise of the wind, like the world was being torn apart. Can terror be remembered from babyhood? I'd like to think not. Yet I think I remember my terror.

Jean Walker dying in a car crash. Another Englishwoman abroad, like Pat Lindsay, who'd married a Scotsman and come to live in Motherwell. Three couples, close, all an Englishwoman and a Scotsman. I remember Jean, alive, wearing a white dress with blue flowers in Dior New Look style, with a wide skirt, smiling. Then Jean was dead and Win was crying. Comprehension of the shock to my mother this loss caused? That came later.

My dad, trouser leg rolled up, bare foot in a lemon plastic washing-up bowl, sitting by the fire bathing a mess of red and purple, half healed, from his injury at work. There was a towel under the bowl. He winced with the pain. Later I learned that a long, thin ringlet of planed-off steel, like a wood shaving but as sharp-edged as a scalpel blade, had been left on the factory floor by some careless workmate, had caught round John's ankle and cut it to the bone. He'd been off work for ages, and according to Win hadn't been given nearly as much compensation as he should and could have got.

This was the time at which Win had seen an advert in the paper for jobs in the Highlands with the Forestry Commission. 'We could have got out,' she'd say, 'had a different life. But he wouldn't have it.' For years Win spoke wistfully of this different, better life that had slipped through our fingers: 'But your dad wanted to be near his precious Fir Park and his precious Shotts.'

This was before Dad had started taking me to Fir Park, the Motherwell football ground so close that we could hear the roar of the crowd. But I knew all about Shotts. Shotts golf club, the easy-to-get-into club that was in a fairly re- mote former mining village that tended to get snowed in in winter. My dad had taken up golf shortly after I'd been born, and Win was furious about it. John's obsession with golf was something Win tolerated resentfully for the rest of her life. 'That golf. That Shotts.' As she was dying, she told me that everything in the house would be mine and David's. 'There isn't much,' she said. 'Any extra money we got was spent on your father's golf.' It wasn't true. Any extra money they got was spent on their endless succession of crap cars.

That wasn't the cause of my parents' biggest row of their married life, though. That row, when we were still in Thistle Street, was because the iron had broken and John had got Win a new one for her birthday. She retold the story many times. 'I could have thrown it at him!' She'd been hurt at the practicality, the lack of romance. 'Is that what you think of me now?' she'd yelled at him. 'Am I your washerwoman now?' Win's great moment of feminism. After that, he always bought her jewellery or perfume.

Being a woman seemed so greatly the lesser part of the deal to me that I used to wish that maybe it was little girls who grew up to be men and little boys who grew up to be women. I knew that wasn't the case really. But I dared to hope.

And there was the social catastrophe – the most significant of my memories of my time at Thistle Street. This, long hindsight has taught me, was the establishing scene, the place where my pattern for interacting with others was set. And it's all so classic, so hilariously Freudian, that it's almost funny.

When I was three years old – it might even have been my third birthday – my dad decided that I was old enough now to 'play out', to get out there on the drying green and amuse myself, meet other kids, have some independence. I have a dim memory of my mother being against it, I think. From what I know of her it's entirely credible. Being against such a thing, it fits with her character. Win was a protective mother. Nevertheless, it may be a memory of being told how against this playing out Win was. It was a story my mother was fond of, because she was the thwarted hero and my dad the insensitive fool. She did that a lot.

There was the story of my naming. Win would put on a moronic, slow voice, a voice my dad never spoke in, and say: 'Ah like L-i-n-d-a', as if calling a child Linda was like calling her Big Fat Jobby. Win had wanted Juliet, which my dad argued would not be at all suitable for the rough and tumble of Motherwell life. Deborah was their compromise.

John always pronounced it De-bra, in an attempt to make it sound less fancy and elaborate. No such modesty from Win, who liked Deb O Rah to be pronounced with just a sigh of H at the end. I was named, I was told by my mother, after the Scottish actress Deborah Kerr. Win loved glamorous movie stars.

I liked being Deborah, but these stories of my father's idiocy made me feel resentful of Win, not John. John, by contrast, would never, ever say a word against my mother. The very occasional, very gentle raising of his eyebrows, a tiny bit of side-eye, a touch of the comic as he warned us to step away from the bureau – these subtle, coded messages were pretty much as far as he ever went.

Anyway, I was duly despatched to the drying green to play, fearful, reluctant, confused.

I stood there, on the edge of the courtyard, where I'd been left like a tethered goat, with absolutely no idea of what I was meant to do next. There weren't any other kids out there anyway, and I don't think I'd ever met any neighbouring children. Before this point, actually, I have no memory that would suggest that I'd ever interacted with another child at all. But I must have. In the Duchess Park. Neil Reid!

Then a local kid, a little older than me, approached and looked me over. The little stranger admired my bracelet and asked if she could try it on. It was my gold christening brace-let, a thin, figured band that expanded as you got bigger. I silently passed it to her. She turned it over in her hands for a couple of moments, slipped it on her wrist, drew a breath and legged it, leaving me gazing after her, dumbfounded, for a few moments before I burst into tears and started running back to the flat to break the news of my first mugging. John and Win met me halfway. They must have been watching from the window.

My parents had conniptions, Win upset and tearful, John indignant and angry. He knew whose child she was and marched me over to the flat of the miscreant to confront her mother with what her daughter had done. The mother answered the door but held it only half open, cocking her head round it. We weren't invited in.

'Look. Your lassie's taken my wee girl Debra here's bracelet.'

The mother denied that her daughter would do such a thing and when my dad pointed out that the girl was standing behind her mother and the bracelet was there on her wrist, the mum just insisted that the bracelet had been given to her daughter on the occasion of her own christening. There was nothing to be done in the face of their denial. The christening gifts of the family's girls were not engraved. John picked me up and carried me home. That was that. My first solo encounter with the outside world.

At three years old, I don't think I learned good lessons from any of this. I had failed to be the daughter John wanted, the daughter who would skip out and make friends. My dad's efforts to make it right for me again and get the bracelet back – they failed too. I wasn't old enough to learn from those security-destroying experiences. So I just internalised them, emotionally, the best way I could. They made me shy and anxious. But they also made me angry, suspicious of others and withdrawn. Which I always tried to cover up by handing over symbolic versions of the bracelet.

I see now that, rather than accepting what had happened and learning from it, I attempted and attempted to defy it. I kept right on putting my faith in others – handing over a precious thing so that the ending could change. One day, I would get 'the bracelet' back, either from the girl (or any woman), who would turn out to be sincere, or via my dad (or any man), who would turn out to be righteous and powerful. 'Share all I have to give, value it, respect it, keep it safe for me. It's my treasure.' My plea to anyone who ever asks anything of me, made so silently that I don't even hear it myself.

I became an adult who strides boldly into situations for which I am ill prepared. I trust people very easily and very completely. I find it hard to show that I'm hurting, until I get so resentful and angry that I lash out. I expect, when I do show my feelings or try to explain them, those feelings to be denied by the person who is inspiring them. I didn't know, until recently, that denying another person their own feelings is the foundation of all emotional abuse.

Another memory, aged about seven: I stood on a concrete platform while other kids threw bricks at me, as a dare. One struck me on the temple, but I wouldn't show them it hurt. It's a habit that gets me into trouble, deeper and deeper, again and again. Anything rather than acknowledge my debilitating fear of the world and the people in it.

I still see exactly how the whole bracelet incident came about, from my dad's point of view. He thought that I was just like him, which parents often do when their children are small. He'd played out at three and therefore so should I. Probably, he hadn't wanted to either. But he had found his courage, or thought that he had. Looking back, though, I see that he coped with the world using similar strategies to my own – by pretending not to be afraid. I never saw John as a fearful person until he was gone. Now I see that his life was governed by fear.

We were alike, my dad and I, more alike than my mother and I, both in looks and in character. Finding fault with my dad was like finding fault with myself. We all have a tendency to feel the most empathy with the people who remind us most of ourselves. Yet I am like my mother too. We are all like each other, the four of us. That's the inescapable fact of family.

3

The Wedding Clipping

The wedding clipping was still there, in the bureau, from a March 1961 edition of the local paper in Brentwood, Essex. A spring wedding. In the photograph that illustrated the piece, you used to be able to see that the couple had foliage behind them. But both ink and paper – the latter as yellow as the roses my mother had carried – are so old now that the background is just a blur of fuzzy grey ectoplasm, from which the two of them materialise.

My dad looks so young, so handsome, with his short back and sides and a shiny touch of Brylcreem on his blond hair. When you see the young faces of people you know best when they are older, those young faces look contingent, inchoate. John looks like that, at twenty-seven a year older than my mother, which, as a marital age gap, is Just Right. I married a man who was a year and three days older than me: also Just Right! John looks a bit tentative, standing there in his pale tie with a pale carnation pinned on his lapel. But he wasn't tentative, not then, not ever. He was always glad to have married Win. He never faltered. I'm sure of that. I think I'm sure.

My mum, who was much shorter than John, who was so tiny at four foot nine or ten, still has her veil on, a short veil held in place on her fashionable dark brown bubble-cut by a pretty rhinestone tiara. Her face looks exotic, all the dark a little more dark than in reality, and all the light a little lighter. The mole on her cheekbone is prominent, the mole that she called a beauty spot and emphasised with cosmetics, the mole that I always secretly considered a disfigurement. Win has the slightest of smiles on her face, which floats in a cloud of starched white-nylon mesh. She looks smug rather than happy, to me. But I would say that, wouldn't I? Anyway, there are other photographs of the day in which both of them look as thrilled and delighted as each other.

The headline the local newspaper wrote still makes me laugh. Difference, even small difference, was so remarkable to people back then. Because John is from far-off Scotland, it reads:

THE BRIDEGROOM FROM
OVER THE BORDER

Miss Winifred Meta Avis, the youngest daughter of Mr and Mrs Avis, of Bird-Lane Gt Warley and Mr John Scott Orr, the youngest son of Mrs Orr of Lanarkshire, Scotland, were married at the Church of St Mary the Virgin, Gt Warley, on Saturday.

The bride wore a gown of white satin brocade and carried a bouquet of yellow roses. The three bridesmaids, Miss Elizabeth Kirby, Miss Jane Kirby and Miss Alice Feltwell, all wore dresses of lilac nylon and carried sprays of violets.

Best man was Mr William Orr and the bride's going-away outfit was a blue tweed suit and white accessories.

The blue tweed suit stayed in the wardrobe for years. Beautiful. Soft, pale eau de Nil, with pink woolly knobbles of slub.

Win may have worn it to our christenings – in Essex and into the Church of England, both of us. Our baptism cards were still in the bureau too. We were Anglican, not Presbyterian. Win had been fastidious about that. I don't know why, really. To please her own mother, I guess. Neither Win nor John believed in God or took part in church activities. They were vehement on that, very sure.

One thing I should probably explain about my mother, before matters get too messy, is that she was amazing. She was accomplished, resourceful, vivacious, terrifyingly well organised and copiously talented as an artist and a crafts-woman. She had a GSOH. She could be great company. She was adored, not just by my father but by her whole, large family in Essex. At my oldest cousin's seventieth birthday party, my only surviving English uncle, Ron, produced some photographs of John and Win's wedding. I'd seen them a million times. But I was caught short by what he and my cousins were saying.

Uncle Ron: 'Oh, just look at her. She was a film star, was Winnie.'

Cousin Jane: 'She was a special one all right.'

Cousin Alan: 'Your dad really got lucky when he married our Win.'

All: 'Yes! He did!'

Me: 'Hey! She didn't do so badly either!'

I was still ready to leap to the defence of my dead dad, still itching to say that my dead mum wasn't as perfect as they all thought. I've often found myself listening to other people sing my mother's praises, while I want to say: 'It's not like that.' Win was praised a lot and Win loved to be praised. She needed it. Sometimes I was too stubborn, too unkind, to give my mother what she needed, and I regret it. I wasn't always like that, though. And when I was little I worshipped her.

When the Royal Mail issued Gainsborough stamps, I would gaze at the tiny red boy on those handwritten envelopes from Essex. 'He looks like you, Mummy. You're as beautiful as he is. More beautiful.'

I think I may even have tried to draw the red boy, who was as glamorous as the film stars my mother admired and had herself loved to draw, before she married. Win taught me when I was small how to draw a mascaraed eye or a lipsticked mouth, patiently explaining the details I needed to get right – how the bottom of the upper lip wasn't a single curve but was three curves, with one at the centre, or how the eye had a little extra bulb at each inner corner that you had to express in the sketch. After she was married, Win would doodle eyes or mouths on the blank rectangle of the newspaper, saved for any breaking news that couldn't wait, while she completed the *Scottish Daily Express* crossword. She almost always drew beautiful women.

I saw very many idealised images of wartime glamour as a small child, as all of us at that time did. Mostly, they appeared in the movies. I had my own private supply as well. My mother had kept a big pile of her sketches and paintings of beautiful women, often in evening dress, sometimes in uniform. Most were pencil sketches on sugar paper. A few were oil paint on greaseproof paper, a nimbus of ochre from the linseed around them. Sometimes the drawing would be on a cardboard rectangle of packing from a new shirt, or a blank page torn from a book. The confidence and certainty of my mother's line, its vivacity – she really had a talent, a gift. When I bought my first flat in my twenties I asked her if I could look at the sketches again, maybe have a few and get them framed to hang up in my new place. I thought she'd be pleased, a bit flattered.

'I threw all those away,' she said, her face angry and closed.

'But . . . why, Mum?'

'They were just old nonsense, taking up space.'

Win really had chucked the lot. None survive. I was disturbed by my mother's act of self-destruction, and hurt. I didn't like the idea that she'd disposed of that part of herself, neither drawing and painting any more nor even keeping the work she'd once been proud of. One Christmas, I bought her a set of oil paints and she looked at them and me in disgust. 'I'm too busy to have any use for *these*.' Later, I realised that she may not have been able to bear the promise that those drawings and paintings showed, that in some part of my mother, stuffed down and denied, there was unwelcome cognisance that her life had been limited by her sex and her class, and her talents were never given room to develop. But she didn't want to look at that, or even at the pile of sketches, ten inches thick, that were its undeniable proof. I am their witness. I remember them.

Idealised images of idealised images. I'd look through those sketches, in wonder, for hours as Win talked about the film stars and about her childhood and her schooldays. Win had worshipped Grace Kelly and Katharine Hepburn. And she'd named me after Deborah Kerr, of course.

She and her school friend, Maureen Rippingdale, had loved the movies. Win went at least once every week, sometimes twice, and she and Maureen spent all their cash on the avalanche of movie magazines that were being published at the time. Maureen would beg my mother to draw this film star or that film star for her. Both girls would study their hair and make-up and copy it. Win looked like a film star because she modelled herself on film stars. Maureen too.

'Film-star crazy, was Maureen,' said my mum. 'Hollywood-mad.'

Maureen dreamed of being such a star herself, dreamed

so hard that she made her dream come true, for a time. She ran away from her Essex home at sixteen, seeking work as an actress in London. Her professional name was Carole Lesley, and she starred in a couple of British films.

We watched Carole, reinvented as a classic blonde bomb-shell, playing Kitten Strudwick in *Doctor in Love* one Sunday afternoon. Not bad. She had talent too. Carole had also starred in *Woman in a Dressing Gown*, which won a Golden Globe for Best English-language foreign film, which can only mean that she'd expected Hollywood to beckon. Mum always wondered what had become of Maureen, why her career had faltered. Whatever did happen, she did not live happily ever after.

Through a newspaper article published in 1974, Win learned that her old pal had killed herself, with a drug over-dose, aged thirty-eight, alone in her suburban bungalow. The poor woman was still enough of a somebody for her suicide to make the national papers. Maureen had come so close, so tantalisingly close, to the Hollywood stardom that she craved. My mum thought that, having come within grasp of her fantasy, Maureen probably found it hard to face reality again. If she'd ever lived in the real world at all. She paid heavily for her few years of glamour, however you cut it. Poor Maureen. In life and death she was a Marilyn Monroe manqué. The movie industry is littered with dead blondes.

So, my mother had these stories, of tragic film stars she'd known from school and *Opportunity Knocks* winners play-ing in the park. It seemed to me that Win really was from somewhere close to the centre of the universe. I couldn't get enough of my mother, of hearing about her life before me in the English countryside. Her triumphs at school, her good singing, her drawing, her youth, her beauty, her eighteen-inch waist, the interest from men she rebuffed as she waited for John. Everything she wanted to teach me, I would learn: how to knit, how to sew, how to cut a dress pattern, put in a zip, how to darn, how to make jam, how to make pastry, how to perm hair. I could literally run the staff at Downton Abbey. I have all of those pre-consumerism household skills.

I loved Win's wide black velvet belt, so tiny, that she kept for years, a reminder to herself of her lovely, curvaceous figure 'before I had children'. I'd stopped being able to fasten it round my own waist when I was about fourteen. But Win's waist had still been eighteen inches on the day she'd got married, at twenty-six. Everyone had worried that she was too choosy and might end up 'on the shelf', a spinster. (Spinster, by the way, was originally the word for a woman so good at weaving that she was financially independent.) Win told me this often, the sense of triumph snatched from the jaws of adversity never fading. But she'd been in no hurry. She'd known there was a man to wait for, a Mr Right who would find her. And he did! He came all the way from Scotland to claim her! Win starred in the romantic movie of her life.

Therefore, of course, Win always talked a lot about her wedding day, the film's climax and final scene. The dress she'd made herself, then sacrificed to make that party dress for me; the short veil, because long veils were old-fashioned and silly, that had been turned into wings for me to be a fairy at a fancy-dress party; the cake she'd made with her mother; the bridesmaids' dresses that she'd made herself; the yellow roses that she carried and that people wore in their buttonholes and on their corsages, because yellow roses were my mother's favourite flowers. Except for John and his best man, my Uncle Wullie, and their carnations.

We often looked at the photographs, some black and white, like the wedding clipping, and some in the exciting novelty of colour. Once, when we were visiting Essex, we made a solemn trip to the pretty church where it all happened. John put an extravagant amount of money in the donations box. 'Worth every penny,' he said, face soft with the gallantry that the situation demanded.

John and Win met, and had their miscegenated, cross-border romance, because of the war. Without the war, I was always told, I wouldn't have existed. John's sister Ellen had been in the forces, had met her husband Cyril while serving and had set up home with him in Braintree, Essex, the only one of the five surviving Scottish siblings to make a life outside Lanarkshire. Ellen had persuaded John to come to England and live with her, at a time when he was feeling lost, or trapped, at home and wanted to escape from the work in heavy industry that had been expected of him. He got a job as a postman and met my mum at a dance at the Ilford Palais. The first time she rode on the back of his moped he roared off, leaving her in a heap on the road. They fell in love. They got engaged. They got married.

It was out of character for my dad, though, this move south. I think it was because he'd had a trauma at work that had thrown him off the settled course he'd fully expected his entire life to take, as people did back then. I think he'd been running away. John had left school at fourteen and started at the Lanarkshire, the great girder makers that had been run by the Colville family prior to nationalisation and Ravenscraig. On one occasion a huge, red-hot girder had somehow slipped from the chains that supported it as it was being swung through the air, on to the next process. My dad, young, quick-witted, keen of reflex, had seen the accident unfolding, seen the girder dashing through the air towards another man and had pushed him out of its path. The girder would have sliced through the man's legs like they were nothing more than the air itself. John, in his late teens, was a hero. The man gave him sixpence, which was a lot of money then.

But the incident really shook my father. He didn't feel like a hero, didn't feel like he deserved his sixpence, didn't feel comfortable with being a shop-floor legend. Instead he was terrified, haunted by the vision of what he'd almost seen: a writhing stump of a man, maybe hit again as the girder swung back; or the girder maybe hitting others who had instinctively moved towards their workmate to help him, to try to stop the screaming. Or maybe hitting John, so young still, a kid in this primal, dangerous, fearsome place.

It was huge, in Motherwell, a steelworker losing his nerve for any reason, as bad as a man being unable to face going to war, or developing shell shock afterwards. No one really understood trauma then. John's own dad had died when he was young, having packed in coalmining because of emphysema. John knew what life and work were like, for a man who had had and lost one of the princely jobs of the town. After being a miner, John's dad had been a bin man and a bookies' runner, which was illegal at the time. He'd nearly gone to prison for it – which would have killed him, Win told me. He'd scraped a living. He'd been brought low. He'd died young and left a widow with five children to look after.

Motherwell's was a macho, patriarchal culture. Losing your nerve, getting the fears – it was entirely unseemly. John's act of heroism, or his feelings about it anyway, had given him a sense not of pride but of shame, had shattered his nerve, his fragile identity as a steelman and his place in the pecking order of the town. He admitted as much when I quizzed him about it, on 28 July 1996, the day that they demolished the big edifices of the Craig. He'd always been frightened, in the Lanarkshire, from the very first day. He had always hidden his fear and carried on. Because John knew how lucky he was. Being part of the Lanarkshire – that was something.

I remember the Lanarkshire's remnants, still standing in the town long after the works had been decommissioned. The cooling towers still clustered by the railway bridge at Flemington, not the waisted-vase shape of the concrete cooling towers that the post-war steelworks had but square ones, tapered to a smaller square at the top, wooden, gigantic, the size of thousands upon thousands of garden sheds.

The wood they were built from was black and dull, so black and dull, and some of the planks had been replaced, the pine so clean and bright in contrast. And there were holes, ragged holes, where the wood in places had collapsed. Those rotting, polluted wooden monuments must have stood there, decomposing, for maybe forty years. I don't think anyone minded. We were proud of the Lanarkshire, as a collective, as a town. It was our heritage, part of us, and it made us part of the world. The great black girders of Tate Modern in London were made at the Lanarkshire. That was the single thing that thrilled me most when it reopened as a gallery in 2000, after derelict years as an out-of-commission power station. Reading those words up the sides of the steel. 'Lanarkshire Steelworking Co Ltd'. These girders were something that my community had been part of, that my family had been part of, that I had been part of.

I stood, years ago, on a steel bridge in Singapore and read the letters forged into the metal, telling me that this steel too had been supplied by the Lanarkshire. The world's finest steel travelled far.

The steel travelled better than John did. He hated the way that in Essex he was never allowed to forget that he was a Scotsman, got called Jock and had to put up with endless jokes about being mean, drinking whisky – which he strongly disliked the taste of – and about generally having heather hanging out of his ears. He was homesick. So he and Win sold up, moved to Scotland and stayed with my Scottish grannie, Elizabeth – Lizzie – while they were looking for their own place. They travelled on my dad's moped. Their belongings did the 400 miles in a removal van. And that was how they came to be living in the tenement in Thistle Street.

At first, my dad carried on being a postman. But after I was born they couldn't manage on one relatively small wage. So he went back into heavy industry. Not making steel, but turning steel at a huge company that made coal-cutting machines, mainly for the South African market. Anderson Boyes. That was where he got the injury to his foot and, as Mum always said, the pitiful compensation.

Yet in Motherwell, all was not well with my mother, just as all had not been well with my dad in Romford. I understood this at an early age, in dribs and drabs, as Win would say. I was her confidante when I was little, a receptacle not just for her fond memories but also for her resentments, her complaints, her own homesickness and her feelings of dislocation and fear. She'd given up her job as a clerk in Glasgow when she became pregnant with me, as was traditional for women then. She was hard up. She was lonely. She didn't fit in.

'On my first day, the girls at work asked me if I wanted a ham sandwich. But when it came it was a horrible, greasy old bacon sandwich, because here they call bacon ham. I ask you? The food up here? They eat whiting. Down our way whiting's for the cat. And tuna. They go on about tinned tuna as if it's salmon. Down our way, tuna's for the cat, too. People here, they have no idea about food.' And this was before deep-fried Mars Bars had even been dreamed of.

Or Win would just say, simply and wearily: 'People are very hard here. Very hard.'

As I got older, I began to understand the truth in what

Win said. It *was* hard there. It was hard and it was tough. It was hard just having the Essex accent that you'd picked up from your mum because you had to explain your funny way of talking, your posh accent, and this in turn drew the regular and oddly accusatory question: 'Your mum's ENGLISH?' The Scots hated the English. The oppressors. The killers of brave-hearted William Wallace. The perpetrators of Culloden. The Scots, it sometimes seemed, hated everything that wasn't Scotland. This was very true in my home town.

Motherwell was a difference engine with a difference, calculating everything that might make a person unlike the other persons, then roaring into the sacred work of driving that devil out of them. Conformity was absolutely everything. Failure to conform to the fearlessness of the steelworker had torpedoed my dad's self-esteem. Failure to be Scottish was a problem for my mum in Motherwell, just as failure to be English had been a failure for my dad in Essex. In both places I was a chimerical beast, an oddity.

There was a bloated, strained self-regard about both places that I didn't recognise. Not then, at least. I came to identify the large, fragile egos that stood sentinel over local superiority as a kind of collective narcissism. There's probably a narcissism about every village, town and city – though we call it civic pride. In Motherwell, in all of Lanarkshire, it seemed extreme. Everyone kept everyone else in line, using phrases developed for such a purpose: 'If she wis ice cream, she'd eat hersel'; 'She'd buy tickets to her ain show'; 'She's so sharp she'll cut hersel'; 'She thinks she's somebody'; and, the one I hated most of all: 'Whit's fir ye ah'll no go by ye', which translates as 'Don't embarrass us all by striving for something different. See what you get and be content with it.' Everyone expected everyone else to be their mirror image. Difference was criticism, criticism was unwelcome, so difference was unwelcome. I saw the same phenomenon in England after the Brexit referendum, in a more complex, multicultural iteration.

Multiculturalism, of course, had not quite hit the Scottish Lowlands, not in the 1960s. The different people then were not quite so different, though there was diversity of a kind. The man who went around on a plywood board attached to a roller skate, scooting himself with his hands, because he'd lost his legs in the war. The girl whose hands were where her elbows should have been, because the Thalidomide disaster had recently struck. Lots of kids who wore bottle-top NHS glasses, transparent pink for girls and transparent blue for boys. People with hearing aids the size of a nasty tumour. Cleft palates. Callipers. ('Did you hear about the cripple who got chased by an Alsatian? He ran like the callipers.') Morag at the top of the road, the same age as me, but 'a mongol'. The atypically abled were easy to spot and curiosity about them was naked. Little was known about 'hidden disabilities' such as autism. Stephen Wiltshire was yet to be born, let alone appear on telly, drawing St Pancras Railway Station. *The Foolish Wise Ones*. 1987. *Everyone* watched that show.

In the mid-1960s uncharitable, insecure feelings were voiced in the same way as they are today, though. One commonly expressed feeling was that the English came up to Motherwell 'taking people's jobs' – even though Win had taken someone's job for about six months, until she dedicated herself to the full-time life's work of being my mother. Anyway, back then, in a huge economic boom, the truth was that if you didn't have a job it was usually because you were just unbelievably, *unbelievably* unemployable. Usually for good reason. Not because some English person had stolen *your job* from you.

So there were some challenges on the assimilation front from both sides, Win's and Motherwell's. My mother had good reason to be shocked, even traumatised, by her move there. She didn't choose it. And she'd never known anything like it. Win had grown up in the Home Counties. She was the daughter of deeply rural people who'd had little experience of industry, or of towns and cities. People for whom London, so near, might as well have been Sodom. Or Gomorrah. Great Warley, whence she had married, was unbelievably sleepy. It had wheat fields. It had barley fields. It had *rose fields*. Those Essex farmers might as well have been recreating Elysium. The nearest Great Warley got to industry was the Tiptree jam plant.

England, to me, was the Motherland. Not Motherwell. Win spoke in such glowing terms of England herself. Plus, at that time, the BBC was the voice of the nation, telling us all who we were in the dulcet tones of received pronunciation. The idea of England as Blake's Jerusalem was still projected strongly and remained more or less unchallenged. Also, it was always summer in England, because we'd only ever visit in the Fair Fortnight.

We'd go down to Essex every second summer, my dad driving whichever unreliable rust-bucket he was managing to keep on the road at the time. He was a good mechanic but a terrible driver who conveyed his stress to everyone else in the car with the usual techniques and didn't like using motorways because they mesmerised him. We were always getting lost, with the car running out of petrol or breaking down.

One time, we saw a wheel bouncing ahead of our car just at the moment that our pale green Vauxhall Viva had shuddered to a spark-flying, juddering, slanting stop. Another time, the car was filling with water, and when we lifted the carpet to see what the problem was, that bit of the chassis was revealed as having been made of old beer cans that had been soldered together. Once my dad, body rattling from the pills he'd taken for his tension headache, had to stop the car and vomit at the side of the road from the anxiety of it all.

The odd thing is that these are joyous memories, despite the stress and the terrible seriousness of those journeys. We didn't really know there was any other way to drive to England. We used to love hitting Scotch Corner, because that meant we were nearly in England or nearly in Scotland. Scotch Corner always got a cheer. Scotch Corner could do no wrong.

Apart from my Essex grandparents, Harry and Annie, and, less regularly, the Kirbys, no one from Essex really came to visit us. Uncle Jim and Aunt Joy had expected at least one of their two girls, Susan and Carol, to be a bridesmaid. But Mum had chosen both of her sister Jean Kirby's girls and neither of her brother Jim's. The other bridesmaid, Alice, had been the daughter of my dad's sister Ellen, at that time the only girl of that generation on the Scottish side. I'd be the third. My Uncle Bob and Aunt Daisy had their first daughter, Karyn, between the two of us. She was and is profoundly disabled by cerebral palsy. Or, as we all said then quite happily, she was a spastic. Daisy did lots of work for The Spastic Society. It's now called Scope.

By the time I was sentient, my mother wasn't talking to her sister Mary either. By all accounts Mary had a spiteful streak and had attacked my mother physically over something that was never explained. There was a lot of arguing in the English family, which made visits complicated, not just over who wasn't speaking to whom but over who was taking who's side.

I didn't meet Uncle Jim until I was eight or nine, because of the Great Rift. Aunt Joy, whom I met maybe twice, ever, was a 'good-time girl', my mother told me. Jim was a long-distance lorry driver by the time I was introduced to him, and had stopped off at our flat in Shields Drive to sleep on our couch. He was a skinny, dirty man and he had a £50 note, the first I'd ever seen. He let me hold it – he let us all hold it, this note, so huge, all pink and red and important. Jim, my mother told me, was a bit of a black sheep. Some of the family say he was just a snooker hustler, no harm in him. Others say he was something of a gangster when he was young, into all sorts of crime and violence. 'Well, by the middle of his life he suddenly had a club foot,' one of my cousins remarked a few years back, adding a pointed rhetorical flourish: 'Who *develops* a club foot?'

None of this was known to me when I was little, though. Jim was just a familial wrinkle in the otherwise genteel life of my cut-above English relatives. When Harry and Annie came to visit we'd go to Glasgow Central Station to meet them. Glasgow, twelve miles from Motherwell, was a place we hardly ever went to. My parents hated cities. I didn't realise then that cities intimidated them. So visits from my grandparents were exciting from the start, and also stressful because my dad hated driving in Glasgow, where he'd get as lost as he did on the way to Great Warley.

Harry and Annie came on the sleeper train, which seemed to me as grand and luxurious as arriving on the Venice Simplon-Orient-Express. Glasgow Central Station was magnificently beautiful then – mahogany-panelled walls, so solid, so perfectly crafted, with sweeping, sinuous curves instead of corners. They're still there, but have been supplemented with other, cheaper panels, which tends to lessen the impact. The station's huge, high glass roof meant that it was full of light on those summer days. And it was so full of smart Glasgow people, with their complex bustle, their mysterious but important purpose, their understanding of all those announcements, all those arrival and departure boards. And my grandparents themselves, who were old-fashioned in a lovely way, still travelled in suits – Harry's shirt so white, Annie's skirt and jacket in a powder blue or a yellow ochre and a blouse with a bow at the neck. And so glad to see us! Such hugs! Win was their favourite child, their youngest, the English apple of their English eyes. They adored us all because we were part of her. Mainly, though, they seemed posh because they were English, and Win was always telling me how much more sophisticated England was.

Harry died at the house on Bird Lane in his sleep when I was in my mid-teens. Annie woke up to find that last night's husband had become that morning's corpse. All the grown-ups agreed that it had been typical of spoilt, selfish Harry to drift out of life with such ease and lack of inconvenience to himself. They all hoped that Annie might enjoy life a little bit now, released as she was from Harry's moody demands and expressions of rage. My wonderful grandad? Moody? This was news to me.

Except that it wasn't, not really. Somehow I'd always managed to hold two ideas about my grandfather in my head. He could be kind, loving and fun. He was diligent, a wonderful gardener. He was a good father, my uncles say. He'd work five days a week, and a Saturday morning, then come home and get his last out each weekend to repair the shoes of his family of nine. They were both hard workers. But I'd always heard about Harry's rages too. I'd always known that it was Annie's job to make Harry happy, not the other way around. I'd chosen the version of Harry that I saw, because that was the one I preferred.

When I was very little, I don't know why, I'd called him 'Man'. Probably because since the men all worked, the women all mothered and my parents didn't do much weekend socialising, he was the only man I was familiar with apart from my dad. Once, on a wander around Motherwell, Man had become detached from the family group. I was terribly upset that Man was missing and remember seeing him walking back towards our consternated little huddle. 'There's Man,' I shouted, pointing. 'There's Man,' and ran towards him, desperate to feel his dry, warm hand hold mine. It's amazing how much a child can adore a human being that she barely knows from Adam. Family. Emotional magic. Sometimes dark magic.

Even Harry's shortcomings, relayed by my mother, seemed to me like great strengths. His career had always been presented to me as a tale of self-inflicted decline, the decline self-inflicted for honourable, heroic reasons. He was, my mother told me, too free with the giving-out of pieces of his mind. He'd been a tenant farmer, a dairy farmer, and had lost his farm after the First World War, during the depression.

A few years back, at a party an Essex cousin threw, I'd learned of something strange that I hadn't known about my Essex family before. Harry and Annie had only had their first two kids, Bill and Ron, when they still had the farm. But when they moved from the farm, Bill had gone to live with his widowed grandmother and her second husband, a man called Nash, while Ron had stayed with his parents as they had looked for an estate-management position. 'Well,' I'd said to my Uncle Ron and the assembled company, 'maybe that was something to do with the dates not adding up.'

I'd trailed off. Ron and my cousins had frozen. My cousins' wives, on the other hand, had looked avid with curiosity, asking me what I meant. I'd realised that neither Olive nor Diane, the wives of these men for maybe forty years, had been let into the Big Family Secret, the one that had only emerged after Annie too was dead. Annie, who'd been in service as a chambermaid, had been pregnant when she married Harry. None of the kids had known until Harry and Annie's own hallowed bureau had become open to their generation of children and they'd pieced together, from the various Life Certificates, that Bill had been born very shortly after the marriage.

How strange that all those men – Ron, and my cousins, Richard and Peter – still appeared to carry the shame that Annie should never have had to feel, and chose to keep a century-old family secret a secret still, from their own wives, the women they had shared their lives with. Families. Families are so strange. Anyway, Bill probably went off with his grandmother in case any aspersions were cast, as the couple sought a tied position with a grand house. England's landowners held their staff to a moral standard that was harsh, rather than high. Quietly dispensing with the son conceived on the wrong side of the blanket may have seemed like the safest thing to do. My grandparents' caution paid off, and Harry became the manager of a grand estate.

My mum, like my dad, was the youngest of seven children. When she was little, her family lived in a house in the grounds of Ingatestone Hall in Essex, which is now a National Trust property. Harry's fondness for telling his bosses where to get off had very much extended to the landowner, Lord Peter. At least I thought he was Lord Peter, like Lord Peter Wimsey. Lord Peter had asked Harry to tell his two youngest kids – Win and Tom – to go the long way round when they walked to school instead of using the main driveway, because they lowered the tone. Harry had gone spare, and my mother was still proud of the fervour with which Tom and she had been defended by their dad. Which was fair enough, I reckoned, considering the men were on first-name terms and everything. I'd always assumed that the move from Ingatestone Hall had been something to do with this.

Later, I found that Lord Peter must have been Joseph, 17th Baron Petre, descended from Sir William Petre KG, secretary of state to four successive Tudor monarchs – the first of them Henry VIII – who built Ingatestone Hall in the late sixteenth century. Lord Petre then. Nevertheless, even if you were a daughter of the staff, Ingatestone Hall to Ravenscraig's sprawl is a big leap in twenty years. And neither extreme was actually chosen by my mother, for herself.

Yet Win recast the stories that were written around her. There was a gap in that narrative too, one my mother had made. The reality of how Harry had come to lose his position at Ingatestone Hall, I realised, had always been glossed over. My mother had hinted that there had been other incidents in which Harry's penchant for speaking truth to power had strained the relationship with Lord Petre. The reality had been a bit different.

A bailiff who'd also worked on the estate had hit my grandfather, who had demanded that the man should be fired. Lord Petre had agreed at first, but then changed his mind when he was told about the difficulties that would make for the bailiff's already suffering family. Domestic abuse wasn't a thing that was discussed then, but if a man is free with his fists, his wife and children tend to know it better than anyone else. Harry had resigned when the bailiff was given his job back. Lord Petre, who thought a lot of Harry, had begged him to stay, and also told him that if he was determined to go he could stay in the cottage as long as he liked, until he was set up somewhere else. But Harry had his pride. Or his shame. Shame is an emotion that is often mistaken, by humans, for pride. We tell ourselves that our pride won't let us, when often it's our shame that won't let us. We call it pride because we know we shouldn't feel shame, really, and we're ashamed of that too. It's pretty likely that Harry didn't want to face his staff when they all knew that he'd been punched by the bailiff, and that Lord Petre had backed him, not my grandfather. Harry's authority had been taken from him, which is a horrible thing to take from the man who runs your life and is responsible for your livelihood. So Harry had walked, propelled by his pride, and moved his family straight out of the house.

But Harry had had nowhere to walk to, so the family had been scattered. The older children were married by then but Jean, Win and Tom had still been living at the Hall. Jean had been old enough – fifteen or sixteen – to rent a room for herself in a boarding house. Tom had gone to stay with one of the other married siblings, and Harry and Annie had kept only Win with them. They'd moved in with Ron, his wife Margaret and their two small sons – four adults and three children all living together for months in two rooms in Upminster, above Ron's butcher's shop. Inevitably, under these cramped conditions, there had been some kind of falling-out, and another move, in with other family members, had been hastily cobbled together.

My mother had never mentioned this period in her childhood at all, never admitted how much the family had paid for Harry's principles, never let on that it had actually, at times, all been a bit like something out of a Thomas Hardy novel. Money must have got tight. It had taken Harry a while to find a new position, this time at a farm. Win didn't say much about that place, and I can't remember its name.

She did speak many times, wistful and still indignant, of how a load of stuff from the farm had been thrown, unwanted, into the pond. 'Antiques, they threw in that pond,' she'd say. 'Lovely things. A beautiful pair of Staffordshire dogs. Serving plates.' I'd wish that I could find the pond, dive down and retrieve those things for my mum. I still see that stuff in the green murk of the water, like shipwrecked treasure.

That position couldn't have lasted too long, though, for whatever reason. By the time the Second World War had come the Avises were all in Bird Lane, an end-of-terrace council house: Harry, Annie, Mum, Tom and Jean, who'd also come back home.

Win talked about that time, and about the war, a lot. She used to talk about how the GIs had arrived and how glamorous they seemed. The girls were silly over them, she used to say. Especially Jean, who dyed her legs with tea and got Win to draw on fake seams with an eyebrow pencil to mimic stockings. Sometimes Win would talk about the doodlebugs, and how you knew when you stopped hearing their whine that they had struck. There must have been lots of activity in the sky over Essex, between London and Germany, close to the heavily bombed ports of London's East End. Jean had been waiting, with my grandmother, for a bus outside an Essex pub that got bombed. Glass everywhere. They were knocked over by the blast and cut by the flying debris. The pub had been empty. But how my grandfather had rushed to find them, bouncing along on his bike. He'd thought they were dead.

Harry had lied about his age to join the army for the First World War, just as it was ending. He'd been too old for the Second World War and, anyway, farming was classed as a 'reserved occupation', so necessary to the war effort that it was better not to fight. But he'd taken the Home Guard very seriously. *Dad's Army* was, Win implied, pretty accurate. She loved her dad, but she was scathing about his failure to play a bigger part in either war, just as she'd been scathing about a young neighbour's nervous breakdown when he was serving in Northern Ireland. 'He had to be bought out,' she'd say, 'but he was only a cook!'

People forget how much women colluded in the perpetration of macho culture, and how much we still do. People forget, too, that just knowing that death and destruction is going on around you, even if you don't see it, can burrow into your brain and sicken it. Trauma is a funny thing and it passes down the generations. Your mum and dad may fuck you up, but only because they didn't know how fucked up they were themselves. The generation of men who fought in that war and the one before it – they were all traumatised by it, just as the women and children at home were. They were traumatised further by the knowledge of what had really been going on, which came after. I didn't know until a couple of years ago that Ron had been stationed in Austria as the war drew to a close, and had been in the concentration camps himself, liberating them. People didn't talk about it. They just watched the heroic movies, celebrated the Blitz spirit and buried their trauma.

I knew about the Holocaust from quite an early age. Win told me about it, and about how no one had known about it until the war was over. I didn't really comprehend the enormity of the genocide, though, except for feeling very sorry for Anne Frank. Later, by accident, I saw a bit of *The World at War* on the telly one weekend. I saw clips of emaciated prisoners, and of skeletal bodies being bulldozed into open pits, then sprinkled with lime. Alone in the living room, aged about ten, I stared, transfixed, at moving pictures I've never forgotten. No one forgets them, I imagine.

I was far too young to see such images and be able to process them. If one is ever old enough. People were more careful about what was mentioned and displayed in front of children in those days. Now, you don't even know what your children see, because of the internet. Children probably see far too much. Children today are very anxious.

But that Sunday the telly had just been left on, probably after my dad had been watching some sport. My mum tried to soothe me after I'd seen these things. I remember sitting on her knee and being cuddled, a bit too big to be comfortable any more, while she explained that we'd have been okay if Hitler had won because we were 'blue-eyed and blonde'. Which just confused me more. My mum had brown hair. Wouldn't she have been killed? She explained that it wasn't just what colour your hair was. Dark hair was a hint that you might be Jewish. There was a difference between having normal dark hair and Jewish dark hair. It was a difference I couldn't quite fathom.

People talk about baby boomers now as if they were the blessed generation – the ones who had it all, who enjoyed it, then trashed the future for generations to come. There's truth in all of that. But for the sentinel boomers especially, people in their seventies now, or for people who were little kids during the war, early childhood must have been very strange indeed. Their tender years took place in the overwhelming presence of the war and its aftermath. Yet the defining event of the time was meticulously marginalised in daily lives that were forced always to take account of it, from the moment you got dressed in your rationed clothes and ate your rationed breakfast. Everyone repressed their traumas.

Contrary to the idea that post-war Britain was full of hope, optimism and idealism, adult murmurs wouldn't have encouraged kids to believe that things were going to change soon. The 1950s were much more a time of austerity and struggle than of the renewal and vigour that the legend of the Blitz spirit suggests.

For Win, and for John, in the battle-scarred areas where post-war pessimism was vastly more common than post-war optimism, there wouldn't have been much in the way of counterbalancing enthusiasm about the future. It can only have been a tough business, forging an idea about your place in the world under such circumstances, like trying to do a jigsaw with lots of the most important pieces missing or defaced. That fucking war. The damage it did. The damage it still does. That fucking man. Hitler.

Part of Hitler's early attraction was that he offered a simplistic vision of identity, valorised it and urged people to take pride in it. Totalitarianism needs to cultivate a monoculture attractive to the majority. Totalitarianism also always needs a pathological narcissist at its head, and Hitler is one of history's purest examples of a pathological narcissist taking the malignancy of his disordered personality to its furthest possible extreme – which is attempting to ensure that every single person in the human race reflects your own image of yourself right back at you. If you can't or don't do that for them, truly malignant narcissists will destroy you for it. They will take everything from you that they can. They will kill you if they can get away with it. They will kill millions. Even in a narcissist man or woman far less malignant than Hitler, the dynamic is deeply psychologically dangerous, to both narcissist and victim. It makes everyone unhappy.

It has lately become an intellectual habit for me, parsing humanity to reveal its narcissistic components. It helps me to understand. I understand myself better, my parents, my family, my friends, my society, my world. Sometimes I think my fascination with narcissism is an unhealthy obsession, destructive in itself. Sometimes I think I should just let it all go and walk away.

But I'm narcissistic myself, of course. Far more than my parents were. All writers have some narcissism in them, memoirists more than most. Which is fine. Narcissism exists on a spectrum, and we all need some to get us up in the morning and brushing our teeth. We all need some narcissism so that we can protect ourselves in a scary world, and put on a face to meet the faces that we meet.

Narcissists can be compelling people, talented people. But some of the biggest, baddest shits who have ever walked the earth will also have been narcissists. Warmongers, dictators, fascists, cult leaders. Look inside the mind of any ruthless bastard and you'll find narcissism there in the mix. The dark triad, psychologists call it – narcissism, Machiavellianism, psychopathy. Add sadism, and you're on to the dark quartet. The world's most evil people, the harbingers of terror and chaos. Hitler screwed up the world in other ways, as appalling as the obvious ones. Not only those directly involved in the violence experience post-traumatic stress, not by a long way.

My parents did, and their families. My parents were children during the war, and young adults at the time when the social idea was to wipe away the female liberations that the war brought and guilt-trip women into getting back into the kitchen. Women had discovered that they could work and look after the children without having to care for a demanding and sometimes ungrateful or punitive man as well; that their vulvas didn't fall off if they had sex with a man who wasn't their husband; that they could go to the pub with a pal and have a good time. These were consequences of the war that patriarchal Britain wished to erase. A return to Edwardian values was the formative sociopolitical cause of my parents' late childhood and early adulthood. They signed up. They committed to the project. As the 1960s started to swing, they married and had a daughter. Their part in the post-war project was me.

4

The Dolls

In 1966 my family was drawn into a vast social experiment and everything changed. I'd first got wind of the new life that was awaiting me in fragments, by the usual means that three-and-a-half-year-old children employ – listening intently to what your parents are saying when they assume that you're absorbed in play. At Thistle Street, John and Win had started talking endlessly about 'the compulsory purchase order', 'the towers', 'underfloor heating' and 'our own bathroom'. My parents were being obliged to sell their flat to Motherwell District Council, who would then rehouse them. The bull-dozing of the town's solid nineteenth-century architecture had begun.

Grand-scale post-war modernism, two decades on from Armistice Day, was surging through Scotland and tower blocks were thrusting up into the sky. In five more years, the nation's first home-produced soap opera, *High Living*, would provide gentle observations on the vast social change this new direction in public housing would unleash. The contemporary Scottish comedy-soap, *Still Game*, continues the tradition. A bright, new, optimistic, future-forward so-cial housing crisis had begun. Half a century on and no end to it is in sight. On the contrary.

Back then, my mother's main concern was that we

shouldn't be rehoused in Glencairn Tower. It had gone up, very near Thistle Street, in 1964, two years after I was born. It was quite a thing: a greeny-grey slab block. It was seventeen storeys high and twice as wide as it was tall. It cast a huge shadow. Controversy dogged Glencairn Tower for all of its existence – which, for an iconic building, was short. The social headaches that Glencairn Tower kept on generating ensured that it didn't make it to fifty years old.

It was demolished in 2011, the first steel-framed building of its size to be pulverised in this way in the UK, and perhaps in the world. The collapse was induced by 100 kilos of explosives, set in sixty-four charges. The twisted metal lay in the concrete rubble for weeks, as it all cooled and settled, before the remains were scattered. It was touching to see that surprisingly small pile of debris, touching to see such an imposing monolith brought so low. Even if it had turned out to be a soul-eating monster.

It hadn't taken long for Glencairn Tower to be recognised as one of Motherwell's less covetable places to live. I was never in the building, but I do find myself wondering which side had the more spectacular view. Dead north, over Ravenscraig? Dead south, over the Clyde Valley? Both landscapes, I see now, were special, amazing. But to me, back then, from inside Motherwell's numerous tall buildings? That was just the stuff on the other side of the windows.

By the 1980s Glencairn Tower had earned itself the self-explanatory sobriquet Heroin Heights, and was by all accounts quite the 24/7/365 *Trainspotting*-style kitchen-sink horror movie. Back in the mid-1960s, it would never have occurred to anyone that a malaise as abject as mass heroin addiction could ever take place in the cities and towns of Britain, or would ever be allowed to take place. Some people believe that the insurgence of heroin, in the 1980s, just at the time of deindustrialisation, was a calculated part of the Thatcherist project. They are conspiracy theorists, nothing more. Which doesn't change the fact that unemployment and addiction go hand in hand.

Back in the mid-1960s, though, my mother's particular concern was 'the jumpers'. 'People can't bear living there,' Win told me. 'They hate it so much that they throw themselves out of the windows, poor souls.' I think she said that seventeen people had already done so. I can find no record of these seventeen defenestrators, beyond the imagined visions of them plummeting down to the ground that have stayed with me all my life. We were walking through Motherwell's latest high-rise housing scheme (our own) at the time. Win told me this stuff and I must have been about five. I gazed up at the windows of the nearest building, people, in my mind's eye, tumbling down left, right and centre – not jumping, exactly, but toppling forward from a sitting position, in chairs placed to enjoy those views, tipping slowly and inexorably, almost reluctantly, until gravity did the rest. They were all elderly, these imaginary victims. I guess I assumed that these were the people who wouldn't be able to adjust to the new and modern way of living.

When, early on in the unfolding of the 9/11 atrocities, a television commentator reassured viewers that cladding panels, not human beings, were what could be seen falling from the buildings, I chose to believe him for days. A surprisingly short time after, when *Mad Men* started broadcasting, I simply could not believe that the opening credits included men falling from a tower block. The jumpers. Still jumping. After Grenfell, I found myself wondering whether jumping was preferable to waiting, waiting, waiting for rescue, terrified, only to be burned to death. On the morning London woke up to the Grenfell disaster, I persuaded myself and a number of other people that the occupants of the tower might all have died in their sleep, quietly ushered out of this world by smoke and fumes. This relatively benign vision was crushed by rumours that the mingled remains of twenty-seven or so people were found at the top of the tower, all squeezed into the last room to be consumed. Which seems much more credible. Sometimes, I'm more childish now than I was as a child.

We didn't get an allocation to Glencairn. Instead, we moved into 375 Shields Drive, Muirhouse. Muirhouse was a brand-new scheme on the edge of town, a mixture of tower blocks and five-storey maisonettes, plus rows of garages, to be allocated to the few people who owned their own car and wanted a wee house for it. We didn't have a car yet. That particular arena for familial stress, tension and occasional outbursts of bliss, joy and adventure was, however, soon to come, in the shape of a little second-hand Morris. I think it was a Morris. Maybe a Morris Minor. I'm bad on cars. Like my mother, I've never learned to drive. Unlike my mother, I tried to learn, quite hard.

We were in a top-storey two-floor flat in one of the mai-sonettes, which contained twenty-five flats. Ours was a 'three apartment', as a two-bedroom place was called. It was very bright and white, Muirhouse, with tiny, rough, rather lovely crystals embedded into the pale concrete sides of the build-ings. The towers, with yellow panels under the windows, seemed impossibly high – seventeen floors, like Glencairn, but much more slender and graceful. Up on their roofs – flat, with a central housing for the lifts that was shaped and striped like the black and white Liquorice Allsort – it was gusty and freaky. You'd go up there, full of bravado, heart in your mouth. What if a sudden madness hit you, and you were revealed to yourself, for the seconds you plummeted, the sound of your own final scream all that you could hear, *as a jumper*, like the others?

Access to the roof was soon stopped. Too dangerous for the kids. And maybe for the jumpers. I don't know. But I do know that some of the kids were a menace, to other kids and to the fabric of the place. The elderly were housed at the bottom of the buildings, which seemed like a good idea because there were no stairs to climb. But it was actually an awful idea. They were all down at ground level, where kids ruled the roost and made the lives of the senior citizens a bit of a misery. If pensioners complained to the kids, or about them, they would find themselves subjected to a campaign of hate. Ringing the bell and running away, or, far worse, excrement or burning rubbish posted through their letter-boxes. In the beginning, problems like this generational one had yet to emerge in Muirhouse, although it must have been encountered and ignored already in other parts of Britain.

That's a charitable interpretation, really. Rampaging packs of kids were a long-standing and well-known problem, imported from the tenements, as I'd learned when I was maybe ten, and Valerie Lewis had got to the late stages of a Scotland-wide elocution competition. (I didn't do elocution myself, though I'd have liked to.) Valerie practised and practised, especially her poem, written by Stephen Mulrine. I can still declaim it in my Valerie Lewis elocution voice.

The Coming of the Wee Malkies

Haw missis, whit'll ye dae when the wee Malkies come,
If they dreep doon affy the wash-hoose dyke,
An pit the hems oan the sterrheid light,
An play wee heidies oan the clean close wa,
Missis, whit'll ye dae?

Whit'll ye dae when the wee Malkies come,
If they chap yir door an choke yir drains,
An caw the feet fae yir sapsy weans,
An tummle thur wulkies through yir sheets,
An tip thur ashes oot in the street,
Missis, whit'll ye dae?

Whit'll ye dae when the wee Malkies come,
If they chuck thur screwtaps doon the pan,
An stick the heid oan the sanitry man,
When ye hear thum shauchlin doon yir loaby,
Chanting, 'Wee Malkies! The gemme's a bogey!'
Haw, missis, whit'll ye dae?

But this is still a bit romantic. Some of the problems were very serious. Problems such as local gangs. Early in the life of Muirhouse, graffiti started appearing, proclaiming the formation of 'Muir Toi'. Win told me that she didn't know what the words meant but that they had been put there by vandals who were 'bad boys'. Negative as it may have been, this graffiti was pretty much the first indication that I noticed, really, of any form of community cohesion at all.

'Toi' is a Scottish word for a gang. Tois, at that time, had been a Scottish tradition for about a hundred years. Despite its horrors, Scottish gang culture was quite romanticised. A book that everyone read at that time, including me and my parents, was *No Mean City*, written in 1935 by Herbert Kingsley Long and Alexander McArthur and telling the story of Johnnie Stark, one of the 'razor kings' of Glasgow's Gorbals.

Likewise the Tongs, the teenage criminal gang that operated ruthlessly in the Calton area of Glasgow, were famous, celebrated even, like the area's Barrowland Ballroom. The word 'Toi' had itself come from Calton, where a notorious nineteenth-century gang, the San Toys, had ruled the area with great violence. The Tongs had evolved from that original group, and so had this more general word for a teen gang, Toi. Tois had spread over the west of Scotland, so Muir Toi followed a kind of tradition as it spray-painted its name around the place and made its presence known in other, simple, destructive ways. Calton is still the place in Britain with the lowest life expectancy, at fifty-four. This was the culture that was being acknowledged and venerated in our new scheme by kids brought up to aspire to petty, pointless destruction and keen to make their mark.

Which they did. Hardly anyone had a phone in their home, so public phone boxes were a precious resource. The phones were always being broken and when they did work, conversations were conducted to the background noise of glass crunching under feet. The booths stank of urine. A few months into the Great Experiment, all the sapling trees had been snapped. Muirhouse would be a different place now if those trees were in their fifties, like me, the white towers emerging from a canopy of leaves that would undulate in the wind, like a green sea beneath the windows, or glisten below them in the winter, dark bark shimmering under a white hoar frost.

Funnily enough, the open, grassy place where the largest concentration of trees were planted became the site for a building that should have been part of Muirhouse from the start – a community centre. It opened, named after local councillor Isa Money, maybe as much as a decade after the scheme had been fully occupied, in around 1974, by which time the community was already in some trouble. I once went to a disco there. I found the atmosphere quite threatening. But I found most things involving people that I didn't know quite threatening then. Now, my discomfort around people I don't know is disguised enough for them to be entirely unsuspecting. I like to think.

There have been many other remedial interventions in Muirhouse since: the usual fixes, like cladding, and less cosmetic ones, like sports fields, much needed and much used. However, the marshland that was drained to make those sports fields would almost certainly be protected now as a valuable natural habitat.

The marshland, for a time, was my kingdom. I had many of those during my childhood. Whatever its shortcomings, the truly wonderful thing about Muirhouse was that it was on the edge of lush, rich and varied countryside. I gathered my territories slowly, moving further away from the flat as I got to know this copse, that stream, a hedgerow, a field, a wood. The marsh was an early passion because it was right by the scheme, only about eighty yards from our building. I was probably about nine when I went marsh-crazy.

I spent hours on those few acres, fascinated by something I understood as a world apart, but didn't know then was an ecosystem: caddis grubs, which made little tubular homes for themselves from their own silk and the water's detritus; water boatmen, the long-legged insects that skittered across the surface like a six-armed man rowing a scull; dragonflies and damselflies; diving beetles and whirligig beetles; frogs and newts, sometimes even a great crested. I got all the names from my Ladybird book, *Pond Life*. Those illustrations are printed on my mind.

There were always lots of meadow brown butterflies – masses of them. Bulrushes grew in the marsh, and great reedmace, which people generally call bulrushes by mistake. Once I took some reedmace home for Win to put in a vase instead of the artificial ones I didn't like because they were hard, not soft, plastic covered in nylon flock, in garish reds, oranges and blues. But the rushes made a mess. The big, brown velvety sausages of flower were teeming with meadow brown caterpillars which wriggled about, spilling seeds (200,000 seeds can be produced from a single inflorescence!). Today I have Win's green and brown vase that the reedmace stood in. It's fashionable again, that vase, as all those vintage German ceramics from the 1970s are. Some of them are ugly, but I always thought ours was a particularly nice example. Win had good taste, and in our modernist flat the vase fitted right in, like the bureau did.

The new scheme was a strange place to live, but we liked our flat – living room and kitchen downstairs, two bedrooms, our own bathroom and a big cupboard upstairs. There was a nook under the stairs that wasn't quite big enough to do anything with, although some of the more game families risked breakfast bars at which the unlucky sitters in the low bit had to crouch. We had an immersion heater, which prompted two of the most-heard phrases in the family idiolect. They were 'Who switched that water on?' and 'Who didn't switch that water off?' But nothing was used more than 'Put that light off.'

I still love the joke about the Yorkshireman on his deathbed.

> 'Steven? Are you here?'
> 'I'm here, Dad.'
> 'Mary? Are you here?'
> 'I'm here, Dad.'
> 'Bethany? Are you here?'
> 'I'm here, Grandad.'
> 'Aaron? Are you here?'
> 'I'm here, Grandad.'
> 'Then why's that hall light on?'

John and Win would have been *magnificent* in a post-apocalyptic dystopia. Mag. Nif. I. Cent. Or a war. We were often told by Win about how the privations of the war had shaped her. My brother once dumbfounded a newly married young neighbour by solemnly explaining to her that he knew she didn't take sugar in her tea 'because you've been through the war'. How my dad had developed his own tea-taking habits didn't quite fit. He took two heaped teaspoons throughout his life. Maybe it was, after the war, a luxury he cherished. In Motherwell, taking your tea without sugar was a privation few people had much truck with.

There was great excitement over our 'underfloor heating', which waned as we discovered that you had to put your foot under the rug to know that it was on. And often we weren't sure even then. I can see Win now, one slipper off, corner of the golden rectangle of shaggy rug in her hand, pressing her tan popsocked sole into the carpet and shaking her head.

You couldn't decorate at first, not until the building had 'settled'. But when that day came, Win splashed out on hessian wallpaper with Real String for the 'feature wall'. The texture contrasted with the fun-fur cushions on the sofa, in bright blue, lime green, red and buttercup yellow (they matched the artificial bulrushes). They'd sit in a row, balanced on one of their corners, diamond-shaped. I realised a few years ago that I have pretty much the same four colours of cushions in my living room in London. Mum called the living room at Shields Drive 'the lounge', though. The bureau, of course, was in the lounge. Win did two painting-by-numbers scenes of Chinese seascapes, a pair of long oblongs that hung above the bureau. They fascinated me. The red-sailed junk! The fisherman in his big, wide hat! (In my twenties, I went to Hong Kong and China to see these things for myself. In Hong Kong I sailed in a red-sailed junk.

Some of the landscapes from the train to Guangzhou were pleasingly familiar.) When I was about nine I made a string picture at school, and it was hung over the mantelpiece, above our lamps whose bases were bottles covered by Win in Polyfilla. These things were all the rage, although our great yearning was for a carboy to grow ferns in. John was unable ever to procure one. But, still. The 1970s were coming! Even to Motherwell!

It was at this time that the crockery, the ornaments and the christening silver began moving out of the glass display section of the bureau and the dolls started moving in. At first, there were just a couple of Scottish dolls and a couple of Welsh ones. But this was the time when the package holiday was becoming available to working people, and our neighbours slowly began to venture abroad. My parents were scathing about all this. The Mackies along the landing went to Spain, to Win's disdain. 'So,' she said, upon their return. 'The Mackies are back. They don't look very tanned, do they? Sun was probably too hot for them. Silly. Waste of money.'

To the faces of these intrepid types, though, Win was demurely enthusiastic. She started asking people to bring back a doll, 'for Deborah'. Before long, the Scottish and Welsh dolls were joined by several from Spain and a couple from Holland. Then there was a Portuguese doll, then a doll from the Tyrol with a blonde plait round her head and a braided skirt. Then one dressed in a skirt of violet, with violet flowers on her apron, a straw hat on her head and tiny violets in her hand. She was delightful, but God knows where she was supposed to be from. One arrived from India, in a beautiful, sheer pink sari with a gold border over a red choli, her black hair pinned back, a bindi on her forehead and gold bracelets on her wrists. Then the first of the lady dolls in trousers – and

69

the last. She was an Arab doll with a gauzy blue veil trimmed in silver, a blue velvet jacket and cotton plaid pantaloons. Maybe she was Persian. Who knew? This was all early in the days of Arab nationalism as a major geopolitical force, let alone Islamism.

Soon there was a decent row of dolls, mostly the same reproduction of a slender female, with hair and facial colouring adapted to suit the region from which she allegedly came. I ached to visit all of those regions myself and see these costumes on real people. In the part of London where I lived until recently, it was by no means unusual to see people dressing, on festival days, in Portuguese national costume, like my dolls come to life.

Though from the arms of those living humans, no octagonal black tags dangled. These, on the dolls, were emblazoned with white writing, in capitals: COLLECTORS COSTUME DOLLS BY REXARD. Then in much smaller letters: EMPIRE MADE. I wanted to take these labels off, but Mum said they should stay on, as the collection might become valuable one day. The dolls all came in squishy clear plastic tubes from which we recklessly liberated them.

Then people started buying us dolls whenever they saw them, and we acquired historical dolls too – Mary, Queen of Scots and Elizabeth I, the family resemblance of course being absolutely uncanny. The fabrics became cheaper and more synthetic as time went on. I noticed, but I didn't care. I adored this collection of dolls. Like my stamps – every child collected stamps at this time, pretty much – they connected me to the forbidden and therefore tantalising *world*. And they were so pretty, in their costumes, in their variety and in their essential sameyness.

There were eventually about seventy dolls. I took them from Clyde Terrace when Win had died and they stayed on crowded display in the bureau for a few years, a bit drunken-looking, because when they toppled over no one tended to right them very often. Win had had them all anchored with Blu Tack, but I couldn't be bothered. Eventually, detached limbs and various accessories accumulated in a pile in a corner of the bureau, waiting patiently for the day when I took up the superglue and started renovations. That day will never come now. There wasn't room for them in my new place, so I kept my seven favourites, plus the two loo-roll-holder dolls, and gave the Tudor cousins to Andrew, my friend who'd visited Win in the hospice. All the rest went to a charity shop. I still can't believe that I did such a thing. I'd coveted those dolls for so long.

I'd first asked for them in 1987, when I bought my own flat in Brixton, but Win was always weird about allowing things out of Clyde Terrace, even the sleeping bag my Essex gran had bought me for Guide camp when I was ten, which Mum wouldn't let me take to university. It lay, never used, in a cupboard in Clyde Terrace for years and she finally offered it to me when I was about forty-five and my own kids were starting to go camping. By then, I just laughed and told her that sleeping-bag technology had moved on. A tiny battle, fought over decades. A small victory in a long war. Like with the dolls.

'I wondered if I could take my dolls for the flat, Mum.'

'The dolls? Why would you think you could do that?'

'Well, you know . . . They're mine. You always said they were mine.'

'They were yours when you were little. They're mine now.'

'Maybe just a few of them?'

'That would break up the collection.'

But they *were* mine. I fretted over the fact that Win would neither let me have them, nor share them with me.

You wouldn't imagine that a person could develop such a complicated and ambivalent relationship with a bunch of dolls. But I did. I resented my mother over them. Such a waste of emotion. I like the saying, which was not one of my mother's, 'Resentment is like drinking poison and waiting for the other person to die.' I like it. But I find it hard to live by.

Anyway ... while it sounds petty – resenting people helping themselves to your bits and pieces, or pretending they're gathering them for you when really they maintain psychological ownership – it tramples over your boundaries and tells you in tiny, constant messages that you may be part of them but they are not part of you. I've always had problems with boundaries of ownership, never been sure what the rules really are. I give people things they don't want and advice they don't want. I let people take things too, when I shouldn't. Even small idiosyncrasies in parenting can affect kids for ever. I didn't see that until my parents were dead, and I'd already failed to mother well myself. It's hard to see patterns until you start looking for them. I see them now.

When I first moved in with my former husband, for example, he inspected my collection of books, plucking the ones he fancied out of the shelves and taking them up to his office, along with other little bits and pieces he took a shine to, like a table lighter and a couple of racks of vintage wire in-trays that I'd joyfully found in a skip. He didn't ask, or mention it in any way, and I tried and failed not to mind. And that sense of entitlement wasn't just about things. He once told me, early in our marriage: 'I'm jealous of your thoughts, because they're inside you.' For him it seemed an ardent declaration of love, but for me it was one of the creepiest things I'd ever heard. He and Win were alike in that way. What's yours was theirs and what's theirs was their own. That was actually one of Win's phrases. She'd say it and laugh. 'What's yours is mine, and what's mine's my own.' Ha, ha, ha!

The dolls, though, in the modernist bureau, in the modernist home, from the modernist package holidays? They were kitsch by the time they came to me, old junk really. But those few that I kept have outlasted the confounding relationship that provided an excuse for their collection. They have outlasted my mother. I think they will outlast me. They are still under protective glass, where I see them every day. I even reattached some arms, which don't match the skin tone of the faces. They have also outlasted the flat in Shields Drive in which the first dolls started to form themselves into ranks.

Some of the apartment blocks in Muirhouse have just been pulled down, beyond saving. Others, like our old one, have been remodelled and gussied up. Our entire floor of the maisonette was eventually sliced off, and 375 Shields Drive, Muirhouse, Motherwell ML1 2EF – our address, which we kids had to learn in case we got lost and needed help – became a ghost address.

In the beginning, when we moved in, very few public amenities had been provided. There was a little shopping centre with plenty of slabbed space, I guess in the expectation of a town-square vibe that never coalesced. It was on two levels, with six shops: a draper, a chemist, a grocer, a newsagent, a butcher and a hairdresser. Theoretically quite stylish, in a modest way. I found both the draper and the chemist intimidating. They were silent and formal, and their carefully chosen stock seemed a bit esoteric, the expression of knowledge and expertise. You had to know what you were talking about to buy things in these places. I felt too ignorant, too much of an outsider and an ingénue to talk to the shopkeeper, or even to meet her eye in case she spoke to me. In many respects, shyness is just a debilitating fear of being rumbled. I'd listen to my mother talk to the ladies, all of the women in full command of their side of a bewildering adult transaction, respecting each other's view and enjoying themselves as they talked, expert to expert. Sometimes my mother would speak in whispers and gestures to the chemist. This meant that she was buying Tampax. I'd explored a box one day, in the privacy of the bathroom. But I still had no idea what these little white mice in cardboard telescopes were for. Once, my mum came out of the chemist feeling insulted, having been served by a young woman who was new. 'She asked me if I wanted "super"! The cheek of it. My God. What sort of woman does she think I am?'

I had absolutely no idea what she was going on about and wasn't going to risk asking. Clearly, I was meant to know. Yet I wouldn't learn of the existence of vaginas, regular, super or super-plus until biology class in secondary school. The other girls – for all science was taught to girls and boys separately – were red-faced with their attempts to silence their giggles, even the ones I'd imagined were as innocent as myself, like Daisy, who was often away from school and wore a dark, curly wig. I was utterly rapt, listening closely to every word our teacher, Mr Westwood, intoned.

I never set foot in the hairdresser's. Win cut my hair and she cut her own. Professional hair-cutting was for my dad and my brother, because male hair needed more skilful and complicated cutting. The short back and the short sides, my mother explained, were too difficult for home hairdressing.

We didn't use the shops that much, apart from Tommy's. Tommy was the newsagent and going to buy the paper from him was a Saturday ritual, along with a fry-up and John's visit to the bookies to put that week's bets on, after he'd studied the race card in the *Express*. Everyone loved Tommy's and loved Tommy's penny tray, which would be brought out from under the counter to reveal a cornucopia of Fruit Salads, Black Jacks, foamy bananas, sherbet flying saucers, gobstoppers and jelloid dummy tits. We'd go to the chemist as little as possible after the tampon incident, mainly if we had a prescription to fill, or if Win had earache and urgently needed one of the tiny bottles of olive oil you could buy for medicinal purposes. When I went to university and found that this medicine was routinely used for frying, I was absolutely gobsmacked. For frying we used lard. ALWAYS. It would harden back to white as it cooled, and when there were too many bits in it it would be scraped out and thrown away, wrapped in newspaper. As for olive oil in salad dressings – staggering. What was wrong with honest Heinz Salad Cream, deliciously tangy? Everything possible, I came to understand.

We'd only use the grocer, Jimmy Gallagher's, at a push. I remember being sent to Jimmy Gallagher's on my own for the first time, at about seven years old. Total ordeal. I was so ludicrously self-conscious.

'A plain loaf, please.'

'Whit?'

'A . . . plain loaf . . .' My eyes fill with tears.

'Ye'll need tae speak up, hen!'

'Plain loaf?'

'A pan loaf?'

I shake my head, overcome with misery. Jimmy hands me a plain loaf. Thank God there were only two kinds of bread in Scotland back then.

Of course, a boy offered to check my money for me

outside because, he kindly explained, Jimmy Gallagher had a terrible reputation for short-changing people. He pretended to count it for maybe a second, then legged it. Some people never learn, and I'm one of them. But the boy's story was so plausible. He seemed so concerned. And Jimmy Gallagher *was* a bad lot. Jimmy Gallagher owned lots of property – the adults said he was rich, in a way that suggested that all wealth denoted essential dishonesty. 'He owns that whole row, they say,' I remember Win remarking, nodding in disgust towards a terrace of four bay-windowed Victorian houses across the dual carriageway from his shop, next to the Gulf petrol station. Plus Jimmy's shop was dirty, and uncleanliness was, in the absence of God, the unforgivable sin.

In the presence of God, however, it seemed that uncleanliness was fine. Next door to our flat was Miss Nelly O'Brien's, and Miss O'Brien took her Catholicism more seriously than most. Both she and her wheelchair-bound sister had lived there at first, in a *What Ever Happened to Baby Jane?* arrangement. The other sister had died there, quite soon after we'd all moved in, and the curtains were never reopened after her wake. I associated the fetid smell of Nelly's flat with death.

Sometimes, when I was locked out, waiting on the landing for Mum to come home, Miss O'Brien would insist that I waited at hers – she was very kind and sweet. I'd sit there, marvelling at the filth and untidiness, breathing through my mouth and hoping against hope that she didn't offer to make me another bowl of cream of mushroom soup, an experience that had made me feel that I was eating vomit while trying not to vomit.

The words 'cream of mushroom soup' still give me the heave. When that old lady used to tell us on the telly that with Campbell's Soup, 'the difference was in the thickness',

I would always just think about the thickness, the incredible thickness, of Nelly's dust and how it might creep over a bowl of cream of mushroom soup, given time. Once, I admired Nelly's Mass cards, which were spilling grungily out of a basket under the telly in their thousands. She gave me some to take home, and my father was furious at the invasion of these Papish accoutrements into our own clean, Protestant dwelling. Obviously, he always called her Smelly Nelly. My dad was funny, but his humour was cruel. Everyone had a secret, unflattering nickname. My Aunt Phyllis, on tranquillisers, was Phil the Pill. My cousin Alan, with his almond-shaped eyes, was The Wee Chinaman. A girl in the neighbourhood with a steatopygian figure was known to us as Mantelpiece Arse. (Mantelpiece arses were generally a sign of being a Catholic, but this girl's was a prime example.) No one's frailties or oddities were overlooked. They were seized upon. But we all lapped it up. When John was joking, he was in high spirits. John's high spirits were wickedly infectious. I still treasure my favourites among his jokes. Like on a day trip to Ayr, when an acquaintance had chided him for chucking away a sandwich.

Her: 'There are starving people in India.'

Him: 'Aye. But I cannae throw it that far.'

Or when our dog, Tina, had come into the house and dropped the upper part of a sparrow at his feet, just as the nation was gripped by a BBC adaptation of an Evelyn Waugh novel.

'Birdshead Regurgitated!'

Being kids, we were always asking our parents where things were, and Dad turned his irritation into a joke.

'Where are my pyjamas?'

'In the pyjamerie.'

'Dad!'

'Where's my drawing book?'

'In the drawingbookerie.'

'Dad!'

We eventually stopped asking and found our stuff ourselves.

Jokes and wit are a social currency, which made my father a very rich man, much richer than Jimmy Gallagher.

The grocer's that used to be Jimmy Gallagher's is much bigger now – with a huge front extension into the failed town square – and has been run for years by Scottish Asians, like the corner shop in *Still Game*. There are a few other shops on the scheme now too, mostly takeaways. Such establishments were unheard of in the 1960s, apart from chip shops. The first Chinese place in Motherwell was called the Sha Tin. It was above the Jobcentre. *Honestly.*

There's still no pub on the scheme itself, as far as I'm aware, though the Bullfrog's still there, beyond the scheme's foot, in Flemington. When I was a kid it looked lovely, with its asymmetric sloping roof, like a Swiss chalet, and its zig-zaggy steel balcony and big white bedded-out window boxes. That reminded me of *Heidi*, the children's novel I loved so much. Now it's a grim pub, largely hanging on, sparsely populated by people without much cash, all of its architectural zing rubbed away by the years and its window boxes long rotted away.

There had been a little filling station in Flemington, next to the Bullfrog, a smart little white one, but it had gone out of business with the coming of the Gulf at the top of the hill and been abandoned. You could just walk in. I'd become friends with Jim McCrumb, who lived in the tower next to our maisonette. We'd spend all day together, every day, in the Easter holidays of 1970. I know it was 1970, because the two of us were obsessed with Bible John. Everyone was. We considered ourselves detectives and I'd decorated the cover of a notebook with the serial killer's name, for our notes. All this was a secret from our parents, though if Jim ever did have parents I don't remember them. We combed through the files in the filling station – old invoices, MOT certificates – searching for clues. If we could catch Bible John, we'd be heroes.

It's easy to explain why Scotland, and Lanarkshire in particular, was so gripped by Bible John – and still is. Partly it was just that everyone knew very well what might come. Serial killers were not new to the area. Peter Manuel, just a couple of stops away from Motherwell on the train in Uddingston, had been convicted of murdering seven people in 1958 and was reckoned to have killed two more. He'd already served time for a string of sexual attacks before the murders. He had defended himself in a rape case in Airdrie – basically part of the Motherwell conurbation – and had got away with it.

So, when Bible John started his own little reign of terror – first beating, raping and killing a twenty-five-year-old nurse, Patricia Docker, who'd been at Glasgow's famous Barrowland Ballroom in Calton, where the Tongs had their base, then doing the same to another Barrowland dancer and mother of three, Jemima McDonald – there was a real sense that if he wasn't stopped he would do it again, and again, and again. Everyone was scared and it was contagious.

The press ramped it all up, coining the nickname because witnesses said that the man who had been chatting up Jemima peppered his conversation with biblical quotes. But the police, who had badly mishandled the Manuel case, ramped it up too. They released the first composite drawing of a suspect ever commissioned in Scotland, let it be known that undercover policewomen had been operating at the Barrowland and generally pressed on with the biggest manhunt Scotland had ever seen. Bible John killed one more woman, Helen Puttock, and then it stopped.

The killing stopped, anyway. The fear went on for years. The women he killed had all been menstruating, and the killer had left a sanitary towel or tampon on or under their bodies. It was so obvious that these people had been killed for being women. Even Jim and I, young as we were, knew that he would have done all that to any woman he could, to our own mothers. Bible John's real identity still isn't known. Some people think it was Peter Tobin, who has done time for a double rape and is in prison now for the murders of three women. Others believe that Bible John may have been the Gloucester serial killer Fred West, who was in Scotland at that time.

There are endless theories and there's an endless desire to hear them. I'll never stop wanting to know. I'll never stop knowing that such men exist, and that they kill women to make themselves feel superior and powerful. All women know. We may not know the names of the psychological theories behind the actions of such people. We may not want to. But all women know that, for some men, being a woman is enough to justify annihilation. We know too that there are plenty of other men, far less extreme in their proclivities, who share the same feeling that women are less than they are. Some women even agree, in part because they fear doing otherwise, in part because they want to share that feeling of superiority. Supporting such men in their efforts to maintain the status quo makes the women feel safer and more valuable. People ask why women, in 2016, voted for Donald Trump. That's certainly part of the answer.

The Goldwater Rule, part of the guidelines set up by the

American Psychiatric Association, prohibits speculation on any psychological disorders or conditions a person may exhibit unless they have been professionally examined. Loose talk about Trump's mental state is discouraged. Convicted serial killers like Tobin and West are given no such slack. They are uncontroversially considered to have been psychopaths, which is the popular name for a person with antisocial personality disorder.

This label doesn't quite explain why a person might kill only women, simply because they are women. It's narcissists who belittle others who are unlike them, narcissists who other, narcissists who will destroy people who fail to give them the unconditional respect and instinctive understanding of their needs that they feel they deserve. A person with both narcissistic personality disorder and antisocial personality disorder is called a malignant narcissist. They may not kill. But they will still find a woman to control, abuse and manipulate, with no guilt, remorse or pity. Often, no one else will suspect that the predator is anything other than a wonderful partner and the woman will be made to feel that her unhappiness is due to her own oversensitivity. This is the foundation of gaslighting, the main technique of psychological abuse in relationships.

Some believe that Bible John's campaign of terror may simply have been a series of stag nights in the run-up to his entrapment of the ideal female who would become a long-term victim, running a home and providing children for him as a cover and a bonus. At that point in his psychological disturbance, a woman who appeared to him to be willing to have sex with him would have seemed empty of respect for him as an about-to-be-married man, empty of respect for the woman he had chosen and, of course, empty of respect for herself as a woman too. Killing such a woman would have been a favour to the world in the eyes of Bible John. All girls grow up in the fearful knowledge, conscious or unconscious, that men such as these exist.

5

A Little White Prayer Book

The filling station where Jim and I searched for signs of Bible John is long gone now, a little row of three more takeaways in its place. Red-brick, featureless, functional, with no attempt having been made to create a place where you might want to hang out. But there had been a place in Flemington for teenagers to hang out in the 1960s and 1970s. The Glen Café. On a corner, it was faced on the outside with pale blue ceramic tiles, custom-made, with the café's name in black. Very smart. Peering inside, when I used to pass by, I could see booths and a jukebox, like on a film set in 1950s America. I'd longed for the time when I'd be able to go there myself. But it never came. The Glen Café is long gone too, a road in its place.

There was nothing like that – nothing so stylish and welcoming – on the scheme. On the contrary, the idea seems to have been that places to hang out attract the wrong sort. When I look at architectural models, with their tiny people frozen mid-bustle in the community, I wonder what the planners envisaged for Muirhouse. Something. They did try. But what was the vision? Kids playing peever – Scottish hopscotch? There were certainly enough paving slabs for it, and actually we did play sometimes, throwing an old shoe-polish tin with stones in it. Once, and only once, we got our parents down to watch the play we had created. Our audience sat at right angles to us, on benches. Merryton Tower's sheltered atrium doorway was our awkward stage.

But none of the community spaces in Muirhouse ever worked, all those vast, slabbed emptinesses, with municipal shrubbery round the sides and little concrete benches topped with chunky hardwood planks dotted about. It would be rare to see an adult ever sitting on one of them. I only remember that time when mothers perched and watched the play their children had written. Even the drunks didn't sit on them.

A few months into the move into our new community, maybe a bit longer, it was clear that it wasn't that good a neighbourhood, any more than Glencairn Tower was. Lots of aspects of actually living there hadn't been thought about. Or of dying there. Miss O'Brien's wake had gone without much incident. But in the thirteen towers it was a different matter. The lifts were too small to accommodate a horizontal coffin, so bodies had to be taken down in a chair. If your tradition was to have a wake at home, this was difficult, especially if you were high up. It was very hard on the Catholics.

There were huge bins around the scheme, aluminium, open-topped, on wheels. Looking back, I see that the idea for our three bins was that you'd go up the stairs to the pavilion under the tower next door and drop the rubbish over the railings. But what you actually got was frail widows and spinsters leaving their rubbish at the bottom of the bins, because they were at least eight feet high and you had to have quite a throw on you to basketball the stuff in. Thus: rats. Also, the bins filled with rain, so everything was pretty rank and disgusting, floating in there. You could see in from our flat. It gave you, as they say in Lanarkshire, 'the boke'. How town planners forget about rain in the west of Scotland I'll never comprehend.

Therefore, and in fairly short order, the community room that had been designed into each maisonette had to be converted into a bin room. That was how the concrete platform came to be there, the one that I had stood on in fake nonchalance while kids threw bricks at me. They put in a platform, so that people could stand on it and reach the bins to sling their rubbish in, and made big doors to get the bins out for emptying. The outer wall of the building had been knocked down but the doors hadn't been installed, making something approximating a much better stage than the tower's entrance, suddenly set into the middle of the ground floor of our block. With a big pile of bricks next to it. These were the days before health and safety had been invented by the fiendish Common Market.

Otherwise, and most disastrously of all, kids ruled at ground level, unwatched by their parents high above them. Kids got up to all kinds of mischief – sometimes it was just mischief, sometimes it was awful stuff, like torturing and killing animals. The Toi kids always had something nasty to prove, to themselves and everyone else. At the little playground you'd have to check that a blown-up frog hadn't been smeared on the slide. There were three slabs of concrete under each swing so that the grass wouldn't get damaged. The health and safety of the grass came first, before that fiendish Common Market, once again, bustled bossily along.

In the 1990s, when we were in our early thirties, while the building was empty and before work had started on slicing our two floors away, David and I found a loose board and sneaked into our old, empty building and our old, empty home. We marvelled at how big the rooms had been, how full of light it was. Upstairs the raw pine floorboards were still pale, clean and new-looking. They must always have been covered by carpet. The view from the lounge was stunning, not least because one of the maisonettes between us and the Clyde Valley had gone. We had always been able to see a sliver of the countryside, all the way up to the horizon. Now it was a vast panorama, a view to covet.

I remember sitting on the wide ledge of the picture window in the lounge, not long after we'd moved in. Win was standing beside me, holding me in a cuddle, and asking me an important question about a new thing that was starting up for pre-school kids in our modern neighbourhood.

'Do you want to go to play school?'

'No! I want to go to real school!'

I couldn't wait. I loved to draw, but I wanted to learn to write. Learning to write seemed more important than learning to read. I drew lines of squiggles on a little 'magic pad' – a blue plastic screen with carbon paper underneath that you'd draw or write on with a stylus and then clear by moving another piece of plastic, a bit like the reed on a loom.

'Look, Mummy! This looks like real writing, doesn't it?'

'Oh, sweetheart. It's not real writing.'

'But it *looks like* real writing!'

I was hurt that she didn't get what I meant, that I had *the gist* of what writing was. The tiny things that hurt kids and that kids remember for ever. How could a parent know? And the tiny things that delight them. Once, while my mum went upstairs, I swept the kitchen floor.

'Notice anything different, Mummy?'

'Nooo . . .'

'I swept the kitchen floor for you.'

'Oh! I did notice that! I thought it was funny! I thought I'd done it myself and not remembered. Such a good job!'

A kindly bluff I grew up and cottoned on to.

Our maisonette stood at right angles to a T-junction in the road which led up to the hallowed Timbers, where our unknown future awaited us. From the picture window in the lounge you could see the Catholic primary school, St Brendan's, with the Catholic chapel, also St Brendan's, being built beside it. Opposite, on the other side of the road, was St Margaret's Church, which had been there for a while. The old church had become the church hall and a newer, rather stylish modernist church with a huge, fat steeple had replaced it, having been built in anticipation of larger, scheme-based congregations.

I'd go to the church, occasionally, for services with the school, and once I went with my English grandmother, who didn't like the stark Presbyterian vibe. The only time I went with my parents was when Uncle Wullie married Aunt Elizabeth. Elizabeth Gray. They're my last surviving Scottish aunt and uncle. I was the bridesmaid from our side of the family and Myra, who would go on to win medals for Scottish country dancing and appear on *Junior Showtime*, was from the Grays' side. All the Gray sisters wore beehives and wanted us bridesmaids to have them too. This was my first time that I remember in a hairdresser's, and it took hours. At the end, my beehive was fat and Myra's was tall. Win said an emphatic 'No' when Elizabeth, the nervous bride who wanted everything to be perfect, querulously asked if mine could be redone. Win had made our pink satin bridesmaids' dresses, so she was in a good position to draw the line. John – best man – didn't even have to be called upon to appeal. Later, at the reception, while my dad stood at the centre of the guests as they raucously sang 'For He's a Jolly Good Fellow' (the Grays being a rather more sociable family than the Orrs), Win gestured wildly for him to leave the ring.

'What's wrong?' he asked her.

'You looked like an idiot, just standing there – the proverbial spare tit at the wedding,' she hissed, and went off in a huff.

Though this wedding was my only foray into the local church with my parents, I did receive religious instruction there. Mrs Devon and Miss Moffatt, both on the ground floor of the maisonette, had asked my mum if they could take me to Sunday school and I went for a while because you did handcrafts there and I loved the coloured plates in my Holy Bible. I'd wear my Sunday best to go, including my white patent Mary Janes and my white nylon gloves. Sometimes, Win would do my hair in my party style. She'd plait the hair from the crown of my head and pin it into a circle on top. I loved it. It was my princess hair-do. The first time I went to Sunday school, I took my little white prayer book as well as the Bible. Which was probably its only outing. It had been a christening present. It was still in the bureau after my parents died.

I have the book and its presentation box in front of me as I write. The lid of the box is decorated with gold printed over white to make a pattern of delicate feathers. The little book itself is bound in white calf, or maybe fake white calf. It's hard to tell. An elegant symbol, also gold, is all that's on the front. I don't understand it now any more than I did when I was small. It looks very religious and a letter 'S' is prominent. It is, gold capitals on the spine tell me, a book of:

COMMON
PRAYER
HYMNS
A&M
(ANCIENT AND
MODERN)

Inside the paper is thin and Bible-y, also edged in gold.

The little white prayer book has no illustrations, apart from a poorly reproduced little black and white picture of Christ as a frontispiece, captioned 'The Light of the World (Holman Hunt)'. There's a blue biro inscription on the inside of the flyleaf in familiar handwriting: 'To Deborah from Aunt Jean Uncle Bob Elizabeth Jane and John 24/3/63.' So, a christening present from English relatives, but produced, a blue and white sticker on the end of the box tells me, by Collins Clear Type Press, a London imprint of the venerable Glasgow publisher Wm Collins Sons & Co. Ltd. Odd. The Kirbys were no more religious than we were. I'm not religious at all. But the prayer book is something I'll keep. I'm not sure why it feels wrong to let it go, just as I'm not sure what it symbolises. Maybe that period, the period that had spanned my life at that time, in which Christianity became something people saw as important to their ideas about family and culture without actually having faith themselves. Then they even stopped believing that Christianity was important to anything other than the rituals of birth, marriage and death – the Protestants anyway. Nowadays, a passionate belief in religion plays a large part only in politics, ideology and violence. Or so it can seem to us atheists.

It was strange, really, the way that religion was all around us, shaping our lives so much, lurking for ever in the bureau, even though we were an atheist family. Win wanted me to make up my own mind about it all. 'I think Jesus was a very great and wise man,' she told me solemnly. 'But I don't think he was the son of God. At Sunday school, you can decide what you believe for yourself.'

The Jesus stuff didn't stick. There were also a few attempts at Girls' Brigade, another religious organisation for children with a troupe at St Margaret's. But it was too . . . *brigadey*.

Very militaristic. Sashes, standing to attention, marching. Dullsville, as John would always say. The manse, at the other end of the row to the church, was large, quite grand. I never went inside, but I loved the cherry trees in the garden. The daffodils bloomed early there. It's derelict now, that house.

Muirhouse primary school was behind these church buildings, just as St Brendan's was behind the chapel. The two schools, across from each other, had been built simultaneously and to the same design, with a one-storey wing where the offices were, classrooms for the infants and a square, five-storey block for the rest of the classes. The only difference in the two buildings was that St Brendan's had brown tiles, brown being a Catholic colour, and Muirhouse primary had blue ones, blue being a Protestant colour. Not that Muirhouse primary was officially Protestant. It was multi-denominational. Anyone could go. Segregation was the Catholics' fault. We weren't that petty, we didn't think we were so special. All of the pupils at the school were Protestants, however, all being not-special together. Two schools and two narcissistic groups, willed by God.

When I was taken to the school outfitter, the shop assistant did what I dreaded and spoke to me. She asked me what school I was going to, and I replied: 'The Protestant one.' My mother was embarrassed, but the two women laughed. As well they might. Though the absurd situation had been made by adults, not by children. Lanarkshire apartheid.

On the landing below us at Shields Drive lived the Cochranes, an extremely unusual family in that Morag was a single mother. She had two daughters, Eileen and Lynn. Lynn was my age, and we played together before we started our different schools on different sides of the road. Morag worked, so the girls looked after themselves a lot. I remember Eileen opening a tin of beans, to eat cold. She asked me if I wanted any. God, no. I was absolutely horrified. This, then, was how *deprived* children lived. I didn't tell Win about the cold beans. She might not have let me play with Lynn any more.

Win was very interested in Morag, though.

'Morag likes the men. She's man-mad.'

'Morag's blonde hair comes from a bottle. She's hard-looking.'

'Morag likes a drink.'

'Morag's a good-time girl.'

'Morag's husband used to knock her about, I've heard.'

'That Morag. She's a character.'

Win liked Morag, despite disapproving of her, because Morag was lovely. Attractive, intelligent, funny, always friendly, always ready to throw back her head in a big, throaty laugh, any excuse, fag hanging from her hand, gap-toothed grin crinkling her eyes. Spirited. She knew that everyone talked about her and she didn't give two fucks. A Catholic woman living as a single mother back then, living her life as she wanted to – that was remarkable. You had to admire her. I think there was a part of Win that recognised Morag's courage and zest for life, her rejection of shame and regret, and honoured it. Win was well capable of that when it wasn't a threat to her. My mother was not a bad person and never became one. She was just inhibited by her choices, so inhibited that they deformed her, in ways only someone very close to her would ever discern.

After we started at our two different schools, Lynn and I pretty much stopped being friends. We lived under the all-pervasive sectarian apartheid, our paths never crossing.

These were the chants kids sang at each other, right through primary. I never sang either myself, but I was the recipient of such serenades quite a few times:

> Proddy dogs
> Eat the frogs
> Two for tuppence ha'penny
> The polis came
> Took their name
> Gave them back a ha'penny

> Cathy cats
> Eat the rats
> Two for tuppence ha'penny
> The polis came
> Took their name
> Gave them back a ha'penny

The rhymes were the same, apart from the colour of the tiles.

Lynn and I did have one conversation as adults, just as I was about to leave home for university, which was quite unusual back then. Lynn was going on to higher education too, to study pharmacy at Edinburgh. She'd thought about becoming a doctor, but the training took too long. I'd made the same decision about architecture. We had a lot in common, me and Lynn, two girls who lived strictly parallel lives. Maybe we'd have been friends for life if it wasn't for the all-important religious differences that the culture imposed on us, whatever we ourselves might have thought about God and religion, William of Orange and John Knox or the Pope and St Brendan. Or maybe not. During that last encounter, though, I think we both felt wonder at how similarly we had progressed, though we were so far removed from each other. There was warmth there, and regret.

The origins of the virulent strain of sectarianism that flourished until recently in the south-west of Scotland, and still has a firm foothold, are not difficult to trace. My part of Scotland and the north of Ireland were handy for each other, twelve miles apart at the closest point, causing similar conflicts of interest on both sides of the narrow sea. But I didn't know that then. All I knew was that my dad hated Catholics. He had a million derogatory names for them, and claimed he could always identify a Groof/Paddy/Taig/Bog-hopper/Fenian/Left-footer/Papist by his big forehead, his long body, his short legs and his thin lips, 'like he had a hole for a mouth, made by a scalpel'. The aggression with which these words were delivered I found traumatic, let alone their content. Win didn't like it either when John went on like that. She was a much more decent person than he was in lots of ways. This was one of them. She had no time for Scottish sectarianism – she found it repulsive. Only loyalty to John kept her quiet about it, outside the house. 'Oh, John,' she'd sometimes say to him when he started up. 'Oh, John . . .'

Sectarianism, like all othering, all tribalism, is an expression of the 'collective narcissism' that found such devastating expression in Nazi Germany. Why did my dad sometimes revel in hate speech, even against groups that contained people that I knew he personally liked and respected? Theories about group narcissism explain it, even if they don't excuse it. My dad felt compelled to say those horrible things about Catholics when he was most fed up with, and disappointed in, John Scott Orr. Whatever else he may or may not have been, this was a way of telling himself, he at least was a *Protestant*. Better, by definition, than a whole other class of people. The unsettling thing about group narcissism is that there's a level on which it works really well. Group narcissism tends to keep individual narcissism at bay. It helps to regulate the feelings of shame that underlie fragile, narcissistic egos by reminding them that they are not only an individual but also part of something much bigger than themselves.

People regulate their narcissism by being in groups of others like themselves within which they feel validated and valuable, which they care about like they care for themselves. The downside, increasingly, as humans travel and mingle, is that not everyone will be in the same group. Other groups will be denigrated, at times when a group or individual finds it hard to see inherent worth in their own group and themselves. Plus, if an admirable group can't be achieved, then a notorious one will do – like being in a Toi. Attention, of any kind, is always welcome, always needed. Within the family, John's expressions of contempt for others got him lots of attention. But he had our attention anyway, he just didn't realise it. When he was dying, and David and I were beside ourselves with grief at seeing him slip away from us, my father told my mother the saddest thing. 'I didn't know how much they loved me.'

We did, Dad. We did. So fiercely, so strongly. You just couldn't see it. That performative hate, though, against others and sometimes against your children? You hid behind it and missed a lot. You were loved as much as any man ever could be. But maybe you were not loved enough by yourself. Narcissism is not self-love. It's the opposite of that. It's a nagging horror that you are, deep down, unlovable. A narcissist needs the love, attention and admiration of others to survive because he or she cannot produce enough healthy self-respect to be at peace.

John wasn't one for joining – except Shotts golf club – and he wasn't a religious man either. But being a Protestant was the nearest he got to being in a Toi. It all faded as he grew older, thank goodness. But it had a lot of influence on me as a child – not all bad. It was part of my dad that I didn't like, and it's important to see people in full – see that you can still love or like them despite their flaws. If anything, I've tended to look beyond flaws too often in my life, excuse them too much – my own as well as those of others. Which, at times, has made me both vulnerable and isolated. Narcissistic behaviour, of any kind, has a huge effect on others.

It's so important for people to be aware of narcissism, but it's a deeply misunderstood pathology. For this I blame the Greeks. People think narcissism is vanity. But people can be very, very narcissistic about their lack of vanity, if that is what they've found that others admire them for. Narcissus indeed fell in love with his own image. But he loved his actual corporeal self so little that he died from self-neglect – without self-love, he could not drink the water he gazed into. He'd have had to destroy his perfect reflection to keep himself alive.

And the woman who truly loved him and wished to save him – Echo? The tragedy is hers, not his. He died for an idea of himself; she died for him. Narcissists, poor creatures, don't love themselves at all, let alone others. Their dark secret, the secret they can't face, is that they loathe themselves and need constant soothing, endless reassurance that they have worth, a mountain of worth, a universe of worth. This is what makes a narcissist feel like a prince in his or her darkness. All gothic horror, all tales of vampires? They are stories of true, deep, malignant narcissists. Malignant narcissists are truly terrifying.

Even for a relatively benign narcissist – a person that a psychiatrist would diagnose as having narcissistic personality disorder, but not antisocial personality disorder alongside it – seeing the whole of a person, the gifts as well as the flaws, is one of the things that they are unable to do. By the same token, we can all have aspects of ourselves, little dark corners, or big, deeply crepuscular chunks, that are intransigently narcissistic. People can have one aspect of themselves in which their mindset and behaviour is indiscernible from that of a narcissist. And have the same debilitating effect on the person they try to control. As a girl I didn't suspect that my parents had such a chunk in their psyches. But they did. Who was Narcissus? Who was Echo? It took me a long time to work it all out.

6

Gran's Purse

Nineteen sixty-six was quite a year. The new flat in Shields Drive turned up. And he turned up too, out of nowhere. David. Or Vanessa, as Win had wanted to call him if he'd been a girl. 'Deborah means "bee" and Vanessa means "butterfly". I'll have a butterfly and a bee.' Oh. I was already last on the list, and the one with a sting. David, by the way, means 'beloved'. Win had a bee and a beloved.

I'm lucky to have memories going back to the age of three. I'm lucky that I can identify them so easily as Thistle Street memories, not Shields Drive memories. I remember Win in Thistle Street, poring over the little soft-covered book of baby names and their meanings, remember her talking about her preferences both to me and to John. But I have no memories of my mother having a pregnant tummy as she discussed the meaning of the names of her putative brace of daughters, or at any other time. Though, of course, she must have had.

I'd been asked if I wanted a baby brother or sister, and I'd definitely insisted that I most certainly did not. (My own elder son, when asked if he was looking forward to his little brother or sister arriving, replied: 'The baby isn't coming any more. We have put all of his little clothes in the bin.') Yet, despite my own clearly stated preference, talk about the 'stork coming to visit' had continued. I'd probably assumed that if I didn't look at this stuff then it would go away, as small kids do, as small kids think the world disappears if they close their eyes really tight. Yet I also knew that Vanessa would not be delivered by a stork. She would be delivered by Dr Grieve, whether I wanted her or not. Win was pregnant and she knew exactly when she would stop being pregnant, and exactly the day when my younger sibling would be born. Exactly as she had with me.

This precision was all down to Dr Grieve and his strict induction system. Dr Grieve was king at the single-storey Motherwell Maternity Hospital. It was built in 1923 by William Mair Bishop, who had had the building's location and purpose carved out of the hospital's red sandstone. Amazingly, the building survives, unlike Dr Grieve's induction system, although it stopped being a maternity hospital in 1992. It's now called the Airbles Road Centre and offers an in-patient service for people with mental health problems. All deindustrialised towns have more than their fair share of those. Demolishing a town's economy causes plenty of stress and anxiety. Demolishing its identity and the identity of its people along with it – that's a more metaphysical cruelty.

In 1966, though, no one in Motherwell imagined that one day such careless collective violence, material and psychological, would be visited upon us. On the contrary, it felt good to be British and good to be Scottish. It felt good to be from Motherwell. Win and John felt lucky to be around during this dynamic and progressive time, and told me that I was too. They felt particularly lucky to have all the medical care that their family had. They didn't take it for granted. They didn't like disturbing the doctor when it wasn't necessary. But when I had a fever in the night the doctor visited me, reassured my stricken parents, told them what to do to make me better. I remember the doctor coming, our GP – we thought the world of Dr Cameron. I remember bad dreams and cold flannels.

I had a recurring dream throughout my childhood whenever I had a fever, and I occasionally had it as an adult. I think the hysteria the dream induced was the thing that caused my parents to call the doctor. The dream was never distinct but always terrifying. It involved the press of a heavy, threatening, pushing weight and the death or loss of my father. Not my mother. Dad was the one who was special to me. His life outside the home, away from me – this was more mysterious and exotic than my mother's life with me, of constant, unchanging, reliable intimacy that could be taken for granted. It was his attention that I missed, because I didn't always have it. Like I didn't always have Dr Cameron's. All the important people, the busy people, the people who engaged with the world outside, that big scary world that went on for ever, were men. When I asked Mum why Dad wasn't at home more, she'd say: 'He's off earning pennies to buy all the things that we need.' So splendid.

Win particularly valued the intense maternity care that she received – also, of course, from a man. Not long before the Boston Women's Health Collective published the feminist classic, *Our Bodies, Ourselves*, Dr Grieve's induction system was considered a wonder of modern medical science. It isn't difficult to see why. To the contemporary eye, Dr Grieve's methods were massively over-medicalised and controlling. And that, I believe, is true. But throughout history, pregnancy had tended to be extremely under-medicalised, with the loss of the lives of mothers and babies, or sometimes of their quality of life instead. The evidence was still all around, even in our own family. My grandmother had lost two babies, after all, siblings John never had, aunts or uncles I never had.

And I dread to think what 'women's troubles' my gran Lizzie quietly put up with as a long-standing consequence of her seven pregnancies.

Win, as she continued with her second and last pregnancy, was – quite understandably – very much in favour of Dr Grieve's controlling innovations, which promised to save her from the physical ravages and emotional losses that Lizzie had endured. Win thought I was mad, more than three decades on, when I had my own babies and sat about waiting for waters to break, like in Dickens. Win knew nothing of my two abortions, although there was a dodgy moment when she looked at my pregnancy notes and asked me what 'primigravida three' meant. So as far as she ever knew, I only had three pregnancies in my life, the last ending early in bloody, haemorrhaging, consciousness-losing, two-crash-teams-at-A&E, near-death miscarriage. Both pregnancies that I carried to term prompted unwelcome and highly familiar lectures on the wisdom of Dr Grieve. Annoyingly, my second son's extreme reluctance to make his debut eventually left me begging for induction myself.

'Oh, Dr Grieve,' my mother would say, her voice soft, affectionate and coated as warmly with respect as when I'd been told the first time. 'When he confirmed that you were pregnant, Dr Grieve would get his chart and plan it all out, right away. Dr Grieve told you when you'd be admitted to hospital, Dr Grieve told you the day of your baby's birthday, and Dr Grieve induced you on that day. You were booked into hospital for a fortnight. Dr Grieve liked to be quite sure you were ready to go home with your baby, when it was time. No waiting around and wondering when it would all start to happen, with Dr Grieve.' 'There's a post-Gina-Fordism joke there, somewhere, Mum. Knock yourself out,' I never replied.

Dr Grieve sounds like he might have had one or two control issues. Women like Win, impressed that their own bodies could be so easily overridden, would have made dear old Dr StrangeGrieve feel very powerful indeed. My mum was the sort of woman who didn't like the sound of lady doctors, then congratulated herself upon realising, many years later and with some wonder, that maybe they weren't so bad. However, a lady GP failed to spot my dad's primary cancer, and spotted my mum's secondary cancer too late. (Although it seems that my mother may have missed some check-ups the lady GP had arranged for her – she'd have taken a man's instructions much more seriously.) There was always an unspoken hint that all this cancer wouldn't have happened with a proper man doctor. Dr Grieve was a proper man doctor. His reign, no doubt unquestioned, came when we were still in the days of the Great Riddle, which could baffle people for weeks:

Q: So. A father and a son are in a car crash. The father dies. The son survives. But the surgeon refuses to treat him, saying: 'I can't perform surgery on my own child.' Who was the surgeon?
A: The boy's *mother*.

The saddest thing about that brain-teaser is that even now, when there are more female medical students than male ones, consultant surgeons are still, overwhelmingly, men. This would console Win, who would always have preferred a male surgeon herself. Having a man in charge felt right to my mother. Having a woman in charge felt like you were submitting to someone who really ought to be your lowly equal. One of the consequences of strict gender-archetyping – a consequence so all-pervasive that it goes almost unnoticed

– is that it encourages men to view other men as their competition and women to view other women as their competition. The upshot, historically, has essentially therefore been that men compete for power and wealth, and women for men. In Win's case, as in general, this was a damaging dynamic. I believe that my mother's basic attitude – subconscious and unknown even to her – was that if she had no agency in the Big World, why should other women have it? Somehow, failing to follow the feminine rules was cheating. Win did have agency over my father, though, and agency over her man was a woman's Great Prize. She didn't want to share it with any other female, even a daughter.

Win took care to explain to me, in her oblique, self-centred way, that this new baby would be no more of a threat to her command over my father's affections than I had been. 'When I was having you, Deborah, your dad said to me, "As far as I'm concerned, the chicken comes before the egg." Wasn't that a lovely thing to say?' For the chicken, yes. For the egg? Not so much. I didn't realise that until later, though.

When I was small, whatever made my mother happy was okay by me. I didn't see, at the time, that Win was jealous and defensive, always getting her retaliation in first. She couldn't see that there needn't be a competition for John's affection, that a man's relationship with his wife and that with his daughter were totally different things, that she and I were not two female parasites desperately trying to gulp down the bigger share of a limited supply of manly love-blood. Over the years, I heard the chicken-and-egg anecdote many times. It never annoyed me, exactly, but I did come to wonder what sort of mentality carried its pre-eminence over its children around triumphantly, like a shining trophy. A mentality that secretly, subconsciously, sees itself as almost completely powerless, I think, and wants to hang onto the power that it does have. It makes me grieve for the lost Win, the bright, talented girl who could have got so much more out of her life, if all of her life hadn't been squashed into the tiny space of husband, home and children.

My mother's whole existence, all seventy-six years of it, was ordered by the choices of men. Their attention, their validation – that was everything to Win. She didn't even think about it, was not really aware of it. Being in the good graces of men, attracting them, keeping the one you chose, your husband, these were the only important ways in which to gauge the worth of a woman. Win's forty-year marriage to my father had been the great achievement of her life. Getting married, being married, staying married. These were things my mother was violently, indefatigably in favour of.

I myself married in large part to console Win. Neither the marriage nor the attempt at consolation worked. Win had been furious, on my wedding day, when I'd casually mentioned that of course I'd be keeping my own name. For Win this was like dropping a psychological hydrogen bomb, and I hadn't anticipated it at all. We were all at a friend's Glasgow flat in the evening, our tiny party of wedding guests. Win heard me say this to somebody else and she shot up like a meerkat, her face a picture of disgust and astonishment.

'No! You are Mrs Self now! You are Mrs William Woodard Self!'

'Please. Let's not argue about it now, Mum. This isn't the time. It's my wedding day.'

'Yes! And on her wedding day the woman takes the husband's name!'

From that day on, every time she sent me anything in the post it would be addressed, in bold capitals, to MRS WILLIAM W. SELF. I'd ask her not to, sporadically. But she always, always did. There are mothers who will never cease to refuse their daughters their own identity, in whatever way they can. My mother was one of them.

I was still MRS WILLIAM SELF when Win died, although I'd had a go at fleeing – without the children, foolishly – the minute she was too far gone to know. Just as well. Ceasing to be thus would have killed her anyway. Or inspired her to kill me, after she'd said, with bitter triumph, 'I knew you wouldn't be able to keep a man.' These were the triumphant words I heard in my head every time I pondered the problem of how to get out of a marriage that you fear the consequences of ending.

The problem of marital unhappiness was not, of course, one that I could discuss with my mother. I'd try, but Win would twist her head away, lower her eyes and say: 'Marriage is hard.' In truth, I'd got exactly what she would have wanted for me – lack of agency, endless housekeeping, childcare only when I was actually working to earn money, submission to a man's career and travel priorities, and therefore to the natural order of things. It wasn't really about me. It was about my gender. My gender, in my mother's eyes, wasn't good enough. I wasn't good enough. She wasn't good enough. Women weren't good enough. That's what keeps patriarchy on the road. For me personally, it meant that I could never come near to persuading Win that I had a right to do things differently to her, all sorts of things. I could never come near to persuading her, at any time, that I hadn't done anything wrong by wanting sex, education, independence, a career. Any difficulties that I had were a result of these bad choices I had made. Though it was John, not Win, who summed up this attitude in an unforgettable sentence: 'Your problems, Deborah, are all of your own making.'

As a family, we didn't socialise with others that much, not family, not friends. But as an adult, no longer living in

Motherwell, I visited home regularly, and Win and I would sometimes run into neighbours and familiar faces in the street. If anyone asked what I was up to, Win would say, with an artificial brightness: 'Deborah's a career girl!' I always took it as a sign that I shouldn't elaborate too much, or say anything that could be interpreted as boasting.

Win kept me posted on Carol Fox, who'd grown up next door but one on Clyde Terrace and had also gone to university, like her older brother Colin. Our families had been good friends, even though the Foxes were Catholics. Carol had gone on to higher education with her parents' blessing, though.

'Carol isn't coming home to live after university. Carol wants to be a career girl too.'

'Carol has gone all feminist.'

'Carol is training as a social worker.'

'Carol has moved to London.'

'Carol doesn't like men. She likes women. Carol is a lesbian.'

'Carol is working for a union. Carol is very political. Colin is very political too. He's in the Scottish Socialist Party.'

Colin, after devolution, became an MSP. Briefly, after Tommy Sheridan had been caught hanging out in sex clubs, he became leader of the party. In the Scottish tabloids he was called Red Fox. All true. Carol had never been a lesbian, though. That was just local gossip.

'Carol is living back in Scotland now.'

'Carol is having IVF. Carol *wants* to be a single mother.'

'Carol is training to be a lawyer.'

'Carol is pregnant. There isn't a father, just a sperm donor.'

'Carol has a daughter.'

'Carol has started her own law firm.'

Carol, and her law firm, won a number of important class

action cases arguing for equal pay in the public sector. She packed it all in to look after her mother, Agnes, when she became old, infirm and confused. Carol's a fucking Amazon.

Nevertheless, I was weirdly annoyed by these bulletins from Win about Carol, because I didn't quite understand the spirit in which this news was being imparted. Was it disapproval of Carol? Or did it come closer to my own opinion, in its sheer wonder at Carol's energy and spirit? I never responded to these highly interesting gobbets of news with much more than mere acknowledgement, in case I found out what Win really did think. Either positive or negative, Win's view would have made me feel a bit horrible. Disapproval of Carol would underline the disapproval of me that I felt so strongly and resented so much. Approval of Carol? Worse. Why do you approve of *her* and not of *your own daughter*?

I still don't know what John and Win thought about Carol, or whether their thoughts about career girls changed that much over the years. In my early twenties, when I was trying to climb the greasy media pole, my parents called it 'always chopping and changing'. If I tried to explain where I was trying to go with this work that was so unfathomable to them, John particularly would say: 'Deborah? You live in a fantasy world.' Or: 'You're always setting yourself up for disappointment. Don't expect us to pick up the pieces.' Such criticisms would hit like a physical attack.

I would have been reluctant to announce to my parents that I was going to faff about with yet more higher education. I didn't call myself a feminist, in case my parents found out about it. I certainly wouldn't have *dared* to declare myself to be a union official aspiring to become a single parent by having a baby via a donor using IVF. Which was quite a thing. Carol was the first single woman in Scotland EVER to conceive a child using IVF and a donor. To achieve her remarkable goal, Carol had to travel to England for treatment. She had twenty-nine cycles of IVF before eventually the procedure worked and she was up the duff. (Needless to say, Carol wrote and published a book about it: *Memoirs of a Feminist Mother*. She *always* gets there first.) That baby, now an adult, was the most worked- and strived-for child since Anne Boleyn got knocked up by Henry VIII. Only with entirely happy consequences. The last I heard, Carol's daughter's first-class master's degree had landed her a job in politics. I'm only glad I wasn't told about that particular career girl via Win.

Because Win so vehemently hadn't wanted me to be a 'career girl', I'd always feel rebuked when she told this to others, as if being 'a career girl' was the most absurd and pointless pretension possible. That made me feel angry for a long, long time. Though it wasn't until Win was dead that I was able even to begin to work out how my own life had really been about just two irreconcilable things: defying my mother, and gaining her approval, keeping the things I did secret when I knew she wouldn't approve. Doing other things, simply because I knew that she would approve. I look back and I'm amazed by how early that pattern is discernible, of hiding things from Win when I knew she wouldn't like them. Such as the pieces and jam which I, aged almost four, didn't tell her about, ever.

The reality of my younger sibling's imminent arrival was brought home to me when I found myself staying at my gran's council flat in Heathery Road, Wishaw, with my dad. Win was finally tucked up in one of Dr Grieve's beds for the recommended fortnight and I wasn't sleeping in the flat in Thistle Street for the first time I could remember in my life. I had been away from Thistle Street. But I only knew that because Win had a story about it. Win had taken me on the coach, as a baby, to be christened in Essex. It was just her and me, because John couldn't get time off work. We'd sat, she told me, next to a black man. 'He was so nice and polite, and his English was perfect. He held you some of the time, to let me have a rest. He was good with you. A complete gentleman. You just can't tell with people, can you?'

Usually, we went to Gran's only on a Sunday, after lunch. She'd always have a few boiled sweets on display in a bowl and I'd always have one, sometimes even two. King's of Wishaw sweets. The local sweet maker. Anything sweet, we had a local maker. Barr's, with their Irn Bru. Tunnock's, with their teacakes. The west of Scotland, Lanarkshire particularly, is a Mecca for sugar cultists.

Later, after I'd learned to read, I'd look forward to getting hold of Lizzie's weekly copy of *The People's Friend*. Even I, in the late 1960s, could see how anachronistic this publication already was. It had a turquoise border, red masthead and a drawing of some Scottish beauty spot on the cover every week, always attributed to J. Campbell Kerr, who I now gather never existed. Which explains why Campbell Kerr's style would occasionally, subtly, irrevocably, change. I loved the short stories. The last one I read, just a few years back, featured a young woman who had found her perfect sweetheart, except that she began to suspect that he was keeping a dark secret from her. Eventually the reader was let in on the dark secret – that he was a morris dancer, and feared that she may not understand. She did understand! They lived happily ever after!

Founded in 1869, *The People's Friend* was published by DC Thomson of Dundee, also publishers of *The Sunday Post*, which carried the behemoths among Scottish comic strips, 'The Broons' and 'Oor Wullie'. At that time *The Sunday Post* had the highest per capita market penetration of any newspaper the world had ever known, being taken by 80 per cent of households. That record no doubt still stands. DC Thomson's grip over Scotland was vast. The company was the self-appointed keeper of the nation's innocence and, auld Calvinist Scots as *The Sunday Post* was, no publication set the company's moral and religious stall out better than *The People's Friend*. Astoundingly, it's still going strong today, cover price £1.30, also available online. The world of the Tois and the world of *The People's Friend* existed in the same space, sometimes in the same flat. I still always think of Scotland as markedly dualistic in its culture. Jekyll and Hyde. 'The Broons' and *No Mean City*.

DC Thomson represented one culture – the strict, re-served, conservative, teetotal culture of the Marcia Blaine School for Girls in Edinburgh, where Muriel Spark's Miss Brodie scandalised everyone with the double whammy of sex before marriage *and* fascism. Though I hadn't heard of Muriel Spark in the 1970s. Francis Gay was the contem-porary Scottish writer best known to me. He was a Thomson contributor whose homilies were compiled every Christmas into a best-selling anthology, *Francis Gay's Friendship Book*. Another regular, David Hope, would publish *The Fireside Book*, with a picture and a poem for every day of the year. Both men, like J. Campbell Kerr, were fictitious. An edition of *Francis Gay's Friendship Book* is still put out each year.

DC Thomson catered to pretty much every demographic. *Twinkle*, *The Dandy*, *The Beano*, *Bunty*, *The Scots Magazine*, *The People's Friend*, *The Sunday Post* and, most influential of all, for a time, on teenage girls of the 1970s like me, *Jackie*. These were the comics, magazines and newspapers that provided my regular, intimate interface with the wider cul-ture. I never got into *My Weekly*. Or I haven't yet, anyway. It still has a healthy circulation. DC Thomson did comics for boys as well, including the little war comic *Commando*.

Thus DC Thomson newspapers and magazines shaped, and still shape, the views and tastes of Scotland and, at times, the whole of Britain. Modest, God-fearing, old-fashioned DC Thomson's was a high-profile and powerfully communicated version of what Scotland ought to be. *Jackie*, for example, which was published between 1964 and 1993, managed both to reflect and deflect the influence of pop culture and 'the permissive society' on young girls. It told us that it was perfectly okay to follow fashion and like pop stars, but totally not okay to have sex before you were married. In certain respects, we were ruled from Dundee. DC Thomson had a lot of soft cultural power.

In 1966, though, I couldn't read, and I was both listless and anxious while Gran was looking after me. She was looking after John too, her youngest son and a man of thirty-one years old, because Dr Grieve's mania for the two-week lying-in didn't quite dovetail with the fact that the men of Motherwell were expected always to turn up for work except at the prescribed holiday times. It was a lot to ask of Lizzie. She was worn out then, already, though she couldn't have been very old. She looked ancient to me, broken. I was told by Win that she'd been beautiful as a young woman, her hair thick, tawny and lustrous. But none of that beauty was left.

Lizzie's hair was steel grey, cut blunt to the length of the nape of her neck, with a kirby grip or two keeping it out of her pale, cataract-clouded eyes. No hairdresser for her either. The ugly, low-maintenance practicality of that hair said everything that Lizzie – maybe in her late fifties at that time – had to say about herself. I never saw my Scottish gran dressed up. She always wore a pinny. Even in the photographs of John and Win's wedding she's wearing a dull, shapeless brown coat. There may even be a pinny underneath. I've never known anyone who thought less about herself, anyone whose self was so irrelevant to her. By the time I knew her, she barely had a sex, let alone a gender, any more.

Anyway . . . Every day at lunchtime my gran would ask me if I wanted 'a piece and jam'. Nothing else was on offer, and this was all quite tricky for me. Win hated the piece-and-jam culture of Lanarkshire (the local jam maker was R&W Scott), so I felt both disloyal to my mother and sorry and embarrassed for my gran, who apparently thought this awful way of living was fine. Win's voice boomed in my head, her Essex accent at its strongest, every time I had to answer the dreaded question.

'A piece and jam. A piece and jam! It's all they ever eat. That and chips. Or "mince and *tatties*".' Tatties would be spat out. The word, that is. Not the boiled potatoes. 'Boiled within an inch of their lives. Overcooked! Everything overcooked! They don't know how to cook here! Cabbage? The smell of it! *Cooked far too much.*' Win wasn't wrong.

Certainly, Lizzie overcooked things. She left the tatties to burn at least once during the fortnight that Dad and I were with her. She put pots and kettles on and forgot them, generally. She was a danger to herself, and John saw what his sister Betty had been telling him for ages while we stayed there. She couldn't live alone any more. That was the beginning of Lizzie's end, really. Not long afterwards Aunt Betty, also a widow and my favourite Scottish aunt, would move in with her to look after her.

'She just wants that council place,' Win told John, as if caring for your ailing, failing mother was the great win in life's lottery. Win always zoomed in on people's possible base motives, even Uncle Bob and Aunt Daisy and their profoundly disabled daughter. Bob and Daisy looked after Karyn from when she was born in 1959 until they died, a few years apart, in the early 2010s. Even when they were in their seventies and eighties, they got just one day of respite care a week. Karyn outlived them. They always loved her and they never, ever complained. On the contrary: Daisy in particular was very involved with the Spastics Society and was a tireless advocate for her own daughter and other children and parents in their situation. Uncle Bob and Karyn's younger sister Laura would come just before Christmas every year, to drop off our presents and get us to buy Spastics Society cards and stamps. Betty would take me to the Spastics Society Christmas fair, which I always looked forward to.

Laura was a tiny bit younger than me. Laura had no brain damage. Laura was fine, better than fine. She's some sort of nuclear scientist now. They were an amazing family, in their quiet, private way. But when they got a caravan, to make it easier to cater for Karyn on holiday, my mum bitterly spoke of how they'd 'probably got help from the council with that too'. A new house – nothing too fancy, but easier with Karyn – and Win again suspected 'help'. It was always a bit uncomfortable for me when Win said these ungracious things. She was mean-spirited when she suspected that people were getting something that she wasn't. When women were. When mothers were.

My mum slagged off women, women she didn't feel superior to who were different to her in a way that made her doubt herself, because she was so invested in the perfection of her womanhood, so proud of it. She said nasty things about Betty and Daisy at the times when their womanly sacrifice seemed so much greater than her own – Betty's as a daughter and Daisy's as a mother. She could relax and like Morag, the single mother who lived downstairs in the maisonette at Shields Drive, because Morag was an unmarried mother, and there was no question that Win conformed to, excelled at, the womanly ideal so much more perfectly than Morag did. Her own high-achieving daughter, who wouldn't follow Win's rules for the woman-club at all, was her worst nightmare. Unfortunately, for both of us. But all that came later.

John, in 1966 and in a bold show of resistance, was noncommittal about Betty, just saying that 'someone had to look after Lizzie'. As for living in Gran's far nicer flat, which was downstairs in one of the pebble-dash houses and had a garden, that seemed to me like a good solution to one of Betty's own problems, not something to hold against her. Betty lived in a one-room tenement at the end of Gran's road, where we hardly ever visited her because, frankly, it was too depressing. Her bed was in a recess behind a curtain, and I think my cousin Jack's bed might have slid out from under it. Eventually, Betty's flat and all the other upstairs flats in the terrace would be made into a nightclub, The Heathery, that I would go to regularly in my late teens. Which was weird.

I'd never known Betty's husband, my uncle, like I'd never known my Scottish grandfather. I never even saw a photograph of my Scottish grandfather until after my mother was dead. He's in a three-piece suit and looks like one of the scarier extras from *Peaky Blinders*. He also looks old and ill. Lizzie, as my mother said, had been beautiful. I've never seen a picture of Betty's husband at all. I think both my grandfather and my uncle were called John, like my dad. I'm not sure. They'd been long dead when I came along, and no one talked about them much. They didn't have the time for memories, really, the widows. Or the energy. Lizzie and Betty always worked, Lizzie in a factory that made girdles, Betty as a wages clerk. The idea that there was a time when women didn't have jobs is a myth. Their work just wasn't taken seriously, as their poor pay reflected. This made things all the harder for the many women who were obliged to be the family breadwinner because their husbands were no good, or ill or dead.

I did find out more about my grandmother's 'women's troubles' as time went on and she became really ill. I know they must have been painful and debilitating because when I was in my early teens, Lizzie's uterus prolapsed to the point where it couldn't be supported in the way it had been in the past any more, with the insertion of a ring to hold it up and in. For me, all this just sounded like part of the absolute nightmare called 'womanhood' that lay in wait for me, still in my future but absolutely guaranteed to get me in the end. One cause of prolapse is difficult childbirth, and the condition gradually advances, over decades, until the pressure on the digestive system and urinary tract from the downward droop of the organs above gets so bad that it can't be fixed. Lizzie probably suffered constantly, and in silence, for much of her life. Christ knows how she managed not to smell of wee, God bless her. She had more pressing matters of personal hygiene than hair-dos to attend to.

Lizzie's life had been tough. She'd been left a widow young: she had been the wife of an ex-miner with a debilitating lung disease, whose ability to earn dwindled and dwindled as the war raged around their family and he sickened and sickened until he died. My dad remembers his dad with a cigarette in each hand, one to soothe his craving for nicotine, the other as a medically approved medicament for the purifying of his lungs. That was a hard, hard gig for all seven of the family, most of it performed before the welfare state was established. It left its mark.

Lizzie saw out her last years in hospital, her various sons and daughters going to see her on a nightly rota on weekdays, mostly spent in silence. After a while, John and Win said that me and David shouldn't go any more, at which we were relieved. Lizzie was just so used up, so far out of the world, that attempted interaction with her was painful. *Coronation Street* was her only pleasure and her only conversational topic. John and Win didn't want coping with that to be a weekly duty for us children – particularly as we didn't even watch *Coronation Street* at that time. It was all the more miserable because there was such a different scenario in the next bed. That old lady was vivacious, grasping life, relishing it, the vigour of her irrepressible personality far outlasting that of her body. Loads of people would visit her every evening, in and out, up and down, high-spirited and raucous, smoking and drinking as you used to be able to do on a hospital ward. When visiting time was over, the old lady would be tearful. 'Thanks fur coming,' she'd tell all of her reliably present guests, with passion, every time. 'If yous hudnae ae come, Ah'd a hid naebody.' Still makes me laugh, the celebratory absurdity of it.

It was very unusual for Dad to come into my bedroom at Clyde Terrace. But he came in to tell me when Lizzie died in hospital. I was fourteen years old. John told me not to be upset, that all she'd had left was suffering and that this was better for her and for everyone. I sat on the green studio cushion I'd made for myself out of old curtains, with its appliquéd home-made Snoopy patch, surrounded by a hard-won row of posters that were really Holly Hobbie wrapping paper, and played the saddest singles from the record collection that had been passed down from my cousin Jack, along with his ancient Dansette. It wasn't so hard to follow John's instructions, but she had been my gran, a constant in my life, the mother of the dad I loved so dearly. What seemed most astounding was that my grandmother had *existed*, in body, in mind, in thoughts, in memories, a human person, with all the complexity that implies for even the simplest soul. And that then she did not exist. There must have been one moment, one split second, when Lizzie crossed the line, moved from being to being part of the past. I did cry, but I think it was for myself. I had come face to face with human mortality. And I had no Scottish grandparents left.

Lizzie had very few personal belongings. But I got her old purse, a keepsake to remember her by. It was still in the bureau on the day we emptied the house. I have it now. It has a simple brass frame and clasp that still snaps firmly and strongly, almost aggressively. A black pouch is suspended from the frame, nicely grained leather, almost like shagreen, but worn through in places. A soft flannel lining, honey-coloured, hangs ragged out of the holes in the corners of the leather. Sometimes a metaphor can be too disturbing.

The purse was empty, but I remember when Lizzie used to give me a penny from it to go up to the local shop and get something from the penny tray. And I remember having Advocaat and lemonade – a snowball – every New Year's Day when we went to visit when she was still at home. I always got Lizzie a pot of Pond's cream for Christmas and her birthday. That's what she said she wanted. I like to think that she enjoyed just a smidgeon of vanity, and that it resided in the rubbing-in of some Pond's cream. The particular sort of group narcissism that we call 'femininity' had little grasp on Lizzie. She was not in the least like her daughter-in-law. Perhaps, in a different life, she'd have liked to wear pretty clothes and make-up, keep her figure trim and girlish, dye her wire-wool hair and have it washed and set for her each week. But she made do with what she had, which wasn't much.

People. We are so tough and so fragile, both at once, we humans.

At the time we were preparing for my younger sibling to

be born, though, Gran was just an adult, therefore powerful, therefore put on this earth to look after me. So I'd eat the piece and jam Lizzie made me. Actually, I'd enjoy it very much. It was *delicious*. But I'd feel guilty about it, like I was betraying my mother. I never told about the pieces and jam, as long as Win lived. I don't know if Lizzie prepared Dad's piece and sugar, before his shift, like Win did. I guess she must have. For his piece, John always had white sliced buttered bread, sprinkled with sugar (Tate & Lyle sugar, Abram Lyle being a shipping magnate from down the road in Greenock). Sometimes, he would wash out an empty can of golden syrup (Lyle again) and put a wire handle on it when the old one was knackered. The men would have tea with their piece, but not out of something so namby-pamby as a mug. Real men were not mugs and they did not drink from mugs. Not when left to their own devices anyway.

'Why don't you take an old mug in?' my mum would ask John sometimes.

'Och, I'd never hear the end of it from the boys.'

But my gran's less than perfect granning was spotted any-way. The pieces and jam stayed secret. But another failure properly to nurture a respectable child had been overlooked.

I had a pinny myself, like gran's pinnies, which I loved. It was tabard-style, like hers, in blue and white cotton, a small houndstooth check. It had red piping all round and red ties at the side. Best of all, it had a red umbrella, which served as a pocket, stitched onto the front. I think my Aunt Betty had given it to me as a gift. After the baby came, when Win and David were fit enough to receive visitors, we all went down to Motherwell Maternity. It probably wasn't the first thing my mother said, but that's how I remember it. We were always letting her down. You waited, really, to find out what obscure and overlooked form your latest transgression had taken.

'John. You've got no idea. She's still got that pinny on. You've brought your daughter out in a pinny. Lizzie should have taken that off her. You should have. Take it off her NOW.' I remember looking down at my lovely pinny – which I'd been wearing constantly, for *days* – and feeling crushed yet defiant. No one but Win could see why it mattered. We didn't understand the demands of respectability with the encyclopedic certainty that Win did. Knowing how to present yourself and your family in public was part of being a good wife and mother too.

7

Harry's Silver Cigarette Case

The thing about Win's outbursts was not that they were frequent. On the contrary. Most of the time my mum was loving, attentive, fun, busy, creative, curious, good company. That was what made her outbursts so scary. It was like some completely different person had suddenly possessed her. And sometimes, after the initial anger, it would take a long time for that other person to leave and for Win to be Win again. I think I learned fairly quickly to try to understand what might upset Win and avoid doing it, or just avoid telling her about it. But there was always stuff that slipped through, like the pinny. Sometimes it was hard to predict what might set her off. By the time I reached adulthood, there were few aspects of my life that I could offer to my mother uncensored. It was always best to keep her knowledge, let alone involvement, to a minimum, just in case. But I'd make mistakes about this too, mistakes that continued through the years and were still being made when my poor mum was in the hospice, barely able to move. Sometimes a relatively small mistake would thoroughly taint quite a large, positive thing.

My first memory of this particular phenomenon, when something you think is wholly positive becomes, when seen through Win's eyes, something wholly ugly and horrible, is an early one, from when I was still an only child. I was on my dad's shoulders, up so high, and he'd been carrying me like this for ages, for maybe the longest time ever. We'd just met Win, as arranged, in Merry Street. She'd asked us what we'd been doing and Dad just told her, all innocence. I didn't listen. I knew where we'd just been, after all.

John had taken me, up on his shoulders, to a more old-fashioned post office than the usual one, shabbier, with wire grilles instead of glass. It had been interesting, this new place, with an atmosphere I wasn't used to. It had been interesting to see my dad doing the stuff with paper and pens and clerks that I usually did with my mum. It had been interesting to see him so relaxed and confident as he did this administrative stuff that he didn't usually do. Mum's expression suggested, however, that this was all far too interesting. She rose to anger in seconds, her face red.

'That betting shop? That den of iniquity? How could you take your daughter there?' Dad didn't even protest. He just dipped his head and looked sheepish. I didn't know then that my dad was a connoisseur of horseflesh, a racing man, a gambling man. I didn't know that this particular thing my dad had done was something that a lot of God-fearing people would consider wrong or sleazy. I just knew she must have him bang to rights. Win would be so sure and so ap-palled when she started on you over your transgressions that you'd simply assume that her feelings – so powerful – could only be right and appropriate. I'd had no idea what a betting shop was, or what betting was. Iniquity hadn't seeped into me. I was being walked around on my daddy's shoulders, so tall, with such a high-up, panoramic, startling view, seeing Daddy do things. It had been great. The world was much bigger than the tiny bit of it that I got to see with my mother. My dad's world was bigger than my mum's. As I grew up, though, I wanted my world to be bigger than Dad's as well. I wanted, as they say, to have it all. But it caused such friction.

Even when I did things that I thought would please and mollify my parents, things that I thought they wanted very much, it didn't always work out. On the day of my wedding in 1997, when I was thirty-five, Win had offered to pick up my marriage certificate from the registry office in Mother-well, after the calligraphy that I didn't even care about had been done. I'd forgotten the whole thing. I called home when I got back from our honeymoon – a fortnight of touring in Scotland, with me the stressed-out, pregnant Boswell. But Win's silent, terrifying rage pumped out at me from the end of the phone.

'You must spend a lot of time thinking about ways to humiliate us,' my mother interrupted, as I tried to babble through the dead air about Skye, Orkney, Shetland, etc. She was deploying *that* tone, cold and deadly, that I dreaded. 'But you've surpassed yourself this time. Why is it that you never tire of hurting us? You never miss an opportunity, do you?'

I had no idea what Win was talking about. But gradually, my crime was revealed to me. She and John had gone to pick up the marriage certificate – after his early retirement they were, apart from golf and the bookies, inseparable. Win had read it, on the spot, and had seen that I'd put my father's oc-cupation down as 'semi-skilled labourer'. 'How do you think that made us feel? Will put his father down as an academic and writer. It makes us look like the poor relations.'

I tried to explain that I hadn't known what to put, that I'd chosen the occupation from a list on the instructions for how to fill in the form, that I'd remembered Dad, one time when we were getting a new telly from Radio Rentals, giving that as his occupation himself. 'Semi-skilled labourer,' he'd said, with charming self-deprecation. 'I was trying to think of a fancy way of saying it. But there isn't one.' I had the memory and I saw the phrase on the list. Anyway, I was proud of him. Proud of how he'd earned his living, as I'd been brought up to be.

'Lies. You're a liar.'

I continued trying to explain myself. I'd been flustered. No one likes filling out forms and I'd been under a great deal of pressure when I was filling these ones out. I'd been pregnant. I'd been working full-time. I'd been trying to sell a flat and buy a house. I'd been building a relationship with two young stepchildren-to-be. I'd been trying to deal with the fallout from a tabloid drugs scandal in which the father of my unborn baby had taken heroin while on the private plane of the then prime minister, John Major, during a freelance job he was doing for the company that employed me, the Guardian Media Group. Which, as they knew, had compelled me to tell my parents about the father of their grandchild's history of drug addiction before they read it in the papers. Meanwhile, his latest novel was late, so he had to spend all of his time doing that while trying to get off the crack and heroin I hadn't even known he was still using. And I'd had to have my honeymoon in fucking Scotland, because the smack incident had left my new husband afraid of flying! And I was sorry. I was so, so sorry. I was full of regret. Couldn't I be given a break here?

No dice. 'You're always full of excuses! And lies! Excuses and lies! Why do you never stop lying to us? They understood how we felt at the registry office. They're doing it all again. Engineer. Retired. That's what it will say. Your father was an engineer.'

John wasn't an engineer, though. There's no doubt that he had the intelligence and the ingenuity to have been one. But he wasn't. He'd had none of the training, none of the education and had gained none of the qualifications. He did not have a profession. That didn't stop me from absorbing the sheer strength of my mother's feeling as a kind of truth. Those words on that piece of paper – a piece of paper since seen only by divorce lawyers – had filled Win with shame and impotent anger. With huge success, she'd projected those feelings onto me. Part of me – the rational part – knows that it was all just Win being weird. Part of me – the part that's all emotion, the part I can never control – still feels sick with guilt at the terrible distress that I caused. Even now, I feel reluctant to tell the truth about what I put on the marriage application. I did think about lying, being the liar Win always said I was, and saying that the words I'd put on the form were 'factory worker'. That's what I'd have put on the form, if it had been on the list. But it wasn't. There was just this phrase that jumped out because of the conversation in the television showroom. The phrase of which I'm still ashamed.

Perhaps that's because I know how mixed my motives really were. I was indeed proud of my dad's no-frills manual work. In part, though, I was proud of what that said about me – me and the distance I'd travelled. Inverted snobbery is a common thing. People often describe themselves as working-class for fairly tenuous reasons – like their parents or their grandparents having started out that way. Win's motives were mixed as well. Part of it was violent snobbery as a defence against a feeling of inadequacy. Part of it was, I think, a deep-seated anger that the errant daughter had managed to get the women's prize – a wedding ring – against all parental warnings.

But part of it was knowing that the two of them were being used in some way, even though Win was never quite able to put her finger on the fact that the motive was my own self-aggrandisement. The more humble my beginnings, the more I appeared to have achieved. I liked to think I'd done well, and I liked it when people understood that. At this time I edited the *Guardian*'s Saturday colour supplement, *Weekend*. I'd been the first woman to have the job. I'd been the first person to edit it, I'm pretty sure, who wasn't a graduate of Oxford or Cambridge. And I'm probably still the one *Weekend* editor whose dad earned his living on a factory floor, as a semi-skilled labourer. I emphasised my lowly parents to feel prouder of myself. Pretty sad stuff. Typically narcissistic.

But all of this, were Win alive to read my opinions, would simply rouse my mother to unimaginable levels of incandescence. I can only say it all because she is dead. Is memoir therapy? Or is it vengeance?

Dad always sided with Mum when big rows with me blew up. But he'd often get the sharp end of Win's tongue himself. He would usually appease and mollify. But he had his boundaries, and all of them ring-fenced his passion for sport. He 'took his telling', as they say in Lanarkshire, over going to the betting shop with his daughter. But he carried on going, he carried on betting and he carried on watching the racing on the telly on Saturday afternoons. If he won, we'd know, because he'd go up to the bookies when the races were over and get his cash. Also, he'd have been shouting 'C'mon How Green Was My Valley, C'mon ya beauty! Yes! Yes!' at the telly.

John didn't have a gambling problem. His thing was outsiders, trying to spot the 300–1 shot who would triumph and winning a big purse from a small stake. So he didn't win that often. However, he'd throw out these rules if we'd had an unexpected expense, and do a few safe bets each way. Plus, Win knew that he didn't spend much on gambling, because he'd hand his wage packet to her each week, unopened, and she'd give him his personal cash for the next seven days. Win came to be more indulgent of Dad's gambling on the horses than she was about golf. It was less expensive and sometimes it brought in some much-needed profit.

'Oh, the gas bill after that cold snap!' she'd say. 'We'll have to see how your dad does on the horses.'

'The car's failed its MOT. We'll have to see how your dad does on the horses.'

John's bets got the family out of a hole sometimes. Other times, his esoteric fancies did win, and then there would be a little bit of mad money, money you could blow on a treat. Once, I got home from school and Dad said: 'Get in the car. We're going to Hamilton. I'll explain on the way.' Win was working part-time at this point, three evenings a week as a wages clerk, so I must have been at secondary school, maybe twelve or thirteen, and David must still have been at primary school. (She went full-time when he was at secondary too, three years after me.) We had to do our errand and get back before it was time for John to go and pick up Mum, he explained. Time was tight. He'd had a win on a midweek race, and he knew precisely how to spend the money.

We'd been over to Marks on the previous Friday, which we did sometimes if we needed special clothes or Win fancied a more thrilling food shop. (Gala pie! Chocolate eclairs! A pineapple! We all loved the M&S food weeks.) That week, Win had tried on a grey wool winter coat with a fur collar. It had fitted and suited her perfectly. She looked wonderful in it. Win had loved it and Dad had tried to persuade her to buy it. But she'd said it was too expensive.

We went there, John, me and David. We bought the coat, full of excitement, took it home and laid it out on the couch for Win. Dad picked her up, brought her home and when she walked into the living room we kids were watching the telly like there was nothing unusual happening while Win just stared, then gasped, then picked up her coat and put it on. We all explained in a wild babble, telling her what had happened, while Win protested: 'You shouldn't have! You shouldn't have!' with a radiant face that told us that John had done exactly the right thing. Such a great family moment. There were lots of those. I wouldn't want anyone to think that there weren't.

John's betting habit was an asset to the family economy, not a strain on it. Also, it connected him to his own father, whom he'd lost when he was so young. One of the few things I knew about the grandad I'd never met was that he'd had a passion for horses and racing too. Win had told me that my grandfather had narrowly avoided going to prison, for running an illegal betting book. She'd said that with my grandfather's health in the condition it was, he could have died in there. When I asked Win about this years later, she said she had no idea what I was talking about. Her father-in-law had liked the horses. And the greyhounds. He had indeed been a bookies' runner, which indeed had been illegal. But there had never been a tangle with the law. It had been one of Win's romantic embroideries, one she'd forgotten or had decided she didn't like after all. You never knew, with Win.

The one item that my father possessed which might have given a clue to his love of the horses was a silver cigarette case, decorated with a horse's head, which had previously belonged to my grandfather. But the case, there in the bureau, hadn't come down from my Scottish grandfather, whose love of racing his son had inherited. It had come down from my English grandfather, who had adopted the same indulgent attitude to John and his highly controlled horse-betting habit as my mother had. Harry had always said that he wanted John to have it when he died. John, the good husband to his adored youngest child, who smoked roll-ups and loved horses. It was a nice thought about my dad, truly affectionate, and that's what the case, above all, represents for me: the way that John was loved by his in-laws, loved by Man. Annie and Harry didn't bet themselves, or approve of it. But they viewed my dad's predilection for the horses as special – fascinating and glamorous.

For me, the cigarette case represented a harmony between the two different families I was from, the country people – for whom horses were part of working life – and the industrial people – for whom horses were a vice and a passion. Plus, it's a nice thing and I like nice things.

The silver cigarette case has a sturdy hinged lid, with an inlaid round centre, into which the shape of the horse's head has been worked. Rounded corners, so that it feels good in your hand and is comfortable in your pocket. Dad used it briefly, but went back to using his Golden Virginia tin. It was what he was used to, and anyway, if the boys at work sneered at a mug, goodness knows what they would think of a very lovely decorated box. It's David's now.

I don't remember seeing newborn David on that visit to Motherwell Maternity, the visit in my pinny. I don't remember ever holding him when he was a baby. I remember David being with us when we went to look at the flat that was about to be our new home, though. I think. I definitely remember, after we'd moved in, my little baby brother in the big Silver Cross pram in the living room, the pram that had to be bumped up two long flights of stairs to the flat. I put a pink bank-deposit slip from one of the bureau's pigeonholes over his mouth, just to see what would happen. Suffocation, say.

'What are you doing?' asked my mother, as she came into the room and caught me.

I still remember the absolute shock of discovery. I knew I was doing something transgressive and bad. Something dark.

'Nothing. Just showing him this.' I held up the pink paper, all innocence.

I was so jealous.

I probably did want to go to real school, not playschool, like I'd said when I looked out of the window with Win. But I didn't want to cede my territory to the baby either, and let him have our mother all to himself. I loved it when Win stopped her housework for *Watch With Mother*. We didn't need to buy the merchandise that was beginning to feature among children's toys. Win did an oil painting for our bedroom with Big Ted on Andy Pandy's back. She knitted me my own Looby Loo. We loved *Camberwick Green* and *Trumpton* too: 'Pugh, Pugh, Barney McGrew, Cuthbert, Dibble, Grubb.' We would sing, from *The Herbs*, 'I'm a ve-e-e-ry friendly lion called Parsley.' *Bill and Ben*, the flowerpot men, were great: 'Flub-a-lub. Flub-a-lub-a-lub.' I always felt secret disappointment when *The Woodentops* were on. Win liked that show more than me. She was such a good mother. It all flooded back to me, when I had my first son. 'Ride a Cock Horse to Banbury Cross', sung by Win as she held our hands and bounced me, then David, then her grandsons on her right leg. Making pom-poms. Making dollies out of wool. Drawing. Tickling. Limericks. Jokes. Doing tongue-twisters that made you say what sounded like Bad Words.

'I chased the bug around the tree.

'I'll get his blood. He knows I will.

'Oh wouldn't it,

'Oh, wouldn't it,

'Oh, wouldn't it be funny.

'If ladies all had wooden tits.

'Oh, wooden tit be funny?'

Flashing her Monster at us, which was a big mole on her side. As with the mole on her face, she was unconcerned about it, considered it an asset. Our delicious fake terror at the advance of Mum's Monster – especially my wee brother's, which could tip over into real hysteria when he was tired. Blowing raspberries on our tummies. Riding on her back.

When we were older, and more complicated, Win would say: 'Oh, you were easier when you were little.' Or sometimes: 'If I had my time again, I wouldn't have kids.' It seems so petty, nursing this stuff. But it was always like a slap. When she did slap me, Win would be upset afterwards – cuddle me, tell me she loved me and ask me to forgive her. Which I was glad to do. I preferred the occasional slaps to the more frequent harsh words. I'm a doler-out of harsh words myself, when the mood takes me. And sometimes a mood does take me, like I've been inhabited by a furious, hateful version of myself. A mood took Win that way too. One of the hard things about seeing the woman behind your mother's mask is that you have to look at yourself as well. I am my mother's daughter.

Of course, I had to go to school, had to leave *Watch With Mother*, the tongue-twisters, the wooden tits, the Monster and all the rest of it to Win and David. The new flat at Shields Drive, in the new scheme, was the place from which I made the strange adjustment to starting school, which actually leavened the stress of making the strange adjustment of having a new life in a new flat with a new sibling. Though there were still difficult moments. Like the time, before Christmas, when I'd poked about in my parents' room to find my hidden presents. There was a huge set of felt-tips, four times bigger than any I'd seen before, with amazing colours. I couldn't wait to get my hands on them. But on Christmas morning, having feverishly unwrapped all of my gifts, I hadn't found them. I was in a tight spot. How could I ask my parents where the pens were without letting on that I'd peeked? Then

I looked up. David had just unwrapped them. They were his. Unbelievable. The thing I wanted most was for him!

I'm glad I have a sibling now, even though our lives are almost impossibly different and our extreme ups and downs are exhausting. It's a good lesson for life, discovering that you're not the centre of the universe after all. Oldest or older children learn about what it's like to shove up and make room for another child. Only children never do, or youngest children. My parents were both youngest children. So, of course, is my brother. There were no more babies for Win and John, just one 'scare' not long after we moved to Clyde Terrace, signalled by the crocheting of several matinee jackets which were washed and hung out on the line to dry as soon as they were finished, all clean for the baby that wasn't.

The experts say that human character is formed a great deal by where a person falls in the sibling order. I don't doubt it at all. It was such a shock, the baby turning up. Such a shock. It's probably better to have your kids close together, so that the first one doesn't remember what it's like to be the only one. You never quite get over the level of usurpation. I didn't, anyway. It had been me, just me, for almost four years. It was what I was used to. Thistle Street and being the only child. And not going to school. I was used to that too. Everything changed. Every. Single. Thing.

Plus, I was not my mother's favourite child, which she pretty much admitted to me. 'You're my firstborn, so you'll always be special to me. Nothing can change that. But John didn't want another baby, like he wanted you, so I've had to have a special soft spot for your brother, to make sure he's as wanted as you are.' Crap. The real reason for the soft spot? David was male. David got to be loved for who he was. I got to be loved because my birth was significant to my mother's story of her life. There was no need for my mother to show her favouritism, no need to explain it to me, and no need to tell me that it was all my father's fault. She just couldn't help herself.

None of this made me resent my mother, though, not consciously. I liked being her confidante, after all. It made me all the more keen to prove myself to her: to be helpful, biddable and accomplished. I tried so hard. I tried too hard. But I saw their kisses and cuddles, David's and Win's, saw her proud gaze on that beautiful, lively, confident, popular child, and knew that I would never measure up.

Despite their almost cloying closeness, David too was subject to our family's strict discipline. I've always said that my childhood was like growing up in a religious cult without the religion, and it felt very harsh at times. But also, until I started mingling with the middle and upper classes, this seemed to be fairly normal. Some of the punishments my parents meted out were clichés, constantly referred to in popular culture, forever cropping up in the DC Thomson comic strips, cartoons as expressive of the nation's collective identity as 'Oor Wullie', who sat on his bucket with his bum smarting several times each year.

My brother and I shared a bedroom, and we always continued with the combative to-and-fro of our competitive, resentful relationship after bed. John would shout up, angrier and angrier, until we'd hear him leaping up the stairs, four steps at a time, his anger propelling him so fast that you'd only have a few seconds to regret that you'd provoked this – again – before he'd grab us out of the bed by the shoulder, one at a time, and thrash our arses. The grip of his hand was like being in a vice, the blows like being hit by the bough of a tree. We'd cry ourselves to sleep, vowing never to be so naughty again.

Not that we'd say 'arses'. Bad language of any kind, we

knew, was not to be tolerated, outside of the tongue-twisters (that's what made them so thrilling). Lynn Mackie's mum – the Spain-going mother from along the landing – had told Win that she'd heard six-year-old David saying the worst bad word, and Win had washed his mouth out with soap so that he would never do it again. And, to stop me from doing it for the first time, I had to watch. I stood in our kitchen while Win thrust carbolic soap into her golden child's gullet, his bawling face as harshly pink as the brick of Lifebuoy, his mouth – in a strategically flawed reaction – a vast volcanic opening, spewing out hellish noise and tragicomic bubbles which mingled with his tears.

The episode was horrific and it had a profound effect on us both. We are terrible swearers. We both find it almost impossible to open our mouths without saying fuck, fucking, fucked, fucker or fuckwit. Fuck, fuck, fuck, fuck, fuck, fuck, fuck. Cunt. Bastard. Tit. Arse. Knob. Wank. Fuck you. Fuck you, Mum. There's a bit of me that will always be an angry nine-year-old, furious and disgusted on my brother's behalf – because I loved him, I did and I do. My nine-year-old self likes nothing more than defying her mother and enjoying the sheer, liberating thrill of saying FUCK! in all its endless variations absolutely whenever she wants to.

Punishment with a public-shaming aspect was frequent, maybe because Win struggled with the idea of public shame herself. Once, wild with excitement because there was an opportunity to get 'squiggle' on a triple-word score, I was caught peeking at the Scrabble tiles, trying to find an 'S'. I was younger than ten, because we were still at Shields Drive. But Win made me a big badge saying 'I am a cheat', fastened it to my coat with a safety pin, and all four of us went into the town centre so that my humiliation could be observed. We saw no one from school, to my eternal gratitude. I've never cheated since. Not at Scrabble, anyway.

These punishments seem small, the complaints of some-one who had a perfectly nice childhood yet still wants to wring misery out of every little thing she didn't like. In the past, as I contemplated my feelings of dysfunction, the dreadfulness of my family relationships, the way I got on so badly with mother, father *and* brother, I'd dismiss the idea that anything from my childhood was bad enough to damage me. (Inner voice: YOU WERE NOT SEXUALLY ABUSED BY YOUR PARENTS.) For a time, it felt like only sexual abuse and serious neglect could have a negative psychological impact on a child. A psychoanalyst told me, when I was fifty-five, that it was the little things that you needed to watch out for, and I was straightforwardly grate-ful. These things did leave their mark. I felt the shame and the malice of Win's punishments very deeply, because I tried so hard to be good. Also, when people told me later in life that I was the problem, I'd believe them. I, after all, wasn't even liked by the closest people in the world to me. Being disliked, or held in contempt, being considered to be of little value by the people closest to me was what I was used to.

In fact, until I was fifty-five I knew next to nothing of nar-cissism and the trauma bonds that narcissists use, sometimes instinctively, sometimes deliberately, to bind their victims to them. Or as a narcissist thinks of his or her victims: the people that he or she loves. I was just endlessly confused. Involvement with narcissists is, above all else, confusing. Not that my mother was necessarily a narcissist: strictly speaking, that's a person who displays half a dozen of the checklist of symptoms for a diagnosis of narcissistic personality disorder. My mother was just a strongly committed member of a nar-cissistic cult, one that coloured the way she saw life and her role in it – that didn't just colour it, but totally dominated it. The cult is a gender cult. The cult is femininity. While feminism has broken much of its spell in the West, the femininity cult remains extremely powerful around the world. The narcissistic behaviours that can be seen in my mother's attitudes are the consequence of her beliefs about what it was to be a woman, not about what it was to be Win.

A technique that narcissistic people use, to keep people on their twinkling toes, dancing away to the narcissist's tune, is triangulation. From early on, I could see that our family's dynamic was odd – two units, me and John, David and Win. That's not so unusual – a daddy's girl and a mummy's boy.

One of the many things I didn't see about my family was that there were not just these two units in it. There were also several overlapping triangles: John, Win, the kids; Win, David, John-Deborah; and John, Deborah, Win-David. These triangles – in which any number of people can play and exchange three roles – are always at the heart of interpersonal psychological dysfunction. So goes the theory anyway, and I find the theory persuasive.

The concept of drama triangles was developed by Stephen Karpman, while he was a student of Eric Berne, who developed the psychotherapeutic model, transactional analysis. The school of thought is controversial – dismissed as 'para-Freudianism', which it is, really. Nevertheless, drama triangles work as a way of spotting poorly functioning relationships and people.

The idea is that in toxic relationships people play the victim, the persecutor and the rescuer. There don't have to be three people. The same person can switch roles many times in the course of a conversation. But it's in three-person relationships that the dynamic can most easily be seen. For many years, as an adult, I was involved in a drama triangle with two other women. One of us particularly enjoyed playing the victim and trying to elicit sympathy from one of her friends, the rescuer, because the other, the perpetrator, was being so awful to her. Then the rescuer would start feeling persecuted by the victim's endless demands for her to sit around agreeing about the awfulness of the other friend, so she'd feel persecuted by the erstwhile victim, seek rescue from the former persecutor, and on and on and on to the point of total exhaustion and misery. This was one of a number of relationships where I've had to ask myself what I thought I was doing by staying in it.

Anyway. Our family was like that too.

Win was always switching between these roles – though she'd never be able to see herself as a persecutor – and John, her rescuer, would always back her. Unless she was cheesed off with him. Then, she always expected me to back her against him, which I was never quite able to do, thus increasing her victimhood. David would become Win's rescuer, just by existing. Which strained the father–son relationship too. On and on it went, in jagged, three-pointed circles.

The strict punishments for wrongdoing made things all the more toxic, because they raised the stakes. I avoided punishment by being good. David had a different strategy. At some point, quite early on, my brother realised that Win would always disbelieve me when I told a truth against him. Sitting back and waiting for our mother to provide an alternative narrative which made whatever had happened my fault became a habit with him. Like the time, when I was about ten, that Win told me to take David, his pal and their bikes down the woods with me. (By then, I'd taken the obsessive nature studies beyond the marsh.) They insisted they were going to take a shortcut, even though I told them there was a burn that they wouldn't be able to cross. They knew better. Ten minutes on, and they were yelling for me. They were stuck in mud.

Slithering down the steep, deep ravine to the burn, the mud and their plangent voices, in the yellow Marks & Spencer trousers and yellow Marks & Spencer blouse Win had insisted I should wear, I found them thigh-deep in stinking black slime, bikes held aloft, saying they couldn't move, demanding to be rescued. If they lifted one leg the other just sank deeper. I progressed towards them by digging one foot out with my hands, then the other, until I'd got them out. We all trailed back home, shocked, tearful, covered in oily, stagnant filth. Win was furious. I had been responsible. Look what I had done. And I'd ruined my lovely outfit. (Which I hated anyway. I'd wanted jeans and a T-shirt with something – anything – written on it. But Win was still choosing my clothes at that time, and she'd continue to do so until I was sixteen.)

I tried to explain that they wouldn't keep to the road, that they'd tried to wade through the burn, that I'd had to rescue them. David denied it all.

Her face intense with what felt like loathing, Win told me that she knew exactly what I'd been doing. She'd told me earlier in the week that a local branch of the Scouts had done some cleaning-out of the burn, which was full of run-off from Ravenscraig as well as sundry dumped items. Their efforts had featured in the *Motherwell Times*. I – newly a Girl Guide – hadn't been able to resist going there to see for myself what they'd achieved, my mother decided, and now I was trying to put the blame on my little brother, which made my behaviour so much more despicable. I don't remember the punishment I got, just the misery of it all. And David's smirk. My mother's story became the true story of what had happened that day, to get three kids covered in mud. Because

Win was in charge of the household's words.

Even quite shortly before she became ill and started to see both of us as conspiring against her, my mother would dismiss any protestation that David could ever be at fault in all of our many fallings-out with: 'There are two sides to every story.' Even when I'd tracked him down after he'd been out of touch with all of us for three years, I got the distinct impression that it had been right that I'd fixed it, because, somehow, I'd broken it.

I don't think that it did my brother any good, that un-shakeable maternal belief in his childish fibs. It did me no good either, always being branded the liar when I knew I was telling the truth. For me, it feels normal to be doubted. It feels normal always trying to prove that I can be loyal, trusted, honest. A straight talker. A truth teller, the more brutal the truth the more obvious its integrity. I'll blurt out the truth – or my own idea of what the truth is, anyway – when absolutely no one wishes to hear it. A bad habit, not a good one. As for other people's lies? I'll always forgive them. Or I did, before I realised that my life had become overrun with lies so elaborate, so long-standing and so manipulative that I thought the knowledge would drive me insane. Or kill me. Before I became aware that a whole chunk of my life had been built on lies.

8

School Reports

I remember a lot of my first day at school. My first day at Real School in my Protestant uniform at the dark-blue-tiled Protestant school in the town my mother hated, in 1967. It was a sunny day, I was nearly five and – bizarrely, really – I was wearing a striped tie: black, gold and blue. Only for school, ever in my life, would a tie be something I was expected to wear. Men's clothing, for schoolboys to become accustomed to. But for schoolgirls . . . why? As a daily reminder that school had originally – had fairly recently – been only for boys?

My mum and I met Marion Welsh, by chance, on the way in. Her gran lived in one of the ground-floor flats on our block, so we'd played together before. She would be my contingency school friend and I would be hers. By definition, it wouldn't last.

I remember virtually nothing substantive about Marion, beyond that day, except that she had beautiful dark brown eyes, one of them slightly lazy (again, routine operations to correct this had yet to arrive) and that I'd been to a couple of scrambles with her. Scrambles happened after wedding services at both the church (Protestant) and the chapel (Catholic), although Protestant kids, on the whole, went to the Protestant ones and Catholic kids to Catholic ones. The groom would throw a big handful of change to the waiting children, who would scramble to get a coin or two. Marion and I had a strategy of staying on the periphery and finding the coins that had bounced, rolled or been kicked away. Not unsuccessful. A good number of thrupenny bits and a couple of sixpences, at the very least, were requisite. The really happy couples would even include a shilling or two. People who threw mostly coppers at their wedding were considered the lowest of the low. Which was one of my mother's favoured sayings too: 'They're the lowest of the low, that lot.'

Marion and I, along with eighteen or so other infants, were in room one. Room two started at the same time as us, I think, and we would eventually become one large class, in Juniors. Rooms three and four had the kids who were six months older, who would become a single class as well. Those kids would remain, to us, an impossibly sophisticated elite all the way through primary school. In room sixteen, Robert Westwood would become the School Dux, officially the cleverest person among our year's leavers, and his name would be painted on the board in gold, like that of all the other boys before him.

I assumed – we all did – that Robert's intelligence was preternaturally stratospheric, and maybe it was. He didn't go on to secondary at Garrion Academy (black, red and grey tie), like most of the rest of us. I think he went to Dalziel High (blue and grey tie), which was considered to be the best secondary in the town. Muirhouse, our scheme, was yards beyond Dalziel's catchment area, while the tenement at Thistle Street had been in the middle of it, and Win did express her regret about that. 'Just our rotten luck,' was her verdict. Robert Westwood's family must have moved, though. He is, I think, a solicitor now, living in Motherwell and working in Rutherglen.

In Infants we got milk to drink at playtime, in triangular cartons with a little transparent pink straw, pointed at one end to break the tense, round hymen of that day's virgin carton. The milk was warm, even though it had sat in a sink of cold water, in an orange hexagonal plastic crate, until break. It was horrible, like drinking fetid, watery mucus. One day, one of the highly unusual women who actually combined her all-encompassing gender role with being a politician would snatch the milk from us all, and the vast majority of schoolchildren would be glad.

Our teacher was Miss MacMillan, who looked, with her neat, tight, grey set, like the strict, disciplined but kindly primary school teacher from the Ealing comedies that were broadcast on the telly on Sunday afternoons. Miss MacMillan was generally heathery – springy, fragrant and tough. She always – to my own recollection at least – wore a tweed plaid skirt, lambswool jumper and pearls. She was formal, as befitted her dizzyingly high status. Sadly, of course, she was *a spinster*, as a career teacher of five-year-olds was wont to be at that time. There were never at any point any male teachers at the school, although the headmaster, Mr Main, was our remote and terrifying patriarch. Our main man, if you will. The janitor was a Mr Dakers, shiny-bald, wiry, bespectacled, always sweeping, in his blue drill overall. Needless to say, he appeared to loathe children.

There was a tiny sandpit in the classroom, complete with little spades. This struck me as wondrous.

I liked the novelty, the avalanche of information and the busyness of that first day, though I looked forward to seeing Win, putting my little hand in her bigger hand, always with rings on which would hurt her if I squeezed, and going back home. She'd been more upset when we'd parted that morning than I had been. Which made me feel tender and protective towards her. Gradually, I realised that everything was always worse for Win.

Many years later, when Win was in her mid-forties, she would phone me at my London flat – she hardly ever phoned me, because it was my job to stay in touch as I'd been the one to leave home – to tell me that the doctor had diagnosed her with arthritis. She was in a terrible state about it, almost hysterical. Her sobs and moans went on for ages, reaching a crescendo when she wailed: 'Why me? WHY ME?' My sympathy curdled, as it often did in the end. Why *not* you, I wanted to ask her. Why fucking not?

But Win was not a stoic. She was not that sort of person. She wasn't even stoical about the mishaps of others. If you told her you had cancer, she'd want you to reassure her that she would find the strength to cope. It wasn't until I did have cancer that I realised that a lot of people I knew were like this and that it's actually a pain in the arse. Your crisis is always their crisis. They have to show you how distressed they are, how huge they know this is, because, one way or another, everything always has to be about them. You'll tell them about something grim that happened to you, and they'll rush to tell you that they know just how you feel because a similar but worse thing happened to them.

I'd rather liked my first day at school, strange as it was. But even if I hadn't, I'd have tried to protect Win from that knowledge. I protected my mother from much knowledge over the years. There was a lot of stuff that Win just didn't want to know and that, once she did know, would become ten times worse than it had been before she knew.

Back then, though, she was just my mum. Just, for me, the most important person in the world. Win loved that – being the most important person in the world. Later, when she felt that this status was slipping away from her, she fought and fought to maintain dominance.

I realise now that my mother's main trouble was her pathological inability to understand at all that I was a separate entity from her. She wanted to keep me with her, in the same way as she wanted to keep her arm with her. My brother, a male, was too different to her for her to want to subsume him in this manner. She almost said as much, in different ways, many times. The group narcissism of femininity forced Win to believe that the two of us, mother and daughter, were indivisible. Every time I did something that Win wouldn't have done, it was as if she'd lost control of a part of herself. But I didn't see that, not while Win was alive.

Maybe a wise child, a nearly-five-year-old master of psychology, could have softened the blow my mother sustained when I swanned off to school with barely a glance over my shoulder back at her. She enjoyed soothing me when I was upset, far more than John did. Which was not at all. Upset kids just irritated Dad. Mum was the one who comforted.

When the bell rang, theatrically anxious Win, bug-eyed, hands fluttering, was waiting for me at the white school gate, near the big silver water tower, the reservoir-in-the-sky, as she'd promised earnestly in the morning. The bulb of the reservoir-in-the-sky had Muir Toi daubed on it in huge, white-painted letters, 100 feet up. Impressive. Menacing.

A row of elegant Lombardy poplars was planted next to the water tower, as a windbreak. Fabulous. I loved trees, the distinct shape of each type contained within a little nut, growing from a two-leafed seedling into a giant with the power to herald a new season. Later, when I could read, the *Ladybird Book of Trees* would become an excellent guide.

Did Win seem almost disappointed that it had all gone fine for me, that I had liked my day, had been excited by it?

That I had managed without her? Perhaps. It's hard to know what's a revelation of hindsight and what's a projection that helps you to bolster your own story.

What I remember most about that first day at school is the feeling of being wholly *there*, in the world, of starting to step out into autonomy, independence. I was present at school from the start. There was no upset, no tears, no fears. No trauma. At last, in my fifth decade on this earth, I know which of my memories are traumatic. It's so handy.

I recall my traumatic childhood memories as if I was watching myself going through all these motions, as if my own avatar had been sent in to replace me, while I look on at myself, beady but unobserved. I recognise now that I have this feeling quite often, and that I always have. It's a coping mechanism, a reasonably successful one. Most people experience it sometimes, but it isn't a healthy response.

Dissociation. The temporary retreat of the mind from reality. In your memories of such times, if you can access them, you'll see yourself from the outside, as if you're looking at yourself, looking in on a scene from which you're detached. Because you do detach yourself, psychologically, and pretend as best you can that this is happening to somebody else. As I did the memories of my bracelet being stolen, or the bricks being hurled, or the change from the bread being swiped. Or turning up at the hospital to pick up Win and my new brother.

In my memory I stand on the pavement in my pinny (which I couldn't have been wearing again, after we'd been told it shouldn't be worn outside) looking at David in my mother's arms, but not seeing Win and David, just myself, from their perspective. My recall is of an image of myself looking at him, which of course I couldn't have seen, unless someone had inexplicably placed a mirror in front of us all in the street. I know how to stop those memories now, as they are forming. Feet on the ground and a few good bangs to my chest. Maybe a couple of beta-blockers. Deep breaths. Always with the deep breaths.

Yet, my memories of that first day at school? I remember them all through my own eyes. Seeing Marion skipping in front of me, in her white shirt and grey skirt. No blazer. It was too warm. Seeing Miss MacMillan, at the front of the class, in her purple lambswool. Seeing the sink, and the milk. Seeing the glorious sandpit. There was a bit of initial shock at being separated from Win for so many hours. But I loved school from the start. I loved learning to read. I loved learning to write. I loved drawing. Every morning, we had to draw a little picture in our Busy Book. Later we'd be expected to write a few words about our weekend or the evening before as well. It was so exciting when you actually had something different or interesting to describe. John called these little jotters our Busybody Books, and said we were encouraged to do them so that the authorities could sneakily monitor what was going on at home. I remember him telling me this and feeling shocked. He probably wasn't wrong.

At times, there was plenty to report. Win was not happy in the scheme, which was, it has to be admitted, a bit on the lively side. We couldn't really play out with our toys. I'd had my Barbie doll taken, which had caused me to cross the portal into hysteria. I'd wanted her so much, she'd come for Christmas and I absolutely adored her. She'd been abducted by a Big Boy and I was beside myself. As with the bracelet, attempts to rescue her came to nothing. We knew the family in question. Unfortunately, however, they were 'the lowest of the low', very much the same type as those who had broken all of the sapling trees into stumps and Muir-Toi-ed the whole place. Windows got broken. Landings got urinated on. There was constant low-level disruption among all of these nice families, getting on with their lives. Also: chip-pan fires. It was not unusual to see a ball of chip-pan fire being launched out in a graceful arc from one of the landings of the maisonette at ninety degrees to us and thumping onto the grass in front of it. Mrs Adamson, along our landing, had had a chip-pan fire and Win was very proud of the fact that, after a couple of manly neighbours had dashed in and thrown wet tea towels over the pan, John had sauntered in and turned the cooker off. *Everyone* knew that you shouldn't throw water on a chip-pan fire. This came very much in the 'early learning' category.

Also, our block was on a hill. At one end it was four storeys high, and at the other end five. Every so often there'd be a craze for a kind of home-made skateboarding. We'd put a book – the annuals all the comics issued at Christmas were the perfect size and shape – on a roller skate, sit on the book and whoosh down. There was quite a busy road at the bottom so it was ridiculously dangerous, which kept Win in fear of a child dying, as terrible for her as it would be for the child and its parents. David and I could only do it when Win wasn't looking, which wasn't often. Jim Imlach, who was in my class at school and lived in the next block, had been run over by a car and had been off school for a year.

Interestingly, Jim's dad was Hamish Imlach, folk singer and leftie. Imlach was on an influential anti-Communist blacklist, it was rumoured. But no one cared. Everyone in Motherwell was Labour, at the very least. Motherwell had been the first constituency in Britain ever to elect a Communist MP – Walton Newbold in 1922 – and the first to elect an SNP MP – Robert McIntyre in 1945. Keir Hardie, founder of the Labour Party, had grown up in Holytown, which was one of the vast number of burgh villages that circled the town. Basically, Motherwell *invented* Labour. My parents, I would eventually discover, were Tories who would vote enthusiastically for the milk-liberating lady to run the country. But that bombshell lay far ahead of me at this point.

Win's entire being was at that time focused on getting us out of Muirhouse. She was a formidable warrior. She haunted the council offices, trying to do the impossible – wear down bureaucracy. Bureaucracy was having none of it. In order to get out of the flat, we had to find someone willing to do a swap. This involved going to see various flats in various schemes that were more run-down than ours. We would all go, all four of us. At one notorious place, The Loaning, which had obviously been named by some major existential joker, we went to see the flat of a very nice, very desperate woman who seemed to have some difficulty moving out of the corner of the room she'd planted herself in when we'd arrived, slightly early. Eventually, my brother – aged four or so at this point – had just peered round her and yelled: 'Look! A dead mouse!' We made our excuses and left. The various other potential swaps would end up offering similar difficulties. This was frustrating for me too, because I wanted a bedroom of my own, away from my brother. But I also wanted something really good for my Busy Book, which I took quite seriously.

One of the reasons why I loved school so much was simply that I was good at it, and the feeling of being good at something was soothing balm. It's a narcissistic memory, if ever there was one, but I remember so well the first time I was praised before the whole class, the delicious surprise of it. And it was a surprise.

As a conscientious child, I always prepared the next day's reading aloud, about Dick, Dora, Nip and Fluff. Everyone had to prepare, because no one knew which of the boys and which of the girls would be asked to read aloud that morning. But one day – sod's law, as Win would say – I didn't, and this was the day that Miss MacMillan alighted on me as the girl who had to read the passage out to the class. I burned with embarrassment as I read the new, unfamiliar words, so painfully slowly, longing for this torture to end, raising my head reluctantly as the torture did finally end, feeling so embarrassed to be caught out so completely. Miss MacMillan was beaming. 'That was perfect reading, class,' said Miss MacMillan. 'At exactly the right speed. Not too *fast*, children. Take your time.' Triumph from adversity.

There were less ambiguous triumphs too. I was still with Miss MacMillan – still in Infants – when I won a prize for poetry. Our theme was spring, and the competition was staged across Scotland, by Platignum Pens. I still remember my poem, entitled 'Springtime', which is no great feat of memory:

> Birds are singing in the spring
> Very sweetly too
> I love to hear the birds sing
> Very much. Don't you?

There was a general feeling among my bitter classmates, some of whom had written *Beowulf*-length epics, that this tiny scrap of doggerel was an unworthy winner. Win seemed puzzled too. She suggested that it was the nice drawing of birds in a nest I'd done alongside it, not the poem itself, that had clinched me the prize – a certificate and, of course, a fountain pen, slate grey and shiny chrome, that I used for years, until one fine day I stood on it.

The knowledge that my mother was on the side of the girls I saw sneering and shaking their little heads, even just a bit, was deflating. Yet it was hard to complain about it because it seemed so innocent, so patently not meant to wound. I no longer believe that it was an innocent remark. I think Win did want to knock me off my pedestal. Win's praise was never, ever unqualified. She could always see my insecurities and find little ways to prick at them, make them flare. It was almost an instinct for her.

It took years to piece all the tiny, toxic fragments together, years to accept that I had tolerated digs and prods from Win all my life, and from others as well, because being undermined, little and often, felt familiar to me. That was what happened with people who loved you. Complaining about it was not on. Complaining would be something unfair that you'd be doing to people who loved you, because *you* expected too much of them. Anyway, complaining tended only to bring further and deeper criticism. It was best to tell yourself that the harm hadn't been meant, or even been real. Once, fed up with always having to reassure Win that she looked nice ('How do I l-o-o-k?'), I vouchsafed that she had been putting on weight. Which she had. 'At least I'm not plain and ugly, like you.' I accepted that if this was my own mother's opinion, then I must be very plain and ugly indeed.

Do I see myself and my mother, in the living room at Clyde Terrace, as she spits this at me, as if I'm a third person, watching? I do. Of course I do. I always will, I think. It still makes me feel hopeless, thinking about that moment, thinking about that comment. I came to realise that I wasn't plain and ugly. But I just had to live with the fact that my mother would lash out with the most hurtful comment she could think of if she was ever criticised rather than lauded herself, and make sure in future that I thought twice about inviting unwelcome truths about myself by criticising her. A lesson learned. A lesson, unfortunately, about how to treat my mother, not about what level of insult I should accept from other people. That's how control works.

Yet the certificate I won for the poem was still in the bureau, alongside two others from secondary school – the Burns Federation prize and the Livingstone Memorial prize. There were other mementoes, of a number of other seemingly unsung triumphs. There was a poster-paint portrait of Guy Fawkes, for example, that I'd done at school around the same time as the controversial 'Springtime' and had been declared by Miss MacMillan as the best in the class.

Fawkes, faded now, appears before a Houses of Parliament skyline – a familiar scene from the little black and white photo on the HP sauce bottle. A gunpowder barrel floats to his left, a stamped, addressed letter to his right. Win praised the picture when it came off the wall at the end of term, to be borne home in triumph by myself. But she laughed at it too: 'They didn't have stamps in those days, silly!' Deflated again. Yet, all those years she kept those things, despite the little, niggling darts she couldn't resist shooting. She was more proud of me than she ever let on. Which I'd always hoped.

I always told myself that Win and John just didn't want me to get big-headed, this child who tried so hard and even succeeded sometimes. I think they found my appetite for achievement exhausting. But I learned from the contents of the bureau that those moments of competence did mean something to my mum and dad – maybe a lot. Their efforts to staunch my conceit, though, made me all the more eager for praise – hungry for it, yet simultaneously distrustful of it. I wanted to be conceited and I wanted to be utterly relaxed about being conceited.

What I wanted, really, was to be self-confident and self-assured. Which I'm still not, though I've learned how to look like I am. Every compliment, welcome as it is, still feels like

I've conned somebody, particularly as I tend to fish for them. The ambivalence, the inability just to be grateful that I have some competencies, the endless, forever unfulfilled desire for unconditional support is what exhausts me and the people around me. The narcissist's burden. That's what my mother carried too.

It's sad to relate, but as David and I went through the bureau after my mother had died, I found my old school reports. There they were, tucked into a pigeonhole, thin as tissue, so that each report would be easily copied through layers of carbon paper as the teachers pressed hard with their ballpoints. My heart actually leaped as I saw them – my pleasure at the thought of rereading those early confirmations that I was a good student and a good girl was tragically immense.

But as I unfolded the sheaf and ran my eyes across the report on top of the substantial pile, all anticipation of retrospective glory drained away.

'Easily distracted.'

'Prefers to be the class clown.'

'Could try MUCH harder.'

'Potential being squandered.'

The horror of it all must have been pasted on my face.

'That's my report!' David said, laughing his head off and snatching it from me. Relief flooded through me. And guilt.

It was hard for my brother, starting at the same school four years after me – so conscientious, so keen to please, so thorough – then having to go through the same process again at secondary. Pretty much all of his teachers had taught me before, and some of them were not afraid to make comparisons in which David was found wanting.

It became obvious, pretty early on, that David was not as temperamentally suited to school as I was. Win even told me, very solemnly, that it was a great shame that I was the one who shone, because doing well at school was so much more important for a boy. I remember the moment so well – see myself and my mother from above as I'm told this. I was utterly speechless. The observation seemed so cruelly unfair. To me and to all girls. None of it did anything to soothe the jagged, eternal criss-cross of the jealousy all four of us felt, me against David, David against me, John against David, Win against me.

I was good at school. But so were others. I'd never come first in the end-of-year exams. I was usually third, sometimes fourth. One year, Gillian Fisher suggested that we should swot and try to be first. To me it seemed like cheating, but Gillian did it, and I didn't see much of her for weeks. I remember the smooth, tanned backs of Gillian's knees above her white socks as she approached the front of the class to get the book that was her reward. Her arms were held out from her body, just a few unnatural inches, slightly awkwardly, because she'd become so aware of herself that she didn't quite know what to do with them. Otherwise, she seemed collected. She had done what she set out to do, and it was so *wonderful*. I loved Gillian. She was my best friend. Her mother was from Shropshire, so we both knew what it was like to have foreign blood.

We also, from the age of about ten, knew what a semi-erect penis looked like as it was being stroked and fondled in the hand of the man attached to it. We'd graduated from the marshland to the edge of the woods – the woods where, in a few months, my brother and his pal wouldn't stick to the road. There was a particular yew tree we liked to climb – we hadn't been the first because there was a smooth, varnished plank nailed up there already. The great thing about this tree was that up at the top all the branches stretched out, so you could sit inside this fragrant cone of sunshine and no one would know you were there. Or so we imagined.

One day, we were lounging in the tree when a young man's voice shouted up to us.

'You two need to be a bit more careful. You could break your necks. That's right. I can see you. Come down from there.'

We stuck our heads out from the branches and looked down.

He was young, a skinhead, dressed in denim jacket and jeans, double-denim not being the fashion crime then that it would become. He continued to berate us – for our own safety – and tell us to get out of the tree. Except that all the time he was gently wanking and not – to his small credit, I suppose – getting very far. We stalwartly refused to get down. Eventually, saying that (by some miracle of investigation) he'd tell our mums if he saw us up the tree again, he left.

'Did you see what I saw?' asked Gillian, once we were sure he was gone.

'Yes,' I replied, rapt.

Gillian: 'It looked just like a big sausage.'

Later, in Gillian's kitchen, which was exactly like mine, we sat at the table, unable to stop giggling because on the sideboard there was a large Cumberland sausage on a plate, covered by an upturned glass bowl. We couldn't tell our parents what had happened, though, because they were always going on about 'bad men' and wouldn't let us down the woods any more if we did. And I loved those woods. To me, they were arcadia. Not being able to go to them? That would have been the worst thing possible. Worse than being banned from going to school. Worse than being 'on strike'. Strikes were all the adults seemed to talk about.

9

Dad's Work Reference

In the Shields Road flat some of the greatest excitements of 1970s childhood took place. I adored the power cuts and the preparations for them too. We'd bought a camping stove, early on, and lots of gas canisters. When the candles ran out at the shops, John made candles from flimsy, plastic tubs of margarine. Not an unmitigated success, but, still. Primal. We were basically living like cavemen, on our wits, on our ingenuity, on our own resources. Sitting in the dark, the four of us, playing word games, eating tinned stew, resplendent in our blankets, *surviving*. It was intoxicating.

I was only dimly aware of the political events behind things like power cuts, the three-day week, the telly stopping at some early point that was still way after my bedtime and Dad not getting any overtime. He usually worked a Sunday-morning shift, but now he was home all weekend and had more time to take us to see Motherwell FC at Fir Park or up to Shotts golf course to practise our swings. We kids had a couple of tiny clubs that John had cut down at work.

I was totally unaware that this was what a 'national state of emergency' looked like, and anyway, in Motherwell the politics were pretty simple. In Motherwell we backed the miners: because we'd all had miners in our family, like I had my grandfather; because all those little villages around

Motherwell – like Shotts – were mining villages; because we all knew how hard, dangerous and health-breaking mining was; and because without coal there was no steel, and without steel we were nothing. Which was unthinkable.

Once, at school, we'd been asked to draw a miner mining as homework, and when John had seen the picture I was carefully drawing, of a man standing up, daintily pick-axeing a vast coalface, he'd been quite stern. 'It's not like that. Men lie down, in cold, stagnant, stinking water, with rats in it, twist their bodies to reach narrow seams. They ache. They hurt. That's what your grandad told me.' John's mum and dad had very much not wanted their sons to mine.

And there had been the Aberfan Disaster when I was four, which was the first news story that got into the marrow of my bones. A bing collapsing onto a school, smothering all of the children? There were slag bings all over our bit of Scotland. And schools.

Aberfan. A mining village, like our mining villages.

And *all* their pretty ones?

One hundred and sixteen children, all at their desks at school at the start of an October day in 1966. I can still see some of those children, the ones that took up residence in my mind back then, in their grey uniforms, heads bowed over their desks, which were yellow, varnished wood, set in rows. I see that avalanche of wet, black filth hit them like a vast, infernal bullet, see it slam them into nothingness in a second, see it engulf them all in dense, thick, stupid muck and in the implacable laws of physics. Twenty-eight adults too, five of them teachers at the school. Wiped out. Literally. Wiped. Out.

Here was quotidian cataclysm, darkness visible, a crude, effective recipe for disaster, whipped up from carelessness and rain. Half of the surviving population of Aberfan went on to be diagnosed with post-traumatic stress disorder. The rest, I'd imagine, didn't like going to the doctor's. There were a number of other bings around that village, and it took a lot of pressure from the remaining residents before they were eventually removed. The people of Aberfan had been expected to carry on living among the grimy, towering piles of mining debris that had killed their children. This life. This was the life that miners wanted a decent wage for living.

As for the oil sheiks who cropped up in the news so often? Well, Arabs were from abroad, so there was no point at all in even beginning to try to fathom them. No point at all.

But while family concerns rarely strayed beyond Great Britain, John and Win kept a beady eye on British politics and current affairs. They took a daily newspaper – *The Scottish Daily Express* – and the *Sunday Post* (like everyone else) and the *Sunday Mail* on the day of rest. They watched the news every evening, and David and I both understood that talk about anything other than the news in question was not to be undertaken. They muttered to each other often about various politicians. My dad was fond of saying that they were all as bad as each other and that no matter who you voted for, you still got the government. Harold Wilson. Ted Heath. Barbara Castle. Denis Healey. Occasional outbreaks of Jeremy Thorpe. These adults seemed to me like far-off giants. Demented, slightly comic giants, but giants all the same.

And they were so very far off. In Westminster, hundreds of miles from our local concerns, a place I knew best from the label on a sauce bottle. In general elections, a lot of people were voting Scottish Nationalist. A chip-on-the-shoulder pride was rife. Scotland the brave. Scotland the ingenious. Scotland the clever, the lyrical, the industrious, the beautiful, the romantic. It was easy, growing up in Motherwell, Lanarkshire, in the 1960s and 1970s, to feel fierce pride in the great achievements that littered our small nation's past: the inventors, the engineers, the medics, the scientists, the philosophers, the writers, the architects, the politicians, the economists, the explorers . . . The evidence was rife: it was special, being Scottish.

But it was easy too, in the 1960s and 1970s, even as a small child, to note uncomfortably that such riches were not nearly so apparent in the present. Who was today's Robert Burns, Walter Scott, Robert Louis Stevenson? Who was today's James Watt, John Logie Baird, Alexander Graham Bell? Who was today's Adam Smith, David Hume, James Boswell? Who was today's Alexander Fleming, Joseph Lister, James Simpson? And so on, and on and on.

It was bewildering, this duality, this constant keeping of two flames, one of Scottish victimhood, the other of Scottish superiority. So much past, so little present . . . the actor Sean Connery was the colossus among Scots in modern mainstream culture, towering above the Bay City Rollers, Jackie Stewart, Billy Connolly, Andy Stewart, Stanley Baxter, Rikki Fulton, Neil Reid, Sydney Devine, Barbara Dickson, the Krankies and Lena Zavaroni (another graduate of *Opportunity Knocks*). There was Rod Stewart, forever dangling a tartan scarf from his wrist. But we knew he wasn't Scottish, not really, the fraud. Even Connery didn't actually like it here. He was a tax exile. 'Oor Wullie', symbol of our nationhood as he may have been, was a cartoon.

And we knew too that, truthfully, some of that Scottish star list was scraping the barrel, their celebrated names symbolising a terrible paucity of modern achievement, not an embarrassing wealth of it. In 1980, when Sheena Easton was featured on the music reality show *The Big Time*, Win would tell me she was related to John's cousin George, over in Bellshill, so she was a cousin of mine as well. This seemed legit. Easton's name before she married was Sheena Orr. It also seemed like something that it would be wisest to keep quiet about, due to its unbelievably vast post-punk naffness. (Motherwell was and is good at talent show breakthroughs. Susan Boyle, late of *Britain's Got Talent*, may herself have been from Blackburn, but both her parents were from Motherwell.)

Of course, once Sheena had really made the big time and was recording with Prince, my relation to her became more interesting to me. But when I asked about it again, Win had no memory of making any such assertions at all, as with my grandad and his near imprisonment for running for the bookie. Win had these romantic fantasies, told you all about them, quite vividly, then forgot she'd ever said anything at all. We all do, I guess. Never mind. At least Sheena definitely *was* a Scot, recording with Prince, even if she wasn't actually related to me. Or was she? I still don't know.

I was a kid, and didn't know that plenty of Scots were out there making a mark in Swinging London and beyond. I hadn't heard of R. D. Laing yet, anti-psychiatrist, poet and darling of the London media, or of Alex Trocchi, a situationist and a giant of 'the counter-culture'. But my sense that Scotland itself was in the cultural doldrums was real, if exaggerated. It hurt, that nagging feeling amid the patriotism that contemporary Scotland was maybe a wee bit embarrassing. We did need change.

John's blanket disapproval of politics and politicians afforded me a handy place into which I could project my own assumptions about change. I knew that John did not like his work. I knew it left him utterly exhausted. I knew he had to work six days a week and undertake a punishing shift pattern to keep the family modestly afloat. I knew that Win worried constantly about the bills, and that John was very much to be respected for what he did as a breadwinner.

We'd all been to an open day at John's factory, Anderson Boyes, whose huge coal-cutting machines were mainly sold abroad. (British mines, with their typically long, thin and twisting seams, weren't suitable for these giant machines. They were just as my father's father had described them.) But what struck me most as I stood on that cavernous factory floor, so tidy, with milling machines laid out in a graticule, was the heavy, insistent, physical, pressing force of the noise. It struck me almost physically. 'It's so loud! How can you bear it?' I yelled in John's ear at the top of my voice, above it all.

He did a double take, his face full of disbelief and wonder, then started laughing. 'Only one of each type of machine is running, and there are twelve of each machine in this department.'

This unbearable cacophony, this merciless auditory assault was to him, to all the men that worked there, virtually nothing. To exist and to concentrate, to look at engineering blueprints and drill perfect holes again and again, accurate in situation, size and internal thread to a thousandth of an inch, within a wall of sound so fierce, so strong that it felt like a living, malevolent force? I couldn't comprehend it – this was surely a kind of hell. Hell, surely, was empty. All the devils were here. No wonder John came home every evening grey-faced, with a pounding headache. My only ambition for the future, from that moment, was to get paid to do something I liked, something I'd want to do anyway even if I wasn't being paid. It still is.

So, my own assumptions were that, politically, my dad was on the side of the workers. On the rare occasions when my parents went out in the evening to a social event, I'd sometimes ask Win if they'd had a good time. 'We had been,' Win would often say, 'until your dad started arguing about politics.' Somehow, despite all the evidence, I convinced myself that John must be much more radical, much more left-wing than the rest of the people of Motherwell. There could be no other explanation for these arguments that kept happening.

Yet I also heard John complain about how shit the union was, how he resented his obligation to be in it at all and to have to pay for the privilege, what a negation of his freedom to choose the closed shop was, how the men were drunk on ideas of their power that didn't exist, how they were obsessed with fomenting strike action, how he hated to be obliged to strike with the others, how the shop stewards were rabble-rousers and troublemakers, how they defended men who constantly threw sickies (John NEVER missed a day's work), who got others to clock them on every day, because they spent their working hours in the pub and didn't care that it was men like John who did their work while they took the money for it. These last allegations seemed unanswerable, because the pub outside the factory gates, perfectly brazenly, was indeed called The Cleekim Inn. The Clock Him In.

The day of rest started for John at 5 a.m., like every working day, when he got up for his overtime shift at the factory – Saturday was time and a half, Sunday double time. John got the best overtime slots because he was diligent, reliable, never ill, never late, never unpredictable. In the bureau, to my disgust, was a work reference from my dad's last boss, at the time of his redundancy, saying what a solid, reliable and generally brilliant worker he had been, how anyone would be able to count themselves lucky to employ him. Employ him? A sixty-year-old man who'd worked in heavy industry all his life, in a town, a region and a country full of unemployed folk? Words. Just words. Win had kept this letter because she was proud of it, proud of him. They both took pride in being good workers. I threw the letter away, like my good-worker parents had been thrown away when there was no longer money to be made from them.

I remember perfectly the moment when I realised that John got into arguments about politics all the time because he was a Tory. And that my mum was a Tory too. Win was more liberal than Dad. If the John who existed back then, in the 1970s, was around today he'd be alt-right. He had that US-style belief in total independence from the state, in fierce pride in your virtually nothing because it was ALL YOURS. Mum, on the other hand, hated the flat that was ALL HERS and the scheme that fell further and further into disarray. She had tried. But there had been no luck with getting a swap.

10

The Smiths Watch

It was bureaucracy that rescued us in the end. And rules. And points. It took a while. After six years in Shields Drive, and five years at school, I was past my ninth birthday. It was considered wrong and indecent for a girl aged ten to share a room with a boy, so we got extra points, which meant that the council was under an obligation to rehouse us. The trouble was that if you refused two offers, you had to take the third one. Win was in a race against bureaucracy *and* time. I remember going to see the first of the places, a flat which did have a phone – hurrah! – but also had shit smeared all over the walls – boo! My parents were furious at the insult – you could eat your dinner off their toilet seat. But they also realised that they were in serious jeopardy. We had to find a place we wanted, before we were forced into a place that was like the one we'd just seen.

Win began wandering the streets (with me in tow, for company), noting down empty houses then going to the council offices and asking why we hadn't been offered a look at them. It was all a fix, she would tell me. The relatives of the people at the council always got the good places. There was probably something in that too. Anyway. That was how we got Clyde Terrace. Win heard that its occupant had died, and pretty much went to the council offices every morning, first thing, until they agreed to make it their second offer. Heroic, really.

And it didn't stop with the house, which had a phone and a garden and a back and front door. We were now in a position to get a dog. John and Win had always told us it was impossible, because we lived in a flat, so it would be cruel. But, what with the new place, the excuse had been invalidated. There was one false start. My dad went out one evening after work, which wasn't like him. When we asked where he was going he replied, as he always did, telling us that it was none of our business: 'I'm going to see a man about a dog.' But he really was.

John came back with a pink-nosed mongrel, white and dirty, about a year old, who looked a bit like a bulldog. We children were ecstatic, but it was clear that Win wasn't happy. Then she started itching, great welts appearing on her tummy.

'It's that mutt, John. It's got fleas. You'll have to take it back.'

John took the dog away, while we children wept.

Win, trying to persuade us that we'd get another dog, a better one, said: 'That dog's got a pink nose anyway!'

'But we could take it to the dog hospital and get a new nose for it,' my brother pleaded.

Win laughed. John went off again a few days later and came back with the sweetest, most adorable puppy that any child could wish for. She was so young that her eyes were still blue.

I was nearly as thrilled at the thought of my brilliant Busy Book entry as I was that we HAD A DOG. She was a Border Collie cross called Sheila, a name Win changed to Tina with amazing speed. In my Busy Book I drew her little face, with her patches of black over her eyes and her alert black ears. It was a moment of Busy Book bliss, a perfect Busy Book entry. Sheer joy.

After we'd moved to Clyde Terrace, not long before I finished primary school, a general election was called. We'd had four years of Ted Heath, with his miner-bashing and his inflation, and Motherwell had high hopes for Harold Wilson's return. I'd come home from school for lunch – I had for yonks at that point, because I was being bullied a lot at school and was keeping it a secret from my parents. (I'd just told Win that I wanted to come home at lunchtime because I loved Clyde Terrace so much.) I was sitting at the kitchen table while Win stood by the sink with her back to me, shelling eggs. I watched as her hands went limp in the basin and she began to stare into space, perfectly still and quiet, for ages.

'What is it, Mum?' I asked her, becoming alarmed.

'Oh,' sighed my mother, after a final dramatic pause and a little shake of her head. 'I'm just thinking about how terrible it will be if that awful Labour get back in.'

Gosh.

That awful Labour didn't exactly get back in. The February 1974 election delivered a hung parliament and a minority government led by Wilson. In another election that October, Labour gained a majority of three, the unions started striking like there was no tomorrow, and Motherwell, steel town, started sliding towards 1979 – the start of the Thatcher years – and our doom. But we didn't know that then.

John and Win voted for Thatcher in the 1979 and 1983 elections. By 1987, even they had wised up. Hardly surprising, since everyone in our family had by then experienced unemployment and the grind of searching for work except John, and he lived in fear of losing his own job as round after round of redundancies hit his firm too, which had fallen to a three-year hostile takeover by a group called Charter Consolidated, despite a split decision by the Monopolies Commission against the merger.

Win's own working life had recommenced once I'd started secondary school and was old enough to look after David when we'd both finished school for the day. Aunt Betty had got Win her part-time job as a wages clerk at Smiths, where Betty worked full-time. Win would go in three evenings a week to work on the gigantic new wages computer. Not many other staff were in the building at that time, but Win used to joke about a man she called Cricklewood, who she said had 'the glad eye' for her. Maybe, she said, 'she'd run off with him'. John tried to be indulgent when she said these things, but he usually only managed to look miserable.

Because the Smiths factory was near my new school, and because my social problems had largely gone there with me, I'd go down to the factory at lunchtime to eat with Betty in the works canteen. In the bureau there was a little Smiths watch that had once been mine, one of a couple of surviving timepieces from the days when Win worked there and every surface in our house – including the walls – had a Smiths clock on it. The staff discount was IMMENSE.

Smiths had long been a giant of British industry, watchmaker and supplier of aeronautical dials to pretty much every plane on the planet. In Tate Modern in 2018, I sat among steel girders from my father's factory, watching the ticking of clocks from my mother's factory, in Christian Marclay's twenty-four-hour film *The Clock*. But by the time Win started at Smiths in 1974, the company had been hit hard by the decline in British manufacturing.

Even I, aged twelve, could see that the designs were outdated. I was particularly horrified when Win brought home, with great pride, a tablet-shaped wall clock with a green fake

Wedgwood depiction of the Palace of Westminster, with a tiny real clock in the tower. The complaints department, Win admitted, was always very active. The stuff was no longer reliable. There were many rounds of redundancies here too, Win going about five years after she'd become full-time in the wages office. She was utterly devastated. No one had ever been made quite as redundant as Win was. There were a number of other jobs over the years, and a number of other redundancies. This was a source of constant anxiety and worry. Win found rejection of any kind unbearably hard.

As for the eventual closure of Smiths, the factory lay empty for a long time before two kids crashed through its high glass roof, their lives saved only by the growbags full of cannabis plants inside. The place, from then on, was known locally as Spliffs Industries.

At that time, though, no one knew that – once a huge number of people had been left with nothing else to do all day except find ways to forget all about their various pre-dicaments – drugs would become part of the fabric of life. Despite the strikes, despite things like the sugar shortage – which stopped Motherwell from functioning more com-pletely than any strike could – the 1970s seemed optimistic. There was little doubt that better times lay ahead, that we were valued, the people of this fortunate country, and that everything would work out fine.

That was the promise of the post-war settlement, after all, and it seemed to be going smoothly, give or take. Ordinary people did appear to be getting on in life, more than they had in the past. We had cars. We had fridges. We had tellies. We had our own bathrooms. Some of us would even, quite soon, have a timber house with a back and front door and a dog. There were no grammar schools in our part of the world, and there was no eleven-plus. Everyone went to the comprehensive their catchment area dictated, and if some were better than others, well, they were all good enough. And we lived in this great country, Scotland, the great River Clyde on our doorstep, just through the woods.

I still liked the marsh. But, Tina the dog in tow, I'd started exploring the wood beyond it, which was so much bigger and, in terms of plant life, so much more complex. Obviously, I liked the trees, which were a real mixture, pine, yew, oak, chestnut, sycamore, beech, hazel, ash, rowan . . . so many shapes to identify! So many names to learn! Sometimes there would be a tree that was hard to identify, that would turn out to be a mulberry or an araucaria. I didn't know then that the families who owned the estate, the Dalziels and the Hamiltons, had been keen horticulturalists, devoted to bringing home exotic trees from around the world to plant on the estate. Multi-horticulturalism.

I didn't know then that this land had first become a royal hunting forest before the medieval period, in 843. I didn't know that 'forest' was a word for a place where deer lived, nothing to do with trees at all. But it was obvious that some of the trees were very old, one of them, an oak, so old that it had spread wider than many of the trees were tall. As an adult I learned that this tree was called the Convenanters' Oak, because a group of John Knox's followers had met here to hold services in the seventeenth century, when Presbyterian Protestantism was banned in Scotland's churches. There's a sign by the tree now, telling people this stuff. There are also wooden stanchions holding up its weary old boughs, offering the ancient tree some life support. But none of this was there when Motherwell was a place with a future. The heritage industry moves in when people don't know who they are any more and have to focus on who they were instead.

I saw the trees as a community, a more calmly interdependent community than the one at my school, one that would host me and let me be. I understood that the trees and plants were all in some sort of complex symbiotic relationship, even though I wouldn't have been able to put it into words, let alone into scientific parlance.

Scientists only found out in 2019 that the apples that don't fall far from the tree are bad apples. The seeds of a parent tree do better the further from that tree they fall. I didn't know either that trees trade via a fungal internet that connects them underground, allowing one tree species to store excess nutrients and swap them with nutrients that other tree species have a different superfluity of. No wonder similar species don't like to grow too near each other. Too incestuous. Too little opportunity for trade in times of hardship.

But I liked what I saw. I liked the various ways in which the plant life under the trees had adapted to the environment, rich in the nutrients provided by the deciduous trees and their leaf mould, yet limited in terms of sunlight. These woods were called the Dalziel estate and, like many places in Scotland, were perfect for rhododendrons and azaleas. They thrive in soil that has coal in it, soil that has conifers on it, soil that has weathered the sulphur dioxide that heavy industry pumps out. Acid soil. The landowners who had lived there, before nationalisation prompted a move to Surrey, had made their fortunes and planted the estate from the wealth created by their investments in coal and steel in the first place, so there was a pleasing circularity in the way that the plants carried on without them. In late spring I'd comb the margins of the woods, keen to spot the rhododendrons that were out of the ordinary, not bog-standard purple – lovely as those were – but crimson, peach, pale pink, pale lemon, the ochre colour of honey. Each new find made me feel I was David Livingstone, charting a jungle unseen by a single soul, apart from all the souls who had seen these things before . . .

Bluebells are the most obvious among plants adapted for woodland survival. They bloom in that brief period when the weather is warm but the trees haven't come into leaf. But the wood anemones do that too, covering the woodland floor in midnight starlight weeks before the bluebells cover it in bright spring sky. The ransoms are around at this time too, their white globes of flowers and garlicky smell declaring that they are wild alliums. Alliums were not fashionable plants in the scant gardens of Motherwell. We'd only see those purple flowers when onions grown for their bulbs were 'shot' – had been left too long after they should have been harvested. I wouldn't have dreamed of bringing some ransoms home for Mum to cook with and she wouldn't have dreamed of taking me seriously if I had. Wood sorrel? So pretty, its leaves so light and effulgent, its little white flowers so delicately traced with their lacy network of purple veins. I still don't know if eating it would delight or poison. Delight. I think.

The ransoms, though. Now, these plants are more widely called wild garlic and are seasonal staples among foodies. I dare say you can actually buy it. Lots of restaurants fall over themselves to serve it in spring. As for actual garlic, we did have a little jar of garlic salt in among the other grungy jars on the pair of Schwartz spice racks. But garlic in a bulb? That was a continental thing that made European breath stink, especially the breath of the French, who also ate horses, frogs and snails. Disgusting. Abroad was still for other people. Abroad, with its awful food and its too-hot sun.

II

Queen's Guide Award

Lurking people – lurking men – made the woods dangerous, despite their bucolic pleasures. The wanking skinhead incident hadn't even been my first encounter with a bad man in the woods. And it wasn't at all the scariest. I'd gone to play and explore there with a new friend, Marilyn, a year or so before, when we were eight or nine. The woods were part of an old estate, the Hamilton estate, and had an abandoned Scots Baronial mansion in the centre, Dalziel House. (It was sold by the council in 1985, for a penny. It's luxury apartments now.) The River Clyde provided a boundary to the woods, and a water meadow stretched from the river to the house. The two of us had been picking wild flowers, we'd reached the meadow and we were trying to get up a tree to get some horse chestnut blossoms. This was before you were told that you shouldn't pick wild flowers.

As Marilyn punted me up the tree, I saw a man, smartly dressed in a brown suit, walking quickly and purposefully along the fringe of the woods at the top of the meadow, away from us. I pointed him out to Marilyn and said: 'That might be a bad man.' She dismissed my worries and got on with the task of thrusting me into the chestnut boughs. Suddenly, like a pheasant breaking cover, the man came rushing towards us. By now I was up the tree, and I saw his pale face with its black eyes fixed on me, his Brylcreemed dark hair falling in a lock over his forehead, his white shirt and dark tie so incongruous in this suddenly perilous situation. I glanced in panic towards Marilyn. She was already a tiny, running figure at the far end of the meadow.

As I scrambled down the tree to escape, he grabbed me round the waist with his unyielding arms, holding me fast. I kicked and flailed so hard that he lost his grip for a second and I skittered out of his arms. Bizarrely, I remember calculating whether I had time to pick up my bunch of flowers and decided that I did. Grabbing them, I ran too, like I've never run, before or since. I felt so strong that it was almost like flying. When I ran towards a barbed-wire fence there was no hesitation. I'd be too scared to attempt this at any other time, but on this occasion I sailed over it. Adrenaline. I caught up with Marilyn, who was cowering in the trees, waiting for me, shaking with fear. She relaxed as she saw me: 'Didn't you pick up *my* flowers?'

That was the worst of many weird encounters in those woods, though it didn't stop me going back, again and again. Marilyn and I agreed not to tell our parents, but she never played with me again. I think I just reminded her too much of how close we'd come to something truly terrible.

I don't know if I'd have told my parents about this even if there wasn't an important practical reason – fear of banning – for concealing the experience. It was all too awkward. Warnings about bad men tended to be coded. Everything tended to be coded. There were lots of public information films on the television at that time, films about protecting your personal safety. In one, the pretty girl got snub-nosed Mike because he 'swims like a fish' instead of the Adonis who'd been trying to impress her poolside in his tiny swimming trunks. In another, you were told how to inflate your trousers to save yourself from drowning. Water was a big danger. Even the need to lag the pipes so that they wouldn't burst in winter was communicated to the nation by a friendly man with a posh English voice.

And there was a cartoon warning against going off with a man who offered you sweets or asked you if you wanted to get into his car to go and see some puppies. No one had much idea of what the bad things the bad men did once they'd got hold of you actually were. Only that they were so bad that they were literally unspeakable. Innocence in children had to be preserved. Not long before I saw my first penis, a girl in class asked me if I knew what a penis was and I told her authoritatively that it was a man who played the piano.

If my parents had told me, at primary school age, what a penis was I wouldn't have known where to look. Kids were generally taught that sex was dirty and dangerous, not to be spoken of. Or, at least, I assumed that's what they were generally taught, because it was what I was taught. The things that we vaguely knew might have happened to us with the bad men – they seemed like sex at its most dirty and dangerous, worse than death. The culturally inflicted shame was huge. Sometimes, however, the details of things that had happened to children did become common knowledge – usually when there had been no actual sexual assault.

One boy from my class – I see him now, skinny, wavy, dry brown hair with golden flecks, dry skin, pale green eyes, a terminally runny nose (really mucusy), always smiling, an imp, but I can't remember his name – had been subjected to a weird kind of torture in the meadow. He had been told by a man with a knife to strip naked, and the man had thrown all of the boy's clothes into the cold water of the meadow's pools and swamps and made him go and get them, again and again.

Something like that wouldn't go in the local paper. And you would only find out about sex attacks if there had been a conviction. That's how we knew about the girl who'd been raped and murdered, by the side of the Clyde but further down towards the foot of the town, under the bridge when the little strip of motorway from Motherwell to Hamilton started. For years after this crime, it seemed, Win would say, 'Oh, that poor girl', whenever we passed. At that time I'd only got a bad feeling about the poor girl. I didn't understand the specifics of what had befallen her. I asked Win when I was older who the poor girl had been, and got the whole story – as much as Win knew, anyway. Later, I realised that the sites where women were murdered often became places of silent warning, like smashed-up cars being left at the side of the road in Mexico, with signs nailed to them asking drivers to reduce their speed.

The inability to speak of these matters – it left children extremely vulnerable, as continued waves of revelation about historical child abuse would eventually illustrate pretty starkly. As for the men who stalked the woods for boys, not girls – like the man who had tortured my classmate – that also led to a long-standing general confusion, whereby homosexuality and paedophilia were linked in the public mind, when they were of course very different things.

Even in Motherwell, faint sounds of the reports from battles to own and define one's identity – as a woman, as a young person, as a gay person, as a disabled person, as a child – were springing up all over the place. We didn't have much truck with that stuff, though. We had being a Catholic or being a Protestant to provide us with any identity needs we may have had. And, of course, we were all the people of Motherwell, Lanarkshire. People of steel. There was a lot of wanting to be tough. Hard as Lanarkshire steel. To paraphrase Hitler.

In the playground, this meant such things as The Dumps, which I think all schools have a version of, for birthdays, when the lucky celebrant would be suspended by her four limbs and thumped down on the tarmac of the playground for as many dumps as her years of life. If your birthday fell in the school holidays you counted yourself lucky.

There was the general drama, of course, of 'outside the school gates at four', which meant a fight about something that had blown up at school, literally thrashed out yards beyond the physical and minutes beyond the temporal jurisdiction of the teachers.

And there was The Piano, which wasn't as melodic as you might imagine. The Piano was a mass punishment in which one child – usually a boy – was pulled or knocked to the ground, while other people – usually also boys – kicked and kicked him, all the while singing to the tune of the chorus of the French song 'On y Va':

> Pia -
> Pia -
> Pi-a-no.
> Pi-ano. Pi-ano.
>
> Pia -
> Pia -
> Pi-a-no.
> Pia -
> Pi-a-no.

The girls tended to provide the audience. I don't know what provoked a Piano, or what the rules of The Piano were. These were things I was keen to have absolutely no involvement with, as they all seemed very sore. The boys were traumatised too, in the cause of masculinity, in different ways to the girls. Both sexes were hardened in their different ways.

I still wonder now how the hell Miss MacMillan, and all our other teachers, did it. Twenty four- and five-year-olds – the number of pupils doubling once we were in Juniors – no classroom assistant, and worse, *no photocopier*. There was a thing called 'the banda printer', which worked on a similar principle to carbon paper, only providing many more copies. A master copy of what you wanted to reproduce was created on a sheet of waxed paper and then printed out from a whirling drum until the image became too faded for any more copies to be squeezed out. But it was used only rarely. The endless worksheets of today's classroom were at that time still an impossible dream-stroke-nightmare.

On the discipline front, the ever-present threat of corporal punishment certainly helped to keep us in line, though the humiliation and unfairness of it hurt so much more than the pain. I don't remember Miss MacMillan ever actually using her belt, though it was always there on her desk. It was just a two-tonguer, brown leather. Mr Main was rumoured to have had a ten-tonguer. The tongues were the smaller divisions that ran up about a third of the strap. They made the sting harder, I think.

While I remember the first time I got the belt, and why I got the belt, I don't remember who administered the punishment. It smarted, not that hard – not as hard as my sense of injustice. That's still with me more than fifty years on. I hadn't been at school for long, and I was in the white-tiled Infants' lavatory, desperate for a wee, waiting for one of the stainless-steel cubicles to be free. Finally I got one, and the bell rang while I was still inside.

'No one should be in the lavatories after the bell has rung,' snapped a teacher through the door. I came out, trying to explain, and was shouted down. Zero Tolerance had arrived at Muirhouse Primary quite some while before it hit New York. I was sent somewhere to be belted and I still can't believe this was done to me. Other times I got the belt I sort of deserved it, like the time in Juniors when Bryan Nelson kept turning round and banging my desk with his fist, and I eventually put a sharp pencil under his hand so that it stabbed him. Which was a spur-of-the-moment thing I regretted, not only because Mrs Mullen belted me in front of the class, saying: 'I expect better from you, Deborah', but also because it really injured Bryan. Sorry, Bryan.

Everyone preferred the belt to lines, though, because it was over quickly and your parents didn't get to know about it. There was so very much that your parents didn't know about.

Mine, for a long time, didn't know about the bullying. I was too ashamed to tell them. I knew it was bad to have enemies instead of friends, to be unable to get on with others. It got so bad, over long months, that even Gillian didn't speak to me any more. She'd been the last holdout, the only person in our class who'd stood by me. But she caved in in the end as well. I don't quite know where Margaret Simpson had sprung from – she hadn't been at our primary school until quite late on. But after we'd moved to the Timbers Margaret and I had fallen into the habit of getting each other home after school, because she lived in Kirknethan, the next scheme along from our new one.

Margaret was stout, with wavy fair hair in a 1950s style, red broken capillaries across her cheeks and a thin little mouth, the sort of mouth that would be described in a cliché as 'cruel'. Somehow I managed to think of her as beautiful, although I did need some help in this endeavour.

Me: 'Mum, do you think that little red squiggly lines on someone's cheeks can look nice?'

Win: 'Broken veins? Oh, no.'

Margaret seemed to me like a character from an Enid Blyton – we were all Enid Blyton-crazy at that time. I found her enthralling. I looked forward to our chats, and I think I started waiting until she was passing and walking into school with her too. She'd said she was in a Girl Guide troupe, in town, and asked if I would like to join too. I always joined. Any extra-curricular activity that was going I signed up for and gave it a try.

Guides were on a Friday night and Guides were right up my street. So many badges to earn! So many little round embroidered bits of fabric that you could actually sew onto a garment that told the tale of your many achievements! God, I loved Guides. My Queen's Guide Award – the highest Guide accolade, which involved gaining masses of badges and going on masses of camps – was there in the bureau, along with a clipping from the *Motherwell Times* reporting on the presentation of a grand-looking certificate and a nasty gilt brooch. In the photograph that accompanies the news story I look like a tired, wan, anxious, middle-aged child.

My Guide uniform and hat were still in my parents' house too, inside a barrel my dad had carved a chunk out of, adding a circular, hinged piece of plywood halfway down, transforming it into a rustic seat with storage. It was an outdoor novelty really, but the weather would eventually have destroyed this unique object, of which we Orrs were very proud, just as it had destroyed all the other furniture from John's rustic-furniture phase – which to be fair wasn't merely his own phase but one that the entire 1970s nation went through. Though we did our rustic phase in the 1980s, having eventually given up on the idea of acquiring a carboy to grow ferns in. At that stage, Scotland was broadly about a decade behind London in matters of fashion and culture.

He was good at making things, was John.

Anyway. Guides. At first it all seemed fine. I even vaguely knew a couple of the girls from the troupe, Pauline and Andrea, who were the daughters of my mother's surviving English friend from Thistle Street, Pat Lindsay. These girls all went to primaries that would feed them on to Dalziel High, apart from one girl who went to 'Hutchie', of which I'd never heard but about which the Dalziel-destined girls talked a lot. They mostly lived in the private houses in town – which to me meant riches – and their dads had occupations like 'doctor' or 'accountant' or 'scientist'. Hutcheson's was a posh private school in Glasgow. I'd thought private school was very much a fictional thing from the past, popular in the fantasies of Enid Blyton, like your dad being a scientist was.

Somehow, these girls – who had to promise to replace their continental quilts with sheets and blankets for the purpose of attaining their bed-making badge, whose parents drank *wine*, who were au fait with private school, who had been *abroad* – decided that I was 'a snob'. Maybe I seemed like one. Maybe I repeated things about the town and its people that Win had told me, that I probably shouldn't have. Maybe it was nothing to do with Win at all, and everything to do with me. I just don't know. One thing I do know is that Margaret agreed with them, and went off to spread the glad tidings at school. A group of three or four expanded until most of the girls in the class were involved, and one or two of the boys. It got quite nasty. At one point a group of them attacked me in the school library and stripped me down to my vest and pants. I see myself cowering there, behind a folding bookcase. It's all I see. All I feel is shame and misery. Different girls did the same thing at Guides, on a camp.

Every girl in the world, it seemed, wanted to see me in my vest and pants.

I dreaded going to school after that. I'd arrive as late as possible in the morning, go home at lunchtime and spend the two 'playtimes' surrounded by jeering, shoving, sneering girls. Sometimes there would be a note stuck on the inside of my desk when I went back into class. 'Bons', one said. It was 'snoB' written backwards. Once, after a classmate had seen me taking our white, fluffy dog home after she'd rolled in cow shit, the note read: 'Your dog is dirty and smelly.' Weirdly, that hurt more than anything, maybe because Tina had become such a comforting friend and companion to me. I spent most of the weekends and school holidays alone, walking Tina in the good weather, in the woods and fields around the town. It soothed me so much. That was the only thing that made me feel halfway normal. Even with my family there was pressure, the pressure of having to pretend that everything was fine. My parents didn't know that I'd been engulfed by bullying. Of this I felt deeply ashamed too, although I didn't quite understand why. I think I do now, to some extent.

I didn't fully realise at the time that a lot of the animosity being expressed was the animosity of young women towards one of their number who was still a child. They all lived now in a world of periods, hormones and the terrifying possibility of pregnancy. The ravaging of young women's bodies via starvation – anorexia nervosa – hadn't become a well-documented phenomenon at that time. The singer Karen Carpenter would die of the illness in 1983, and everyone would learn all about it. But the ambivalence, the feeling of resentment about becoming a woman – the *fear* of your body's betrayal of the child you had been – that was there. 'They're just jealous,' Win always said when I told her that someone had said a nasty or bitchy thing. In a way, they were.

I'd given puberty barely a thought until one day, at mandatory primary school swimming lessons at Wishaw Baths, Gillian Brown emerged from the changing room in a purple halter-neck bikini, silky, long, ash-blonde hair tumbling over her shoulders. The rest of the girls were in black or navy one-pieces, with the occasional concession to florals and little skirts, and looking like girls. The boys were in little trunks with strings, and looking like boys.

Gillian, however, looked like a Bond girl – that is, like a curvaceous, pneumatic, lounging-on-the-top-of-a-car-at-the-motor-show WOMAN. She would have been ten or eleven. A couple of the boys placed their hands over their crotches, while others turned generally purple, like the bikini. Mostly, the boys just gasped in wonder and exchanged delighted and mildly awestruck smirks. The girls looked on, vaguely mutinous. BOOBS were something that you could write on one of the new, exciting pocket calculators, using the numbers 80085. They were comic. So, what was with the deep, satiny cleavage? What was with the waist? And the hips? Seriously?

Gillian was an adult now, and no longer of our world. She had had greatness thrust upon her. It's short, within the span of a life, just seven or eight years of sentient, continent childhood, and lonely, I guess, when all of your peers are still children. Gillian, I was told, hung out with a much older crowd, mostly male. The information was not related kindly. I, on the other hand, still had years of childhood ahead of me on Purple Bikini Day. Far too many of them, I eventually began to feel.

12

An Album of Tea Cards

During the years when I waited patiently for BOOBS that never came, Win was my stalwart supporter. Most of the conversation was had when we were both in bed together, because Win hated sleeping on her own when John was on night shift every other week, and I loved having Win all to myself. Sometimes we lay in bed and sang together, tunes from the musicals that we both loved – *West Side Story*, *The Jungle Book*, *Mary Poppins*, *Paint Your Wagon*, *Fiddler on the Roof*, *The Sound of Music*, *The Wizard of Oz*, *Oliver!* Sometimes it was Shirley Bassey songs. My parents both loved Shirley and so did I. Once or twice we got carried away and the Ralstons next door banged on the wall to tell us to shut up. The poor old Ralstons.

In Muirhouse, Motherwell, while sectarianism and sexism were facts of life, the community was largely homogeneous in economic terms. This was especially true at primary school, because pretty much everyone rented council houses. The earnings of the small minority of 'breadwinners' who worked in the professions did not seem massively greater than those of the majority, who worked in heavy industry. Or so it seemed to me. Being an able-bodied but unemployed man was disgraceful. The Remploy factory at Flemington provided jobs for the 'handicapped'. Any women and children who were stuck with a poor-quality breadwinner were to be pitied. A woman who had primary-age children, but worked, was clearly being brave in the face of adversity. Mrs Ralston worked as a bus conductress, even though she had three children. Sometimes her husband was out of work. He was, my parents, said, 'Too fond of the pub.' Everyone knew that he hit Moira sometimes. You could hear through the wall. In years to come, there would be a towel hanging outside on their washing line in all weathers.

'We've heard it's something to do with wife-beating,' Win told me. 'Do you know what?' It's so that the man can go outside and hit the towel with a stick when he's angry, instead of his wife. Women 'made their beds and had to lie in them' back then. That's what Win believed. You were expected to accept your lot in life and everyone, on the whole, did so without much complaint.

People did have dreams, though, smaller dreams than the big dream of winning the pools. Win's dream, having gone from life in the country to life in flats, had been a 'house with a back and front door'. Buying had been beyond our means, which didn't make us any different to most other people. But even though the dream of a back and front door had been achieved, we still loved 'going through the bungalows', just the two of us. We'd done it since David was in his pram.

At the bottom of the hill on which our scheme was built there were a couple of streets of private houses. They weren't all bungalows, but a lot were. The great thing about them was that they were all different, with different characters. Their gardens were varied too. We'd talk about which were our favourites, what it would be like to live in them, how this one or that one had had its door painted a different colour and whether it was an improvement. Very, very occasionally there would be a For Sale sign and we'd fantasise about buying it.

Estate agents seemed so posh that when my boyfriend and I first visited one, when I was twenty-five, I asked him whether I should dress up for the meeting, like going to the bank manager. Which, oddly, he found hilarious.

It was part of Saturday With Win, going through the bungalows, long into my teens, like going to the library was. Dad would be at the golf. David, who was a popular kid, would be out playing. If we still had the house to ourselves after we got home from town, which was unusual, we had other rituals to share. Win and I were the ones with the sophisticated palates. So we'd break out the Vesta Curry on these occasions, with its boil-in-the-bag rice and its 'heat gently' sauce. Beef curry was our favourite, although the beef itself seemed decidedly granular and synthetic. Chicken curry at a pinch. Once, we threw caution to the wind and tried the chow mein. Horrendous. Afterwards, we might have a milky coffee. Only we girls liked coffee. Instant, of course. Who knew that coffee came any other way? But we favoured Mellow Birds, 'to make you smile', as the advertising jingle went. Not Nescafé, which was, as Win loved to say, 'common as muck'.

We'd have tea, though, if there was a new packet of Brooke Bond to be opened. It was best to do this when David wasn't around, because I was an avid collector of the picture cards which came with the tea and the slew of information, printed in tiny blue letters, that appeared on the back of them. He'd want them too, if he was there, which caused *trouble*. I'd forgotten all about this until I found *Famous People 1869–1969: Fifty of the Greatest Britons* in the you-know-what. There had been others and I don't remember what their themes were. This was the only one that we'd managed to collect the entire set of. Win used to send off for the albums for me, which were sixpence and, it says on the back, 'offered in the interest of education'. She must have bought postal orders to send off for them. We only had savings accounts – one for John and Win, one each for me and David, all at the Trustee Savings Bank.

Seeing *Famous People 1869–1969* again, it all came flooding back. I'd loved the R. L. Stevenson card, in which he has shoulder-length hair, a droopy moustache and a shirt and kipper tie. He poses against a red and yellow sunset, three palm trees to his right and a clipper to his left, à la Guy Fawkes. I'd read *Treasure Island* and *Kidnapped*, both in Bancroft Classic editions with a red and black spine and a painted illustration on the front. I'd amassed quite a little collection of these – *Wuthering Heights* and *Jane Eyre*. *Oliver Twist*, *Great Expectations* and *A Tale of Two Cities*. *The Last of the Mohicans*. *Gulliver's Travels*. *Robinson Crusoe*. *Lorna Doone*. *The Swiss Family Robinson*. *20,000 Leagues Under the Sea*. *Tom Brown's Schooldays*. *Alice in Wonderland*. *Little Women*. *The Water Babies*. *Heidi*, of course. I got one every Christmas and birthday and if some of them were a bit demanding for me, compared to Enid, well, I didn't let on. I persevered. *Ivanhoe* defeated me though. Sir Walter Scott defeated me. Scotland's greatest prose writer – for shame. Though I also loved my only book of poetry, Stevenson's *A Child's Garden of Verses*, which, I felt, balanced things out.

Though there were a lot of Scots on the list of fifty – even a couple of local boys, Livingstone and Hardie – I was aware that Scottish writers seemed like a glory of the past. I was even more keenly aware that of the fifty great Britons, only seven were women, and that on the whole they were celebrated for things that were strictly part of the feminine realm, lauded in my *Bunty* and *Diana* annuals.

There was Florence Nightingale – nursing and soldier-saving. There was Edith Cavell – nursing and soldier-saving.

There was Dame Alicia Markova – ballet, Kathleen Ferrier – singing, and Pat Smythe – horse-riding. Many of the men were famous politicians, but the only woman who had been involved in politics at all was Mrs Emmeline Pankhurst, who had battled so hard and been reviled so much, just to get women involved in politics at the most crude and basic level. She was also the only one of the fifty whose marital status was signalled in her nomenclature. The most impressive – to me – of the women was Amy Johnson, who had been the first woman to fly solo to Australia. Like Amelia Earhart, she'd died young, crashing in her plane. Both ladies were hero and cautionary tale in one.

That was how girls were still socialised in the 1960s and 1970s: with awareness from the start that the making and the doing in the world, apart from some exceptional labours or talents that were set aside for females, was for the men. Even Ferrier, the note on the back of the card made it clear, rose on the talent of Benjamin Britten, another, greater Great Briton. Sure, there was some reason to believe that all this was changing – a bit. In 1975 there would be a huge fuss about Angela Rippon, female newsreader. Did her voice really have the gravitas and authority to break news? The jury was out. She won everyone over by being a sport, and scissor-kicking her legs for the nation's Christmas on *Morecambe and Wise*. Each year's *Miss World* competition was sacred enough almost to feel like a national holiday. The demonstration against it by 'women's libbers' in 1970 had been disgraceful. No laughing matter. Elsewhere, the woman-driver jokes, the wife jokes, the mother-in-law jokes and the general women-are-thick-and-a-drag jokes continued to rain down. 'Take my wife . . . I wish someone would!' You weren't a sport if you didn't laugh. Women *were* a joke, after all.

The funniest men on the telly – Danny La Rue, Stanley

Baxter, Dick Emery – dressed up as women, as drags. The women in the top-rated comedy of the 1970s and early 1980s – *Are You Being Served?* – were a silly dolly-bird and an old trout with a 'pussy'. Effeminate men – John Inman, Larry Grayson – were a joke too (and a very risqué one, as homosexuality was barely legal and far from accepted). Girls in bikinis were draped over the cars at The British International Motor Show or bearing trays at The Ideal Home Exhibition, both big events that would be featured on the news. Hill's Angels, the sexy ladies on *The Benny Hill Show*, were hilarious.

In my late teens, working at a bar in Teddington Lock, I was told by a cameraman that if I played my cards right, I could be a Hill's Angel myself. I was supposed, quite clearly, to find this offer of exposure irresistibly flattering and offer some private exposure in a nearby copse by way of advance gratitude. Did the sexism – what was coming to be known as being a 'male chauvinist pig' – creep into the heart of your sense of yourself? Yes, it did. Even on *Top of the Pops*, for the young folks, post-sexual revolution, women danced and girls simpered on either side of such marvellous chaps as Jimmy Savile. Young woke women now tell old white feminists that they are out of touch. They have no idea what a toxic patriarchal culture we grew up in, just a few decades ago, or how fragile the gains we have made really are.

Win and I didn't talk about this much. Win believed that a woman's place *was* in the home, and that women found their satisfaction there. Yet she always encouraged me in the things that I wanted to do – nature studies, drawing, reading, schoolwork, endless badge-seeking at the Guides. We'd go to town most Saturdays, to do errands. But she'd always take me to the library first to change my two books, which I'd usually have read during the week. This we had done since I had learned to read.

Motherwell had a Carnegie library, one among so many built by the philanthropist Andrew Carnegie, who had emigrated with his weaver family from Dunfermline when he was thirteen, in 1848. The vast wealth he amassed in the US, largely by developing the steel industry there, he put down to the education he received at a school supported by a philanthropist back home and an uncle who had encouraged him to be a reader. Carved above the front doors of all Carnegie libraries is the motto: 'Let there be light'.

And what doors they were. Tall, elegant, oak, I think, set into a beautiful golden sandstone building. You stepped through the doors into a hallway with marble floors, a dome above, a grand staircase to the left, glass doors to the right and another set of doors straight ahead. We'd always go straight ahead into the main lending library, where the books were arranged in a room with wonderfully high corniced ceilings and wooden shelf after wooden shelf filled with books. To the right was the gramophone library, full of classical long players, which looked even more magnificent, almost hallowed. I never went inside.

I was obsessed with folk tales. It had started with the *Arabian Nights*, intensified via Enid Blyton's retelling of the Greek myths, *Tales of Long Ago*, and expanded to include a compulsive exploration of Scottish folk tales – full of selkies and kelpies – and thence into any folk tale from any place that had them. When I'd exhausted that large seam, I'd started browsing in the adult section, at the back in a modern extension, where coloured-glass windows overlooked the railway line. I didn't think much of it. I'd begun sneaking the paperbacks that were kept in my parents' bedroom. Jacqueline Susann. Catherine Cookson. Grace Metalious. Jackie Collins. They described the life of sex that I awaited with both hope and horror.

Certainly, the sheer work of female adulthood looked strenuous. I'd always been privy to my mother's grooming routines, and some of the activities struck me as extraordinary. She'd sand her legs, for example. She'd buy a pack of three flattened tubes of fine sandpaper, she called them shaving mitts, and she'd scour them over her legs in a circular motion to remove her leg hair. Over the years, these items became more and more difficult to source as such innovations as 'the Ladyshave' and Louis Marcel waxing strips came on the market. Win held out for a long time, but eventually and reluctantly invested in the one electric shaver that lasted unto death. For all of her life she would put rollers in her hair every evening as she watched the telly in her dressing gown, and tie a scarf over her head so that they didn't come out as she slept. Nail-manicuring and eyebrow-plucking would be done on a Sunday. Win would put the rollers in her wet hair on a Sunday evening because Sunday was bath night, for all of us. Win would bathe first, in late afternoon, and I would scrub her back. That routine was sacred.

One warm Sunday evening, though, there was a knock at our front door. My mum answered the door and called to me. As I peered out from behind her, I saw my worst nightmare. Kids. Loads of kids. What seemed like most of my class at school. Kids circling lazily on bikes in the road. Kids holding footballs. Kids with their dogs. I can't remember which two actually knocked at the door and asked if I was coming out to play, just that there were two.

I shrank away immediately, back into the living room. What about my bath? My mum told me not to be silly, that I should go out and play and have a bath later. So I did. I didn't tell her that I'd been being bullied at school for months, that even the kids who didn't take part in the bullying just avoided me, such was the power of that group of girls I'd got on the wrong side of. My former friends.

I just stepped right out there, in absolute terror, to face this latest ordeal.

I was full of dread, but nothing bad happened to me. I don't remember details – it's all a blur, a mass of feelings. Yet the general memory of what happened in the next hour still brings me to tears. We played, maybe twenty of us. And then we all went home.

I didn't fully understand how extraordinary that hour had been for years, maybe not even until I first sat down and tried to put it into words. A load of children, led only, I think, by their good instincts, bestowed on me a collective act of kindness, sympathy and solidarity. Sixty minutes of casual acceptance. Three thousand, six hundred seconds of disorientating, astonishing, healing balm. It's too easy to forget that people can be wonderful.

Soon after that, I told my parents about what had been happening to me. I had to. I just had some sort of breakdown and couldn't really move much any more. My lips became swollen. I couldn't control my bladder. Doctors were consulted, nerves were mentioned, rest was prescribed and Win, armed with all that I'd told her, went to the school to talk to Mr Main about it all. The auld creep said I had to come in too. He stated his displeasure at having to deal with something that 'seems to have started at the Guides', made the whole class line up to shake hands with me, one by one. And that was that. I was gently avoided, or avoided like the plague, depending on level of culpability, until primary school was over. I had done, after all, the thing we children could never do. I had told.

13

Fleming House Badge

My secondary school – the school I'd always known I'd be going on to – well, it wasn't Dalziel High, with its glowing local reputation. Later, after league tables came in, it would emerge that Dalziel High was one of the best schools in Scotland, state or private. It still is. Yet everybody had known it was an exceptional school anyway, without league tables to tell us. No one made that big a deal of it all back then, before 'parental choice'. If you missed the catchment, you missed the catchment.

Anyway, Dalziel High, Motherwell, was old and traditional. Garrion Academy, Wishaw, was new and modern. It was fantastically well equipped: recording booths in the modern languages department, a double row of island kitchenettes in the home economics department, and loads of sewing machines. The shelves of the cupboards in the art rooms groaned with supplies, and there was a kiln. The music department had loads of instruments and a piano in every class.

The sports department had a huge games hall and a lovely, wooden-floored gym. We had a hockey pitch, right by the school, and a football pitch, also marked out for athletics. We had a school swimming pool, in which you had to wear a school swimsuit – no purple halter-neck bikinis here. Motherwell, under an inspirational coach, David Crabbe, had produced a run of Commonwealth and Olympic swimming champions in the mid-twentieth century, and water sports were taken seriously in the town. So much so that on the walls of the room which housed the pool hung two canoes, one red and one yellow. But they were tantalising as they were barely ever used. I don't think our class got our hands on them once.

Garrion also had a technical block, where the girls didn't go. There, the boys did woodwork, metalwork, technical drawing and loads of other things. There was a fake sitting room in which to practise home-decorating. Some of the boys built a car from scratch in there. The boys were carefully trained for their future in the heavy industry at the heart of the town. Much good it would do them.

There were still traditional aspects to the school. There was a house system, for example. Everyone was in a house – Fleming, Livingstone, Scott or Watt. I was in Fleming, named after Alexander Fleming, who discovered penicillin. On our way to the seaside, for family days out, we would drive through the village of Fleming's birth, Darvel, which had once been famous for the lace its factories made. They had all been long closed by my time, though there were still beautiful lace curtains at many of the village's windows. But penicillin and lace are still bracketed together in my mind and I still have a fondness for Dr Fleming. I was pleased to be in Fleming, although – despite my trouble with *Ivanhoe* – I secretly longed to be in Scott, like Gillian, because their little round enamel badges, with a thin border of brass, were a delicious shade of violet, whereas Fleming's colour was yellow. The badge was still in the bureau.

Each house had its own dining room and its own day for assembly. You'd go to your Fleming housemaster – Mr Collins – or your Fleming assistant housemaster – Mr Irvine – if you had pastoral difficulties. Mr Irvine was small and fit. He dressed fairly casually as he was a teacher in the technical department. Mr Collins – who I think taught history, though never to me – was very tall and very fat. He wore a grey flannel suit and wire-rimmed glasses. He looked like a giant schoolboy from *Billy Bunter*. I remember an impassioned speech he gave at one assembly, which somehow involved him actually having seen the lungs of a dead man, all black from smoking. That was as much, really, as the house system impinged upon my consciousness. The real divide at the school, after all, was of much greater significance.

Basically, we had a grammar school within a comprehensive school. Though nobody called it that. It was called the classics department.

In our final year at primary school, completely out of the blue, a man had turned up with a briefcase and our teacher had told us there was going to be a test – right there and then. We were each handed an A4-ish booklet with thin, shiny paper (an IQ test, I later realised), and were told we had a certain amount of time in which exam conditions were to prevail and that we were to fill in as much of it as we could. We did the test, then forgot about it.

Months later, when we all turned up at Garrion, we'd been arranged into classes based on the results of that test. I'd assumed that only the Robert Westwoods of this world would be in 1:1. But I was in 1:1 as well. I could barely believe it. This was *epic*. I wandered alone about the podium – a glassed-off bit of playground under the main building – trying to come to terms with the *honour* that had been bestowed on me. From then on, the people of 1:3 to 1:9 might as well have lived on a different planet to us. In 1:1 and 1:2, you got Latin. Mrs Holmes ran the classics department, and she was something else. Mrs Holmes had a shiny helmet of dark, purple-tinted bob and wore brown lipstick. She favoured very sharp, almost ankle-grazing skirts over lace-up boots and little jackets, almost boleros, over crisp white lawn shirts. She remains one of the most stylish people I've ever known. She was smart and strict. At the start of her lessons she would raise her right hand, and we had to stand and raise ours too.

'Salve, discipili!'

'Salve, Magistra!'

Later I was told that her first name was Margaret, and her maiden name had been Starr. Many, many kids had believed they were greeting their Latin teacher with 'Salve, Maggie Starr!' She was an exceptional teacher. Of course. We in the top classes got all the most exceptional teachers. Miss Stoddart for English. Mrs McNaughton for history. Mrs Mackay for art. We were *la crème de la crème*.

There had been some shocking omissions from 1:1, though. Margaret Simpson, who was very bright, was in 1:3. She got moved up after the first few weeks. Gillian wasn't in the top class either, which she told me, very dismissively, she didn't care about. At secondary school, Gillian hung out with the cool girls from the start. Which hurt me, because we'd been best friends for a long time until that terrible final year of primary school. Now she hardly spoke to me, and I knew that when she did it was when the others weren't likely to see us. At those times, we recaptured some of the old closeness though. The last time I saw Gillian, when she was seventeen or eighteen, she had left school and had landed a plum job as a teller in a bank. She was engaged to a young man who was into 1950s music, style and dancing. We sat in her bedroom, in the maisonette flat I'd spent so much time in as a girl, and she showed me the 1950s clothes that filled her wardrobe – satin circular skirts, little white blouses, tight Spandex trousers and bomber jackets. It wasn't clear to me whether Gillian was into all of this stuff herself, or if she did it to please her fiancé. At that time, she'd just found out that he had been meeting an ex-girlfriend on the sly. She intended to forgive him, and I don't know how things went for them. Well, I hope. For her anyway. She was such an intelligent young woman. Gillian had wanted others to know how clever she was when she was nine. After puberty, her cleverness became something she preferred to hide.

The grammar school within the comprehensive school certainly didn't last, though. By the time David was old enough for secondary, three years after me, there was no more IQ-testing, and no more *crème* to be *la crème* of. Latin was still offered as an O-Grade (as was Greek). But no one got Latin from the start, as we had. Everyone got classical studies instead.

At the same school, only a few years on, David received a quite different education to mine, one that he didn't enjoy and, by the end, when he was sixteen, didn't have much on paper to exhibit as 'achievement'. In the time between me going to Garrion and David starting, setting and streaming had been abandoned and fully comprehensive mixed-ability teaching embraced. Not that anyone had much awareness of what was happening. The 'parental choice' revolution was yet to come. Whether or not mixed ability was fairer, it certainly didn't improve things discipline-wise. Not long after David left, the school erupted into a full-scale riot. After a period of closure it was relaunched as Clyde Valley High in an effort to put its past behind it. That's still its name.

Despite these other changes, which I believe had a strongly negative effect on my brother, and despite our different temperaments and attitudes to life, I carry some guilt about the hugely different experience of education that my brother and I had. Win would often point out to me that it was hard for David, travelling in the wake of his clever-clever sister and with certain expectations thrust upon him. Bright and talented as he was, David was a typical boy: bored when he sat still, having to listen, and reluctant to accept the authority of others – of women. Male teachers might have got more out of him, as a brace of incidents later in our school lives illustrated well.

I was halfway through my O-Grade courses when David started at Garrion, and that year's first parents' evening arrived. They didn't usually – and participation from parents was much less expected back then anyway – but this year my parents decided to attend.

I'd taken physics, which I found an extremely satisfying exploration of how the natural world worked. (My physics notebooks were still in that capacious bureau as well – so neat! This must have been the reason why they were kept. I *always* used a ruler.) Not many other girls did physics, although the coolest girls in our year did: Anne Galway, Karen Drummond and Anne Orr. (There were three Orrs in our year at school, none of us related.) Anyway, because these cool girls – Gillian's friends – were in the class, I didn't participate. None of the cool girls displayed any keenness at school because then they wouldn't be the cool girls. When they were in a class, the other girls tended to follow their lead. So the teacher would ask a question and we'd all sit in sullen silence, waiting for one of the boys on the other side of the room to answer.

'Deborah,' he would say, 'I know you know this. Don't you?'

'Sir. I don't.'

He'd glare at me, exasperated. It really annoyed him.

Anyway. My parents went in to see the physics teacher, expecting the same fulsome praise they got everywhere else.

Physics teacher: 'I think that Deborah does not apply herself in class nearly as much as she is capable of.'

My dad: 'Well, I think maybe it's the singer, not the song. Come on, Win. I'm not standing here listening to this.'

Shortly afterwards, they went to see David's science teacher.

Science teacher: 'Davy Orr? Great kid. Very smart. Good scientific mind.'

My dad, in the belief that the science teacher *had to* be talking about a different child to his: 'No. *Orr.* Davy ORR.'

Science teacher (horrified): 'Yes. That's right. Davy ORR.'

Win told us about it in a you-can't-take-your-father-anywhere way. It was told as a funny story and we accepted it as a funny story. But it wasn't funny really. It was telling. And my mother's telling was telling too. It emphasised my dad's favouritism towards me. It was a joke against him, and his bias against David. Who loved that teacher. Mr Fraser carried cans of beer about in a carrier bag. He was one of the lads, though at the same time his authority was complete. All the boys loved him. They called him Whizz-bang, which he embraced. He had perfect grammar. He'd never say 'This is them.' He'd say 'These are they.'

Relations between myself and my brother were not good. We fought and squabbled a lot. I was resentful because, when Win had started working, after I'd started at Garrion, I'd been expected to help out more around the house. It was my job, for example, to cook dinner on the evenings when Win was working and have it ready when John and she came home. He always collected her from work in the car. Win had never tried to learn to drive, but hated public transport too.

I wasn't very good at cooking dinner. I'd get distracted and go out into the garden and play. Or I'd fart around with my plants. I had my own much-fussed-over plot and was forever planting seeds, attending to my tiny pond – an upside-down bin lid – or making adjustments to my rockery. I'd transplanted lots of the stuff that had been in the garden when we first moved in – lupins, of course, but also tiger lilies, London pride and blue flowers Mum called Jacob's ladder. I'd also poke about among the hedgerows around the fields, where the adult gardeners would dump the plants they wanted to dispose of. I'd take the rejected plants home and repurpose them. It was amazing, the number of these secret little compost heaps you could find if you were looking. I'd check particularly fruitful dumps pretty regularly.

And there was the shed as well. There was always work to be done in the shed. There had been an old corrugated-iron shed in the garden when we arrived, which was allotted to me when John built the garage. I spent hours, days, weeks painting it, scrounging furniture for it, making curtains and thinking of ways to hang pictures on corrugated iron. I wanted to be in the Secret Seven.

I was always very busy, losing myself in whatever fantasy world I'd entered that afternoon. Then the car would sweep into the driveway, with the authoritative scrunch of the gravel alerting me to the fact that I'd left the dinner on the cooker and forgotten it. The potatoes would be burnt and John would be outraged.

'Why doesn't David have to help?' I'd ask.

'Because he's younger than you.'

'But he's the age I was when I had to start helping.'

'Girls mature quicker than boys.'

In the mid-1980s, when Win and John were working, David was unemployed and he still didn't ever have to make the dinner. I asked why, again. Why, even now, did Win and John come home from work and make dinner for an able-bodied young man who'd done nothing but loll about all day? Win shrugged and said it was just much harder to get him to do things than it had been to get me to do them. By this time David had had his own key to the house for years, something I didn't get until Win was in the hospice and I helped myself to the spare, aged forty-nine. They always waited up for me to come home whenever I visited them. I eventually stopped keeping up with friends from home because it was so awkward, having to account for myself to my parents when I got in. Without a key I had no choice but to do so, on the spot, as my tired, irritated mum and dad listened in a silence that suggested that they'd had to stay up for something that was pretty damned trivial, hadn't they? I'd asked Win about that too.

'And why does he have a key to the house when I still don't?'

'He's a man. We worry about you more. You could get pregnant.'

'David could get someone pregnant.'

'That's some other mother's problem.'

Chilling stuff, really.

14

Two Macramé Pot Hangers

At the age of fifteen, there had been absolutely no possibility that I would become pregnant at all.

It was farcical, really, that my burgeoning womanhood had been the single factor that had sprung the Orr family from Shields Drive. At ten, at twelve and at fourteen I was still a child. While other teenagers were getting into punk (or so the television news said), I was obsessed with macramé. There were few things that could be made out of string that I didn't make out of string. My well-thumbed manual, *The Basic Book of Macramé and Tatting*, had survived outside the protective environment of the bureau. Two jute pot hangers had thrived, coiled up inside it. During the height of my craze, you couldn't move in the house for pot hangers. I made papier-mâché bowls for the pot hangers too.

There was no doubt – I was a weird kid. In that, I was indulged by Win, who still went to the library with me on Saturdays, bought me all manner of nature books, plus stationery, art materials (I wanted to go to Glasgow Art College after school) and study guides, which were at that time slender, recondite tomes that you had to go into an obscure academic bookshop in Glasgow's west end to buy. A teacher had told us about them, but I didn't know anyone else who had actually tracked them down.

Win took me into Glasgow on the train to get them. Which was a big thing. The city was twelve miles away, but we only went a handful of times. Driving in Glasgow was torture for John, but he refused to use all other transport, as did Win. But she fostered my boundless enthusiasm whenever she could. I wanted to do *everything*. They drew the line many times – at riding lessons, dancing lessons, elocution lessons, trips abroad with the school. But there was the Guides, the Duke of Edinburgh's Award Scheme (yes, gold), the hockey team, the athletics team and the badminton team.

A certain amount of creativity was deployed to obtain equipment for me. Instead of hiking boots I had men's work boots with steel toecaps that Dad had got from the factory, with which I wore three or four pairs of socks. We had no idea that the point of hiking boots was supposed to be lightness.

When John was on night shift, every other week, Win would let me stay up late and we'd watch dramas on the telly – David would usually go out with his pals after dinner. Often they dealt with quite dark stuff, which fascinated Win as much as it repelled her. A lot of the time I didn't really grasp what was going on. *The Brothers* was mostly boring. *Bouquet of Barbed Wire* – ironically, as it turned out – was baffling. *Pennies from Heaven* was shocking. Though I only saw every second episode, we watched some terrific shows that had a huge impact on me. John Hurt in *The Naked Civil Servant* was mind-blowing. I missed the second episode of the three-parter on Oscar Wilde, and also wasn't allowed to reveal to John that we were watching it at all. He was scathing about 'that pervert'. No one had heard of homophobia, but even though it didn't have a name it was the norm. Tom McLaughlin, at primary school, had preferred to play with the girls and was always called Nancy. I liked Tom. I can still see his red, ecstatic face as he jumped so skilfully over the skipping ropes. Stuff suitable only for nancies and boxers.

At secondary school Tom would gain a great deal of social traction, when the church he'd attended all his life became the one that ran the locally hottest of the discos for schoolkids that had sprung up around Britain. Thanks to my early sympathy with him, I was good for this. It was at the Wishaw Parish Church disco, courtesy of Tom, that I experienced my first 'slipping of the hand' over my bottom, during a slow dance. I didn't want it. But I didn't know how to stop it. Afterwards, I was told that my boundary failure had been noted and that this was not the sort of thing that the parish disco was for. Not by Tom: by another girl. Tom had bigger problems. The vicar had taken to the stage, telling all the kids that it would be nice to see us at church on Sundays as well, and he was mortified.

I had my first kiss at the parish disco too, from a redhaired French boy on a school exchange whose tongue in my mouth was a loathsome surprise, like a warm, slimy slug. This was during a time of rapprochement with Gillian, which the French boy incident brought to a close. She had got off with his friend and was disappointed when I told her the next day that I never wanted to see my boy again. She pleaded, but I was adamant. Boys absolutely terrified me – their hands, their tongues. Apart from Tom.

I thought it was awful that Tom was called Nancy, and so did Mum. Years later, after I'd accumulated a glittering array of gay friends, and they had accumulated a glittering array of successes in equality and freedom, Win told me that her father's cousin had lived with another man, and that Harry not only had endlessly fulminated on how disgusting 'the things they do together' were but had threatened more than once to call the police on them. Win was much more liberal than John, but to a large extent she hid it from him. His long list of prejudices was never challenged, though during our times together when he was on night shift Win would subtly confide that she found all the hates quite difficult to accept.

That's one of the mysteries of my parents' co-dependency. Win had far more empathy for people who were different to her, and empathy is precisely what narcissistic people lack. So in that respect Win was not narcissistic at all, while John was off the scale. Studies show that narcissistic traits are more prevalent in men than in women. Sometimes I wonder, because I have many female friends who believe their mothers to have been narcissistic, whether such tendencies might be something that women tend to unleash only on their own daughters. I was the one person who Win insisted should be exactly as she wished me to be, because anything less was an insult and a humiliation. Otherwise she was pretty accepting, a good, fair-minded, liberal person.

Eventually, even though much of it remains precious to me, I had to re-evaluate even some aspects of that shared time, just Win and me, so intimate, that I had cherished so much. Some of it was subconsciously designed to keep me a child, physically and mentally. Sure, genes were the main culprit. I was tiny. I had to get clothes and, more terribly, shoes from the children's department well into my teens. But I was gently mocked every time I asked if I could have a bra. Gaslighted, really. A low-voiced Win would whisper that I was being quite silly, wasn't I, to think I needed a bra for my 'little bee stings'.

I didn't get a bra for ages, not till I was nearly fifteen. The girls at school and Guides found my vests hilarious, which was part of the reason why I'd been stripped to them both at school and at Guide camp. Even my brother considered my tender, unprotected breast buds vastly amusing. He'd ping them, the little sod, because it was so sore that it would make me yelp. One Saturday morning, while John and Win were having a lie-in and we were watching the terrestrial Gumtree for kids that was Noel Edmonds's *Multi-Coloured Swap Shop*, he did it. He pinged and I pushed him away with my foot – hard. He landed on his bum in a jagged mandala of broken glass and costume dolls. I'd sent him flying into the hallowed bureau. He started bawling, Win started screaming and John came rushing down the stairs. Interestingly, his penis was hanging out of his white pants, bouncing along. My only sighting, ever.

Anyway. It was a nightmare. They were furious. John, in particular, read us the riot act.

'That's junk now,' he said over and over again, 'just junk. We'll have to throw the whole thing away. That bureau's ruined.' The war, and in my father's case extreme poverty, had made them very thing-conscious. The bureau, of course, was the thing among things.

My breast-bud-pinging accusations were swept away by a heartfelt-seeming denial from David. The familiar verdict: I was the oldest; I was in charge; this had happened on my watch; now I was smearing my brother – again! – to avoid responsibility. Clyde Terrace was thick with animosity, shame, bitterness, fear, resentment, tears, sweat and blood. David had a huge cut on his arse.

Later in the day a neighbour came by and waved away the moans of 'junk' and 'ruined' with an airy assurance that these kind of doors just lifted out of the runners and that new glass could quickly and cheaply be cut and ground. The bureau survived, to sit outside my sons' bedrooms, bearer of clean T-shirts and survivor of trauma. Some people can turn a drama into a crisis. My parents could turn *anything* into a crisis, and frequently did.

For me, the longer-term consequence was that I shut up

for a while about wanting a bra. Win always just said that I didn't need one yet anyway, that there was plenty of time to be an adult, and that if I really knew what adulthood was like I wouldn't be so keen to arrive there.

It wasn't until a couple of years later that I noticed that Anne Orr, one of the cool girls in my physics O-Grade class, had very small breasts even though, like all the other girls, she'd been wearing a bra for years. When I went home and told this to my mum she finally relented, and we went to Galls and I became the owner of my first bra – white, padded (Hurrah! Hurrah! Hurrah!) and with little purple and pale orange flowers embroidered on the cups. God, I loved that bra. Eventually – though not very eventually, because Win was a total clean-freak – it had to be washed. When I came home from school Win told me that it had blown off the washing line, that Moira Ralston next door had retrieved it and knocked at the door, saying she thought it would probably be mine. 'I'm sorry. It's so embarrassing for you,' my mother told me, 'what with Linda having those huge bosoms of hers.'

Linda was Moira's eldest child, a year younger than me, and I obligingly did feel the embarrassment I was told I ought to have. Now I wonder if the story was even true, or if Win had simply tossed the bra into the wind in the hope that it would never be seen again. Maybe I'm paranoid. Yet I understand narcissism now, and either of those scenarios is plausible. It sucks to have this kind of retrospective insight – or maybe just suspicion – about your own mother. But there it is. I do. I guess I should add that my mother was very proud of her own generous embonpoint. She'd once told me, back in Shields Drive days, that John was the sort of man who liked a woman to have large breasts.

I guess, also, that I sound less paranoid when I admit

what came at the end of the years of being told that I was better off not having boyfriends, better off staying away from men, better off without children – sentiments that I heartily agreed with at that time.

My first period started a couple of months before my sixteenth birthday, the day after I got my O-Grade results (perfect). Or, as Win said to John when he got in from work, while I stood there beside her in the kitchen: 'Deborah became a woman today.' To which my dad said: 'Oh, aye? Very good' and left the room. The exchange made me feel awkward and obscurely ashamed. What a long saga the securing of this 'womanhood' had been.

On the first night shift after I 'became a woman' my mother delivered an incredibly shocking birds-and-bees talk, one that ensured that I would never again bring up the subject of sex with her. She told me that she'd still been a virgin ten days into her honeymoon, because attempts at intercourse had been so painful and awful. She told me that sex was something that a woman was obliged to do with her husband, even though it was terrible for the woman. She told me that even the nicest of men – like my father – would occasionally impose this vile activity on his wife even when he loved her so much, so very, very much. She told me that I'd be better off learning from her mistakes and staying single.

From then on, I wanted to get away. I got my first job a few days later, three evenings a week and a Saturday, stacking shelves at the new Fine Fare in Motherwell. I'd been waiting to be sixteen and able to work part-time. It gave me space to buy my own clothes, be my own person. The Saturdays with Win suddenly stopped. I made a good friend at Fine Fare, Renny. Complaining about her dad and stepmother one day, she said: 'I mean, he's not going to stop me having sex with Ted, because he's too late for that.' I was dumbfounded. But

I hid it. This permissive society stuff? These behaviours I'd seen on *Bouquet of Barbed Wire*? This shit was *real*.

About twenty years later, Win, in love with her first grand-child, was spending more time with me. Late one evening, after my baby son was asleep, she fired at me, out of the blue: 'You *like* IT. Don't you?' I knew what she meant by 'IT' right away. Wretchedly, eyes cast down, I confirmed that I did.

My parents are dead. But they would die all over again if they knew that this information had been placed by their daughter in the public domain. I have no excuses. But one explanation is that a burden as heavy as that one can only be carried for so long. It is awful to know that there was a vast, sad void at the heart of your parents' happy marriage, to know that they spent their lives as perfect victims of a cruel, joyless, needless cultural repression that damaged their relationship with each other, their relationships with their children and their relationships with themselves. They had intimacy and honesty in all other aspects of their marriage. They had every emotional foundation in place to have a wonderful sex life, a bond that would have made them so strong together and so much less fearful than they were. Instead, they were loyal to each other in their sexual misery and shame.

I know that the shame, fear and disgust my poor mum felt about sex has been shared by many women. I think that many men have been made to feel like monsters for wanting to be a lover to someone they loved. They were not born prudish, my parents. The culture they grew up in made them so. When feminists argue that patriarchy damages men as well as women, the perfect example is here. My mother married a Scot, then spent the rest of her life lying back and thinking of England. Her control over me was a completely misguided obsession with protecting me from being that awful thing – a woman who enjoyed sex and didn't want to live her life having had terrible sex with only one man. I put up with Win because I felt so sorry for her. She never stopped being disgusted by me, because to her I behaved like an animal. To both of them. It is so sad. It's the shocking secret at the heart of my existence. Or it was.

I think I understand why this was all so extreme with my parents. They were part of a brief, unlucky generation who spent their late childhood and early adulthood in the midst of the century's second post-war effort to regain sexual control over the masses. On the home front, all bets are off during the anxiety and trauma of war. But the roar of the 1920s was quietened, and the same trick was tried in the late 1940s and early 1950s. In Britain there was a great deal of pressure on women to return to home and family, and for the respectability of the pre-war status quo to be re-established. The same pattern repeated itself in the US.

The film stars Win modelled herself on, with such success? The movies she loved so much? Their content was strictly dominated by the Motion Pictures Producers and Distributors Association, created in 1922, and reinvigorated as the Motion Picture Association of America in 1945. The Production Code, the system of censorship these groups enforced during the youth of my parents? It didn't fully collapse until 1966, four years into my parents' marriage. My mother grew up in cinemas, watching films in which married people in bed had to keep one foot on the floor and bad women came to bad ends.

As for the secret that Win's parents kept for their whole lives, about the premarital conception of their eldest child? It's hard to imagine that the shame at the centre of their family did not, in certain ways, transmit to their children. None of Harry and Annie's seven children divorced. None of John and Elizabeth's surviving five divorced either. They were the last generation for whom divorce was a cataclysmic last resort. Though, come to think of it, I'm the only person from the generation after that, on the Scottish side, to have divorced. The Kirbys – Jean's kids – somehow give the impression that they've had more divorces than they've had marriages.

In Scotland, though, there was still a lot of Calvinism among the Protestants when I was a kid. For Catholics, of course, divorce simply wasn't allowed. Even though religious belief was on the wane, people like my parents seemed to cling to the moral framework of the religion they'd rejected all the more. The pre-eminence of religious identity in Lanarkshire was one aspect of life north of the border that reinforced poor Win's psychosexual fears. It wasn't that she might even have divorced John. She wouldn't have. It was more that marriage was considered something that you had to put up with. You made your bed and you had to lie in it. Win, she herself felt, very much, was much more fortunate in her choice of husband than many women, despite the horrors of marital sex.

I fully believed, growing up, that sex before marriage wasn't really a thing. Discovering that, for my parents, sex after marriage wasn't really a thing either – it was absolutely fucking terrifying. The realisation that this was the fate my mother expected for me – wanted for me, in fact – more than anything else made me want to run, run like I'd run from the man in the brown suit, run until I'd got the hell out of Dodge. This was not normal. This could not be normal. These two people, my parents. They did not deserve this. And I didn't deserve it either.

Why did Win want this horror for me? Why couldn't she want a happier sex life for her daughter than she had had? Why couldn't she see that the world had changed? Only because she didn't want to. She lived in her own world, and she wanted me to live in it with her. The full force of the narcissism she used as a defence against the idea that she had failed at an aspect of being a woman and a wife was directed at me. I just didn't know how to spot it then. I'm glad I do now, for many reasons.

Because here's the thing. Once you know how to spot it, narcissism is everywhere. Narcissism explains many aspects of human society. It is, I believe, the psychological motor behind patriarchy, behind racism and behind most, if not all, prejudice. The need to feel better than others, or that others are no better than you, whether in a family, a group or in the whole wide world, is a need that many people feel, especially in this age of individualism. Narcissists, from Harvey Weinstein to Donald Trump, thrive in contemporary Western culture. They manoeuvre themselves into power and then exploit the fact that others want to be burnished by association with them.

Identity politics is full of narcissism.

All politics are identity politics.

Politics is full of narcissism.

The politics of my family was full of narcissism too. That's always the case, I guess, to some extent. Maybe even by the time I was old enough to go to school, maybe even from that first day I recognised that school was a place to get away to, to be myself and nurture my own narcissism. And that Motherwell was a place to get away from as well.

15

Silent Monitor

The second-last time I ever saw my mother we spent the afternoon in New Lanark, a place we all loved, the four of us. I'd been taken there on a school trip when I was fourteen and had come home raving about this hidden, desolate village, and how we all had to go. I'd never heard of New Lanark before the school took us and neither had Win and John. Which was a bit odd, because we knew the rest of that stretch of river so well.

Car trips down to Clydeside, as a particular part of the river was called, had always been a feature of family life. Sometimes it would just be a run in the car, along the road beside the river where it passed through the Clyde Valley, market-gardening country, with little hamlets like Crossford or Hazelbank. Tomatoes, raspberries, strawberries and Victoria plums were grown on Clydeside, and I was always told as a kid that these fruits were the sweetest and most delicious in the world. I still think so. We'd go to buy the fruit when it was in season. Sometimes, on hot days, we'd take picnics and sit by the river at Rosebank.

Mum and Dad would have fold-out garden chairs and David and I would have a blanket. We'd take the power-cuts primus so that we could have tea. We kids would wear our swimsuits and spend hours building fish traps, catching minnows or just letting them tickle our feet as they nibbled. Occasionally you'd see the pulsing, silvery-green squiggle of an eel. Or the shimmer of a trout.

Cows would stand in the meadow, swishing the flies away with their tails. Sometimes, there would be horses. Dalserf Church nestled in thick pine trees, looking, again, like something out of *Heidi*. This was Lanarkshire at its most bucolic, so soft, so green, so pretty, so peaceful, so full of histories that reached back far beyond the Industrial Revolution, which dominated our everyday lives so effortlessly, and way back beyond the Agrarian Revolution too. Dalserf Church, it turned out, was thickly screened by trees for the same reason it had seventeen doors. The Covenanters conducted secret religious services there, and the doors allowed them to run out in all directions, surprising attacking state forces – Roman Catholic. That sectarian thing? It had been going on for a while.

There were ordinary houses and gardens that we were all fond of and always checked out. One in particular, on a corner, had an amazing display of bedding plants each year, as many as possibly could be found space for, carefully planned out and tended with exquisite attention to detail. Part of the river must at one time have belonged to a private estate, because there were gatehouses on a couple of roads over it that led, now, to nowhere. These gatehouses, in the Scots Baronial style, with their round towers and conical roofs, seemed to me like tiny palaces from fairy tales. I'd have wanted us to live in one had Clyde Terrace not been so indisputably our One True Home. At these times we were the happiest, most contented, most *perfect* family on earth. Or so it felt.

New Lanark was tucked away, though, off the Clydeside road that swept up to Lanark, the shire's market town, leaving the river behind. That's why we'd never known

New Lanark was there. We knew Lanark, though. It hosted Lanimer Week each year, an ancient fair that we'd never been to, although I listened to accounts from people who had with envy. Lanark had been an important place in the old days. William Wallace launched a successful attack on the English sheriff of Lanark there in 1297 as part of his strenuous effort to free Scotland from its big, greedy neighbour. New Lanark, as its name spells out, was a much younger place. A former cotton-milling village, it was founded in 1786 by the Scottish industrialist David Dale and purpose-built into the sheer, deep sides of the Clyde just at the point where its longest stretch of waterfalls hammer down the mountains. There are several mill buildings, maybe six or seven terraces of flats for the workers, and a number of other public buildings of various sorts. The Falls of Clyde supplied the mills with their power. The waterfalls were what brought Dale to this deep pocket of wild beauty.

I'd only heard of the Falls of Clyde before the school trip because a drawing of them had illustrated the front of the telephone directory one year. I'd always wondered where these Linns were ('linns' being Scottish for waterfalls), because they looked so spectacular in the drawings. Three of them are at New Lanark: Bonnington Linn, Dundaff Linn and Corra Linn. There's another one, several miles downriver – Stonebyres Linn.

It turned out that we were just about the only people in the history of Britain who had never visited the Falls of Clyde. Turner had painted them. Wordsworth wrote a poem about them. Coleridge and Scott had swung by. When it was new, the village had been a magnet for industrialists, social reformers, philosophers and utopians from all over the world.

You can walk right up the Falls by the side of the river,

up, up to the very top, which John and I did many times. Win would wait in the tea room, cooling her high heels. She was not a walker. If there's a finer, more simple pleasure than returning to a beautiful piece of countryside over decades, again and again, seeing what changes, what stays the same, what, for some odd reason you've never noticed before or had maybe just forgotten, then I don't know what it is.

John got right up that steep climb on the Boxing Day of his last Christmas, up to the top of the Falls. Win would always come some of the way, along the early, flat stretch, and turn back. Though she didn't venture even that far after John died. Win was not a merry widow.

But there was no tea room for Win to wait in when we first went to New Lanark. It was an almost completely derelict village, like an American ghost town, dominated by a scrap-metal yard that had been spreading itself about the place for decades. A few people still lived there, hanging on. But it was very cut off. It hadn't been connected to the national grid until 1955. It still got snowed in for long periods in winter.

Part of the magic of New Lanark for us, the Orrs, was that we found it when it was at its lowest ebb, just as efforts to honour and preserve it were beginning. It's now a UNESCO world heritage site, completely restored, austerely beautiful and quite the tourist attraction. There's a hotel now, and self-catering waterhouses which have a front door at the top with kitchen and living room inside, and the bedroom down below. You can lie in bed listening to the roar of the river roiling past on the other side of four-foot-thick walls not far under your window. And I often did, when my children were small.

On that first visit – which we did with the Foxes from next door but one – the main attraction for my parents was the Falls. I'd piqued their interest with my chatter about the abandoned village. But Win had seen that the Falls were in full spate only three times a year, when the hydro-electric power station around a mile upstream was turned off for maintenance. The rest of the time, much of the water was diverted away through pipes to have its wild energy transformed into electricity. We piled into the two family cars and off we went, to find the village teeming with enthusiasts desperate to explain why New Lanark was important and had to be preserved. The Falls were great. But John and Win were enthralled by the passion of the campaigning locals too. They were romantic about the Industrial Revolution, and for them the story of New Lanark was an antidote to the Marx-Stalin-Revolution-Workers themes that, frankly, terrified them. The story of an enlightened boss makes Tory hearts beat so much faster than Labour hearts. And New Lanark had not one of them, but two.

David Dale built the mill and the village in the belief that living and working conditions for industrial workers didn't have to be so inhumane. He'd been apprenticed as a boy to a hand-loom weaver in Paisley before he started to make his first fortune as a linen importer in boom-time Glasgow. He knew the business from the bottom up, which helped. He'd worked as a child as an Ayrshire herd laddie who assisted in the husbandry of cattle, so he had an insight into the cruel robbery of child labour too. Dale's greatest innovation as an enlightened employer was the provision of education for the children – day school until they were six and evening classes after that, because by then they were old enough to work.

Dale funded a number of other mills, including one at nearby Blantyre. The explorer David Livingstone received the rudiments of his own spectacular education there. Dale, like Livingstone, became a leading abolitionist, campaigning against the slave trade from within a city and an industry that prospered from it. Dale's leadership was significant, for these reasons. He broke ranks with the merchants of Glasgow, whose selves and whose city had grown rich from slavery on tobacco, sugar and cotton plantations in America. And by then Dale was a force to be reckoned with.

Dale's model mill village had been a sensation at the time it was built. Among the industrialists and social reformers who visited was a Welshman called Robert Owen, who married Dale's daughter and eventually took over the business. Dale's reforming zeal was nothing compared to that of his son-in-law.

Owen had at first been a follower of Jeremy Bentham, the classical liberal and utilitarian. But he broke with Bentham's free-market ideas and became a utopian socialist, successfully campaigning for improved working conditions and instrumental in the passing of the Cotton Mills and Factories Act of 1819. He was a founder of both the co-operative movement and the trades union movement. Weirdly, John and Win admired these men as much as I did. They saw the existence of such early good bosses as proof that people would do right by their workers without anyone asking. I saw the pair as exceptions that proved quite different rules.

At New Lanark, Owen introduced nurseries for infants, further improved conditions for children, instituted the radical idea of an eight-hour working day, founded the first co-operative shop where the workers could buy their goods (alcohol strictly limited) and taught adults about the benefits of cleanliness, good sanitation and general moral probity. To achieve all this he began the Institute for the Formation of Character (lots of singing and dancing) and invented the 'silent monitor', a wooden block, its four sides painted four colours, with a hook that would hang by each

worker's station. The managers would turn the silent monitor to black, blue, yellow or white to indicate how well the
person in question was living up to Owen's high standards.
We didn't have an original silent monitor in the bureau,
though I'd dearly love to own one. But there was a printed
paper model of one, still flat and waiting to be constructed,
that John and Win must have acquired at some point along
the way.

The whole silent monitor thing sounds impossibly controlling and paternalistic now. But Owen's relations with his
workers were excellent. The families were mostly recruited
from the slums of Glasgow, people wanting to escape the
Tongs of Calton among them no doubt. They were grateful for decent conditions and, probably, clear institutional
boundaries. All this showed in their work and also in their
enthusiasm for Dale's and Owen's ideas. Owen started other
utopian communities, several of them in the US. But none
of them worked like New Lanark did.

I had been taught at school, and saw no reason to doubt,
that there was a great deal of resistance to the reforms that
Dale and Owen started. Friedrich Engels, after all, published
The Condition of the Working Classes in England four decades
after Dale died (though thirteen years before Owen would
die, penniless, back in the village in Wales he had come
from). However, we'd learned about Marx and Engels, not
during our studies of Britain but during our classes on the
Russian Revolution.

Anyway, I knew that primitive factories that didn't look
after their workers had existed very recently, as had child
labour. My own dad had worked in a primitive factory from
the age of fourteen, his education ruined most probably by
his morning hours of work at the baker's before school, from
when he was nine. This came almost two hundred years on

from Dale's first emphasis on the education of child workers. It made me feel disgusted. John never expressed anger about any of it though.

For John, I think, the important thing was to cling onto acceptance. As a psychological coping mechanism he internalised the idea that he was not worth more than he had got in life, not worth educating as a child, not worth training and promoting as an adult. He was wrong about that, so wrong. He was a clever, frustrated man. But he couldn't allow himself consciously to think that way, because then he'd have filled up with an anger against the world itself. He took out his anger on other people instead, slyly, in his rants against Catholics, black people and neighbours from the safety of his comfortable home. And he did appreciate his safe, comfortable home. He valued it as much as houseproud Win did and he was grateful to her for providing its comforts. John's early life, I think, had been so *hard* that his life just a few decades on – wife, kids, house, garden, car, telly, phone – seemed hugely improved, incredibly much better than it could have been. He had started working as a child, after all, war coming to an end around him.

But his daughter and his son had a different life. We had only seen war on television. We didn't know what hunger was. As for cold – well, Scotland is cold in the winter. Up in our bedrooms there'd be frost on the inside of the windows and your breath in the morning would condense in great clouds. I'd dress under the blankets and rush down to the electric fire in the living room. Central heating was one of the things they talked about at Guides. But there was always a room full of warmth. I doubt there had been in my father's childhood. The education I got in the local primary and the bog-standard comprehensive? First-class. The support my parents gave me in making the most of it? Undaunting. Also,

I'd been prohibited by law from working until I was sixteen years old.

The changes in employment law were quite new. That was a good thing. I was fully ready. I loved having a job, loved my three evenings a week at the supermarket, loved my Saturdays there, loved the occasional Sunday stocktaking day. For the final summer after school was done I worked in a laundry too. John and Win didn't charge me rent, as some parents did. They were always as generous to both of us as they could be. We wanted for nothing. In that final summer of childhood, I felt rich beyond the dreams of avarice.

At last, I could afford to indulge in a bit of avarice too. I started going out. To Girdwoods, the notorious underage pub in Wishaw, on Fridays. With Renny, the new friend I made at Fine Fare. She was at Coltness High, a school about which I knew very little, and she hadn't been near the Guides in her life. She was slightly horrified that I ever had. Renny drank – pints of heavy. Renny smoked – Embassy Regal. She was into metal – AC/DC. She regretted staying on at school, but had to get Higher maths so that her dad could get her a job as a bank clerk. Renny had recently broken up with her long-term boyfriend, Derek, known to all as Dozer because he always fell asleep in class. (No wonder. He was the son of a farmer, so rules about children and employment did not apply to him. He just helped out, and always had. There was a lot of helping out to do, before and after school.)

Socially, because I still felt isolated at school, Fine Fare was a fresh start. School was still fine workwise. I was doing five Highers: English, Maths, History, Physics and Art. It kept me busy. But I felt on the periphery of various groups of girls, drifting about between them, fully accepted by none. I lived for Saturday lunchtimes, when Renny and I would go to the Wimpy and SIT IN. For Win and John, eating out was a terrible waste of money. I'd been to a proper restaurant, such as I considered the Wimpy to be, only once before – The Chariots in Romford, with the Kirbys. At the end of the meal, Uncle Bob had plucked a shoebox from under his chair and paid the bill with the luncheon vouchers he'd been saving up for years and with a certain degree of chutzpah.

Renny's mother was dead, and, like many children whose mothers died when they were young, Renny remembered her mother as an archetype of kind and loving femininity, a cut above her husband. Proof of this thesis was Renny's name, a man's name plucked from a series of novels her mother had loved, *The Whiteoak Chronicles*. That was so much more posh than being named after a Hollywood star, even a classy one like Deborah Kerr. Renny had a wicked stepmother, Jean, who was always telling Renny's dad that she was a 'problem', which was a particular shame, because in the days when Renny's widowed father had driven a powder-blue Jaguar he had dated the Scottish singing star Lena Martell. Whom both Renny and her younger sister Holly preferred. They lived in a private house. Renny's dad was a bank manager, which to me was a bit like being an MP or something. All this glamour, all this middle-classness, fitted in with what I'd known from the telly about people who had sex outside marriage, as Renny told me she had already had. It was something that the posher people did. Posher was more free.

I'd think about what Renny had told me, when we both should have been stacking non-food shelves, all the time. 'I mean, he's not going to stop me having sex with Ted, because he's too late for that.' I was pleased with myself for having nodded sympathetically, as if I was used to this being part of the warp and weft of general conversation, when inside I was thinking, and continued to think, 'Oh, my God! OH, MY GOD. I'm right! Sex before marriage does exist in the real world! People do this! People I know! And they are not struck down by a God they don't believe in!'

The Great Sex Revelation, the money, the sense of independence, the idea of change and excitement in the future that staying on at school was bringing, the arrival of 'womanhood'. Everything came at the same time. I was assiduous in ensuring that I'd be coming too. The frigging years had begun. It was time to stop reading *Jackie* and start reading *Cosmopolitan* and *Company*, the magazines that told you that you had a clitoris (who knew!) and schooled you in how to activate your G-spot (so easy when you know how!).

Among the paperbacks that had been appearing in my parents' bedroom for years, almost mysteriously, the result of much passing-on of books people had read and enjoyed to my parents, were my two favourite books for masturbating to: *The Betsy* by Harold Robbins and *Inside Linda Lovelace*. Both books were products of their time, and neither has aged well. Lovelace later said she had been coerced into acting in *Deep Throat*, the porn film that made her famous. Robbins's sex scenes were often rape fantasies. Women hadn't really started tackling the new inequalities that came with sexual liberation – as far as I knew. The uneasy terrain between 'nice girls don't' and 'normal women do': this was simply the landscape that had to be negotiated. I wasn't exactly well briefed.

Yet I threw myself into it all anyway, as best I could. Fine Fare seethed with teenage intrigue. David fancied me. I fancied Douglas. Douglas fancied Karen. I broke the deadlock in the time-honoured way by getting off with Douglas's best friend Campbell, more in a spirit of experimentation than anything else. It all went so much better, once you were ready for tongues. He was a practice boyfriend, if you will. Practice did not make perfect. To Campbell, after much cajoling, I tossed the burden of my virginity, before breaking off with him. I barely remember the great deflowering, in Campbell's mum's high-rise flat, in the single bed in Campbell's childhood bedroom. It was all so quick and so *dull*. So lacking in experience or finesse. Maybe it was his first time too. I don't know. I'd gained the impression from Campbell's general demeanour that he had had sex before and I'd been too much of an idiot to question this. I remember the breaking-up, though. That wasn't as easy as I'd imagined it would be.

Me: 'I think we should stop seeing each other.'

Him: 'Well, I don't.'

Me: 'Well, I do.'

Him: 'Well, I don't.'

Me: 'I really think that it's over even if just one person stops.'

There were two reasons for my jettisoning of Campbell. First, he wasn't very nice. He'd got off with another girl after I'd left a party, which, understandably, I found humiliating. Another boy who worked at Fine Fare had told me this with a certain amount of glee. Plus, after the Big Break-up, the same boy told me with yet more glee that Campbell had told *everyone* I was 'too loose' to be a virgin. I can only blame my trusty bottle of Mum deodorant (shaped like a short, stubby penis) and my less trusty rolled-up copy of *Jackie* magazine. The good thing about makeshift dildos is that they can be imbued with a great deal of irony.

But I'd have put up with the casual two-timing, I think, as I would in the future, many times, if I hadn't had another, much bigger reason for ending the practice-boyfriend experiment. The real reason, the big reason was that having a boyfriend was making life hellish at home. Win hadn't been wildly enthusiastic about the Campbell news. She was sniffy when I told her about it, and pursed her lips in the way she always did when she disapproved. But she had clearly passed the snippet on to Dad.

Neither of them ever met the guy. But John's reaction was astounding. The phone, which had been in the hall, was moved into the living room. If Campbell called while they were at home, I could only speak to him while my parents sat listening. And that was only if I or Win managed to get to the phone first. If my dad picked up the phone and heard Campbell's voice, he'd simply replace the phone in its cradle. He didn't speak to me at all, or look in my direction. He could barely be in the same room as me. John had become my silent monitor.

Renny's father hadn't helped matters. Renny, Campbell and I had decided to go to the Loch Lomond Festival, for one day only. Campbell had driven us, and getting out from the car park at the end of the concert had taken ages. I'd got home at about 1 a.m. to find Win and John in hysterics.

'Where have you been?'

'We thought you were dead.'

'You are not going out in the evening again unless you agree to let your father pick you up.'

'We've rung everyone we could think of. We've rung the hospitals. You could have been in a car crash for all we knew.'

They'd called Renny's dad as part of the general red alert, who'd told them laconically that if he knew teenage girls, Campbell and I would be in a lay-by somewhere. This accusation I'd had to rebut, while at the same time feeling that being in a lay-by somewhere would be very heaven. All I could do was put up with it, rock the boat as little as possible and nurse my escape plan. By my eighteenth birthday, in a few months' time, I intended to be gone from Clyde Terrace.

I hadn't realised at first what an excellent hand in life a clutch of good O-Grade results could be. When, after the results, I went to see a careers officer arranged by the school, she glanced at my file, looked up at me and said:

'Well. With these results you could do *anything*. Nursing OR Teaching.'

'I was thinking about art college.'

'An art teacher, then!'

It wasn't that both weren't great options. It just felt a bit . . . binary. It felt like there were only two jobs that qualified women could do. It was then that I started having second thoughts about art college. If it could lead only to teaching, it was actually a bit limiting. And I'd by then been exposed to the Dalziel kids, at Guides and at Fine Fare, who all talked about university as if it was the natural thing to do. In fact, they seemed so knowledgeable and confident that I didn't want to ask them anything in case I revealed the depths of my own ignorance. But when Mr Collins had said at assembly one day that anyone wanting to apply for university should wait behind for an UCCA form, I picked one up.

I told my art teachers that I was thinking about university and they were distressed. I'd always been good at art, they'd always encouraged me, and for years they'd known that I intended to go to Glasgow School of Art. I had a painful meeting with the head of the department, Mrs Mackay.

'You will miss art if you give it up.'

'I won't. I will always do art.'

'You think that now. But you won't.'

Mrs Mackay gave me a booklet about combining art and academic studies. There was a course at both Edinburgh College of Art and Edinburgh University which offered a joint degree. But it was a six-year course. Six years seemed like for ever to me. The booklet also suggested architecture, which I loved the idea of. But that was seven years. It did give me the idea of contacting universities for literature, though.

I got prospectuses in the post and combed through them. At St Andrews University you could get an MA in three years. Also, we'd been once, when John had a golf tournament there, and I knew the town and the sands were beautiful. It would be so nice to live in a gorgeous, *clean* place, by the sea. Crucially, too, my favourite character from Enid Blyton's *Malory Towers* series, Darrell (everybody's favourite character, because she was meant to be), had finished her time at school by 'going to St Andrews to become a writer'. Becoming a writer seemed pie in the sky, despite my fantasies of change. Writers, to me, were like GODS. But I put St Andrews as my first choice anyway, for English and History. Win and John insisted that I should put Glasgow and Strathclyde on the list too, but otherwise seemed a bit disengaged.

They were distracted by politics at that time, my parents. We were heading into the winter of discontent, when all striking hell would break loose, and strikes made my parents nervous. Strikes, and the laid-back response to them of the then prime minister, Jim Callaghan, provoked them into fury. Plenty of people felt just like my parents about the ever-striking unions. Years later, Win would still quote Callaghan's famous comment – pedantically speaking, apocryphal – 'Crisis? What crisis?' when she thought some problem wasn't being taken seriously enough. Those feelings contributed a great deal to Margaret Thatcher's election win in 1979, including those two votes from Clyde Terrace. When I talked to them about giving up the idea of Glasgow Art School and going to university instead, I'd see them meet each other's eyes, but I didn't know what it meant. Nothing good, I feared. I knew that they found my endless enthusiasms wearing sometimes. 'You're competing with lawyers' daughters, doctors' daughters,' Win once said in exasperation when I asked about a pricier-than-usual Guide camp. 'We can't keep up.'

John and Win did write the cheque that I needed to apply, though, with a sigh or two, because I only had a savings account. Everything was much more cash-based then. John and Win got paid in cash, and hadn't had a checking account long themselves. It was 1979, and cash machines had barely hit Glasgow, let alone Motherwell. I'd first use one at university and later I'd show my reluctant mother how. I don't think John ever used one. But I may be wrong.

When I was offered places at all the universities I'd applied to, it became glaringly obvious that John and Win had simply assumed that the whole thing was a fantasy, a problem that would go away. This was fair enough, in its way. It's hard to emphasise how unusual the idea of university seemed to them, how rarefied. People spoke in awed whispers about folk with 'letters after their name' – intellectual superheroes, their brainpower vastly beyond our ken. No one from either of my parents' huge families had been to university, not their brothers or sisters or in-laws, not their nephews and nieces. None of their friends had been to university, although Colin and Carol Fox were actually at university at that time. Colin and Carol were my ace in the hole, my evidence that such a thing was possible, and that some parents would allow it. I didn't have much to do with Colin and Carol myself, what with them both being older than me and Catholic. But our parents were friends. The Fox family and the Orr family were close. They, in fact, were the only Clyde Terrace near neighbours my parents hadn't yet fallen out with.

One of the excitements, when we first moved to Clyde Terrace, was that Win and John started having parties. Not big parties. John and Agnes Fox would come and so would our next-door neighbours the Duncans, Peter and Margaret, who had a boy and a girl, Alan and Jill, a little younger than us. The three couples would have parties at their homes, on a rota, after the kids were in bed. Exotic things like 'Moscow mules' would be discussed in the run-up to these parties. Sophisticated comestibles like Maraschino cherries and silverskin onions would appear in the cupboard. I remember Win making herself a green trouser suit for one of these parties. Green Crimplene trousers and a jungle-printed Bri-Nylon tunic. Artificial fibres were the in-thing. We had easy-care nylon sheets too. The brushed ones caught your hangnails and the shiny ones slid off. But we persisted. This was modernity.

My dad, apparently, had met Agnes Fox before we got to Clyde Terrace. Agnes was very glamorous. She dyed her hair rich black and kept it immaculate. She always wore a fetching orangey-red lipstick. She was a staff nurse at the Law Hospital and was the only woman in our ambit who actually had a career. She and John remembered each other, because she'd once given him a tetanus jab and he'd been funny and charming. John was the most funny and charming man in the world when he wanted to be. Anyway, I think John and Agnes properly liked each other, but it was all made into a joke. The joke was about wife-swapping. So it was John Orr and Agnes; Margaret Duncan and John Fox; and Win and Peter Duncan. Once, at one of these parties, Win told me, they smoked a dried-up old joint Agnes had procured via a patient at the hospital, and they were disappointed by the lack of a hit. Once, as I heard a song from *The Jungle Book* being played at one of the parties, I came down and found them all doubled over, pretending one arm was a trunk and marching around. 'You didn't know adults could be silly too, did you?' Win said, steering me back to bed. I certainly know that adults can be silly too now.

The whole parties thing ended badly. I'm not sure of the superficial course matters took, or the literal mechanics of the fallings-out. But some things were obvious. John Fox and Win Orr flirted more naturally with each other than either of them did with their designated Duncans, and this, I think, felt more balanced with Agnes and John Orr's real connection. Margaret, my mum thought, had taken things too seriously with John Fox. She said to my dad: 'I think that when she spends afternoons up in that bed of hers, saying she's got a migraine, she's really up there thinking about him.' Like most Victorian moralists, Win had a mind like a sink.

Whatever. The Orr parents and the Duncan parents *really* fell out and we were told not to play with Jill and Alan either. John gave Alan the nickname Zoony, saying he was vacant and incredibly stupid. He had a cruel a nickname for Jill too, who was little still. I don't remember it. John's nickname for Peter was Strawberry Bobber, because he was always hunkering down in his strawberry patch, or Peter Dungcan, because he would get a pile of cow dung delivered to fertilise his fruit and vegetable garden. John would say things about Peter, using the nicknames, when he knew he was crouched down in his garden, near us. 'Be careful what you say. Strawberry Bobber's lurking on the other side of the fence.'

It was actually really nasty, John's campaign of hate, and it went on for years. It was particularly awkward because the houses were close, at ninety degrees to each other, with a shared driveway. There was a lot of hostility about leaving the gates open, or using our fork in the driveway for reversing. Relentless, really. Eventually the Duncans moved to another house, with a smaller garden, further up the street. John and Win literally drove a family out of their home.

They were similarly estranged from the Ralstons on our other side. Again, I don't know the mechanics of the falling-out. But if John saw me or David talking to any of the Ralstons, even twenty years on, he'd be extremely annoyed.

Eventually the Haggertys, over the back, went the same way, although again there had been friendship, parties and pretend flirtations that perhaps became too unpretend for Win and John. I didn't really know that it was weird, to be at war with all your neighbours and give them the silent treatment, decade after decade. Now I see it as typical narcissistic bullying. It was instigated by Dad. Mum went along with it. It wouldn't have been her choice. Mum liked to feel popular, valued, loved. I do think she enjoyed being valued and loved by a man who, as she would always say, 'doesn't suffer fools gladly'.

I didn't know about the narcissistic cycle at that time, or how it ends with 'the final discard'. But I do recognise it in the way John behaved with his neighbours. At Shields Drive, making fun of Smelly Nelly had seemed normal, because she lived in such an unpleasantly alternative way. But we were not, as a family, kind to her and she was a lonely, isolated, frail old lady on her own. I see now that my parents should not have treated her simply as a figure of fun and they shouldn't have encouraged us to do the same.

Peter Duncan, and then Bill Haggerty – these were men with whom John did everything. He treated them like the sun shone out of their arses to begin with, at the start of the cycle, when you are put on a pedestal and made to feel perfect. This is what you seek to regain during the cycles of discard. Then there will be a period of complaint, and a period of friendship, but not as strong. So it would go on until John broke with them for the last time, and the project of convincing himself and everyone else of their worthlessness would begin. John's discarded friends were, to him, beneath contempt. He didn't remember any good times, or kindnesses they'd done him. Everything was black or white.

Having a boyfriend – Campbell – was my first experience of discard from John, and the cold contempt of it induced misery and trauma. I wanted to get back to how things were, which was why I decided that I wouldn't have a boyfriend after all. Only a few months on, though, I was about to receive my second big discard, from which there was sporadic recovery at times, but after which nothing would ever be easy between us, like it had been when I was a child. Not for the rest of my dad's life.

16

The Dope Box

When the letters came, offering me places at university, that was when it all blew up – for ever. When I told Win and John that I'd been offered a place at St Andrews and wanted to accept, they at first warned me that I'd be out of my depth, mixing with people who had very different lives to me, more money, posh, snobs. I wouldn't be able to keep up with them. This, they told me again, had been a perennial problem. I always wanted to mix with people Win and John couldn't compete with, at the Guides, at the Duke of Edinburgh's Award Scheme. I always wanted to join these expensive, exclusive clubs, and this was another one.

'For years, Deborah, it's been art college, art college, art college. This is just another one of your nine-day wonders. College is more suitable.'

'I've changed my mind. I don't want to be a teacher.'

'Why not? That's a very good job. A good job for a woman. For a mother.'

'Aye. So I'm told.'

'Less of your lip.'

The arguing went on and on.

'Isn't it about time,' John said at one point, 'that you started bringing some money *into* this household?'

Win, to her credit, looked at her husband in sad

disapproval. 'Oh, John, no. That's not the reason. You can't say that to her.' I felt so grateful to Win. I can feel the rush of relief gushing into me now, just as it did at that moment.

But Win had not become an ally. She merely didn't like this particular argument. 'We just think that your place is at home with us, until you're married. You've got a place at Glasgow and at Strathclyde. You can easily go in every day, on the train.'

'But Mum. I don't want to stay in Motherwell. You've been telling me how much you hate it all my life.'

Pursed lips. 'This is your home, Deborah. Your place is here, with us. This is where you live, where your family is. We are your family.'

'But you didn't. You didn't stay with your family.'

'That was different. I moved where my husband wanted to go. That's what wives do. When you're married, we won't stand in your way. Of course you must live where your husband wants you to live.'

'But . . . you can't just keep me here, until some man comes along to claim me. I don't even want to get married!'

'You say that now, Deborah. But you'll be glad to have a ring on your finger like the rest of us. I don't want to argue with you any more. Your father and I forbid you from going away to university, and that's that.'

'Forbid me? You can't forbid me. I'm almost eighteen.'

'That's right. You are still a child and you don't know nearly as much as you think you do. You'll go to university in Glasgow, if you have to go to university at all. That's an end to it.'

But that was not an end to it. I'd been shocked by this encounter, dumbfounded really. I didn't understand where they thought all of their encouragement of my schoolwork had been going. I couldn't understand why they couldn't be pleased, like Agnes and John were pleased about Colin and Carol. But I also knew that I was going anyway, and that for all their talk Win and John couldn't stop me. I'd even got quite a bit of money saved up because of the summer job at the laundry, on top of the Fine Fare job. A permanent post at the laundry would be available if the summer job went well. It did not go well.

The laundry job is the nearest I've ever got to working on a factory production line. I worked on the collander, which was a machine that folded the hotel sheets and tablecloths that made up most of the laundry's contracts. You'd stand around for ages, then they'd start coming and you'd have to catch them and fold them widthwise, according to the tastes of the hotel in question. Sometimes there was other laundry to fold as well, small pieces, clothes. But a lot of the time, it was waiting. The girl who worked alongside me, Theresa, known as Tress, was sixteen years old and what was referred to then as 'a bit simple'.

She'd had three children in her early teens – Tress's mum looked after them while she was at work. No one knew who the three fathers were. Tress was an exploited child, and while her situation was relayed about the place in scandalised whispers, people tended to blame her rather than these vile men. School had not been part of Tress's life for quite a while and the work at the laundry was considered to be a kindness, like employing the alcoholics at the steelworks was. God knows what they paid her. Tress was stolid and silent. No fun, unless, I guess, you happened to be fucking her. I hope they've DNA-tested those middle-aged kids by now and shopped the bastards who were responsible for raping and abusing a child in that way. When I told John and Win about her they dubbed her MaTress.

The work at the laundry was ghastly. The boredom was

the hardest thing to cope with. They wouldn't let you read on duty. The bossmen loved their power. They often do, in my experience, even the mildest of them, although I had one boss at Fine Fare who I could see was always trying to stop himself from actually giggling as he carried out his duty of endlessly scolding me. When he heard I was going to university, he came up and shook my hand: 'Well done. Good luck. Best place for you, God knows.' I was and am a terrible employee. I *always* get fired. I've only twice left a job without knowing I was likely to be fired. *Those* were really painful. I prefer the firing. Nice and clean.

Fine Fare was fun because I had Renny and we had all our intrigues with the boys. But at the laundry, with Tress for company, I became a compulsive clock watcher, always glancing up at the all-knowing dial on the wall, thinking it was half an hour since I last looked and discovering, to my very regular horror, that only three minutes had passed. It was a Smiths clock, of course. They all were at that time. People were still buying British, despite rather than because of a campaign to remind them to do so that had started a decade before, in the late 1960s.

That campaign offers quite an insight into Britain at the time. It was the brainchild of five secretaries in the London suburb of Surbiton, who offered to work half an hour extra each day with no pay to combat falling productivity. The media liked the story – five girls doing their patriotic bit – and quickly the nation was sporting Union Jack badges with the slogan 'I'm backing Britain' on them. The prime minister, Harold Wilson, endorsed the campaign. But the unions hated it, saying it placed the blame for low productivity on bad workers, not bad management. Then Robert Maxwell, press proprietor and Labour MP, tried to muscle in. He wanted 'Buy British' as his slogan in his paper, the *Daily Mirror*, and in his political career with Labour. But when his T-shirts were found to have been printed in Portugal, the entire country lost interest. The sentiment endured, though. Princess Diana was criticised, after she married Prince Charles, for having a German kitchen installed. Maxwell, of course, was more dangerous than a few Portuguese T-shirts might imply. He disappeared off the deck of his yacht in 1991, on purpose, it is presumed, because he was found to have embezzled every penny he could from the Mirror Group's pension fund. Flashy narcissists have been a feature of public life since public life became a thing.

Renny encouraged me to get away from home and go to university. So did another man who'd started declaring his love for me, Angus. He'd joined the Merchant Navy, and on his first leave had had the two of us called to the back entrance of the store over the tannoy, which was quite unusual. We could see how he'd managed to persuade them, though, because he was almost hysterical. He babbled about warships in the seas off the Middle East and warned us to flee because a third world war was coming. St Andrews, he advised, was just the place to flee to, away from Motherwell, which would become a producer of munitions. He'd write a few weeks later, saying he'd been sectioned and was in Hartwood, the mental hospital that served the area and was mainly referred to in fearful jokes. He asked us to visit him, and we did. It was terrible, seeing someone of his age locked away like that and tranquillised. I still hear from him now and again.

The laundry, Hartwood, the atmosphere at home – all of it made me more determined to escape. I accepted the place, applied for a grant and requested housing in a hall of residence. When I'd been allocated a room in Andrew Melville Hall, designed by James Stirling and looking out over St Andrews Old Course and the West Sands, I went up with

Renny to scope things out. We weren't organised. There was no open day. We wandered about as tourists and Renny gave me a punt up so that I could see inside the rooms at Andrew Melville. They were very bare and I started thinking about how I could jazz up my room. I asked Win if I could have various things, but she and John just looked astonished by my cheek. My parents were determined that nothing from Clyde Terrace would be going to university with me.

Renny and I loved the place, though, its beaches, its bars, its ancient buildings. She promised to visit, said she'd be up all the time. She did visit. But not that long after I'd gone she was pregnant, not with Dozer, not with Ted, but with another youth. They got a council place and set up home together. But he didn't help her, they rowed constantly and she kicked him out. She wouldn't trust him with her son for the weekend at first, but eventually he persuaded her. One day he and his mother refused to return her toddler, told her they were keeping him. She played a smart game, did Renny, pretending she was fine with this new arrangement, grateful even, until she'd found a swap to a flat in Glasgow and kidnapped her son right back, leaving no forwarding address. Life can be very hard. People can be very cruel to each other. I hadn't known what Renny's future was going to be. But it turned out to be the sort of future that I'd gone to St Andrews to avoid.

I can't even remember if I told John and Win that Renny and I had visited St Andrews. Probably not. The atmosphere in Clyde Terrace, by that time, was pure, toxic hostility. I did try to talk to Win about it all again, on her own. But this time it was even worse. I told her that I intended to go away, but that I'd really prefer it if they would 'give me their blessing'. Win gave the anguished cry of narcissists the world over: 'But what about me?'

This obsession of mine, Win explained, had destroyed all of her ideas about what her life would be like. She and I would be friends. I would get married, I'd have her grand-children, and Win would be around to help me look after them. I told her that I didn't want children either. Eventually, John and Win announced that they had decided that I could go to St Andrews, but 'only if I promised that I would come back home to live when my course was complete'. I made the promise and I knew that I'd be held to it. A kind of peace had been made. Or a bridge had been built at least, one that I'd cross when I had to.

Except the bridge was never crossed, not really.

After I'd gone to St Andrews, there were new secrets to keep from my parents. The secrets kept on piling up. Most stressful was coping with the dark secret that I couldn't let my parents suspect at all. University and me simply didn't get along. It was great to be away from home, if a bit discom-bobulating. But the rest? The reason why I was really meant to be there? The education bit? I didn't get it. What was it all *for*? I was dimly aware that you were there to learn to think for yourself. But I'd never, in my life, been aware that I'd been thinking for anybody else.

I'd intended to study for joint honours in English and Modern History. I'd quickly decided to stay for only three years, instead of the four that is standard at Scottish uni-versities, doing the St Andrews' ordinary MA, which meant that you did lots of different first- and second-year subjects without ever specialising. I was an avid reader of Fay Weldon at that time, and her author biography always said 'she had an MA from St Andrews by the age of twenty'. Me too. I always read that boast and smirked. I met Weldon years later and told her I knew that what had seemed like intellectual precocity had really signalled: 'Fucked up university.' She guffawed. 'Only you and I know that though.'

It took me a long time to decide that university had in fact been the right choice. After graduating I spent quite a while teaching myself graphic design and working in the art department of an Edinburgh magazine publisher, regretting that I hadn't gone to art college. Yet I'd had a grounding in so much other useful STUFF that I'd end up fiddling about with the actual words I was supposed to be graphically designing, or being asked, in emergencies, to write pieces. I ended up in newspaper journalism because subeditors in the 1980s still did page layout as well as copy-editing. If I'd planned to worm my way into newspapers, I'd never have come up with a strategy so perfect.

While I was at St Andrews I did two years of English, two years of philosophy, one year of modern history, one year of medieval history, one year of social anthropology and one year of Arabic culture. The last – which I signed up for as everyone said it was really undemanding – has probably been the most useful. Bizarrely, although I never went to lectures in my own subjects, I'd slip into history of art lectures sometimes, because I could see the point of those. Even St Andrews, so fantastically traditional when I was there that it was compulsory for English literature students to learn Anglo-Saxon, had embraced the Kodak Carousel.

But in general, the students at St Andrews had nothing in common with me, and I had nothing in common with them. There was huge resentment between 'town and gown' and my sympathies lay with town. The loose crowd I eventually ended up in had a mixture of both, some former students who'd never left, some 'townies' attracted in rebellion to aspects of student life – sex, drugs, rock and roll. Also, Barleycup – a vile coffee substitute – plus macrobiotic food, the *I Ching* and shiatsu massage. St Andrews was still very hippy, even in the 1980s. People were always moving out to Crail, a little fishing village along the coast, because the sunrise over the sea was so *amazing*.

The hippies were preferable, however, to the Yahs. This was the name for the very posh English aristocrats who dominated the university and set the tone. It had been explained to me, early on, that St Andrews was full of posh English people because privately educated kids who didn't get into Oxbridge viewed St Andrews as the next-best thing. I'd nodded, even though I didn't know what 'Oxbridge' was. I didn't know what anything was. I didn't know why people kept declaring that they'd 'probably get a tutu' or that they'd 'be happy with a tutu'. It wasn't like everyone was leaping about, doing arabesques. What the hell?

And no one understood a word I said. Overnight, I'd stopped being a person who was teased because of her snooty accent and pretentious ways and become someone whose Scottish accent was 'thick'. I had to repeat everything I said, sometimes many times. More than occasionally, the struggle to communicate would not seem worthwhile.

'No! Really? I thought that's what you were trying to say. But I couldn't believe it. You don't have A PASSPORT? I didn't know that was even *legal*. Surely you've been to FRANCE? ITALY?'

'What? You mean spaghetti hoops? In tins? Oh, no. I don't think *that* counts as pasta.'

'What do you mean, you've never seen a bottle of olive oil this big?'

'Well, that's a bit strange, I must say. You've lived in Scotland all of your life and you've NEVER BEEN SHOOTING?'

Yet, weirdly, even though these people were undoubtedly far more sophisticated than I was, a lot of them also seemed stupid. None of them even knew how to do a pan of chips, let alone put out a chip-pan fire, which as far as I was concerned were the basic survival skills. Their priorities were frivolous, their entitlement baffling, their conception of how the world worked, it seemed to me at the time, hopelessly unrealistic. But what did I know? One young man, who exuded quiet confidence and bore himself as if success in life was guaranteed, turned out to be the heir apparent to the Earl of Elgin. Which he still is. He lived in a beautiful family cottage in Tentsmuir Forest, a beachside pine wood that was first settled by humans 8,000 years ago. Lithographs that I now realise must have been worth tens of thousands of pounds hung on the walls. He travelled into town in a Land Rover.

'What I like about you, Deborah,' Charlie Bruce once said to me, is that you only speak when you have something to say.' I took this as a compliment. But in reply I just laughed lightly. Mostly, I had nothing to say because I was simply gobsmacked by what was coming out of other people's mouths. Later that evening, I was told that this Charlie was a direct descendant of Robert the Bruce. Which rendered me yet more silent. It wasn't true. The most famous of these Bruces is the 7th Earl, who took the marbles from the Parthenon. A different matter entirely, and one that I had to wait for Wikipedia to be invented to discover.

I couldn't sleep at night, for a reason that I'd only pinpoint later. I kept falling asleep in the lectures I tried, early on, to attend. One day another student, posh and English, had had a go at me about it.

'Why did you bother to come if you're just going to sleep? Another person could have your place on this course.'

'I didn't know I would fall asleep.'

Her hostility made me shrink away inside.

I found lectures boring. None of the lecturers seemed

remotely good at public speaking. I realised that my teachers at school had put a lot of effort into keeping us engaged. And there was no interaction between students and lecturers outside tutorials. I'd rather have just read transcripts. Reading. That was the way I was used to collecting information. Lectures, like everything else at this ancient university, seemed needlessly medieval. I stopped going to them at all, not long into my first year. I was unable to face them, yet full of guilt about it. I've had anxiety dreams about missing lectures, failing exams, squandering university, just being in an inescapable mess for all of my life since then until 2016, when they stopped. When I stopped living in a domestic environment where I constantly felt undereducated.

It wasn't until I went home at the end of the first term that I realised one of the big reasons why I couldn't sleep. In bed, back in Clyde Terrace, I could hear the rattle and hum of the Craig, 100 yards away, and the occasional, plangent, sonorous thwang of a sheet of metal on the move. This was the sound I'd fallen asleep to almost every night of my life. Not the oppressive weight of silence. There was a sign up in the student's union: 'Just 0.03 per cent of students at Britain's universities are the children of manual workers.' I know that it was there to point out a social wrong. But sometimes it seemed to be saying: 'Go home, children of manual workers. You don't belong here.'

The other reason why I couldn't sleep at night was because I was worried, frightened and anxious all the time. And I couldn't tell anyone about it. The girl in the room next to mine, Maureen, didn't like St Andrews either, and that was a comfort. But she was organising a transfer to Edinburgh, with the support of her family, and would leave at the end of the first term. I couldn't face telling my parents that St Andrews wasn't right for me, couldn't face the idea of Mum and

Dad trying to persuade me that the thing to do was drop the whole idea, couldn't bear to tell anyone else the bizarre – to all of them, I felt sure – fact that my parents hated me being at university. I just had to tough it out. My pride wouldn't let me admit to Win and John that they'd been right and I'd been wrong. At least, I thought it was my pride. After they were dead and gone, I realised that the reason why I couldn't speak to them was shame, not pride. Corrosive, toxic shame.

So tough it out I did. I took on the persona that was being thrust at me. I started to smoke. I started to drink, heavily. I started to take drugs – acid and speed eventually, but just dope at first. For some reason, probably because it was handsome, Win had hung onto the little hardwood and brass box that I'd used back then to keep my hash in. My dope box. There it was, thirty years on, in the bureau. She'd seen the little box lying on my bed during the holidays and had admired it. She'd asked me what I used it for.

'Oh, nothing.'

'It would be just the thing for my safety pins.'

'Have it.'

It was empty. No safety pins. Did Win keep the dope box just because it was a gift from me? The gift I'd given because I hadn't been able to tell her what I used it for? The most awful secret in our family was the tumult of affection we had for each other. We clung to tiny, sometimes misguided pieces of evidence in order to remind ourselves that it was there.

I also started shoplifting at that time, stupid stuff, risky stuff, that became riskier as I kept on getting away with it. I swore as much as I could. I adopted big hair, prefiguring Joan Cusack in *Working Girl*. I was never seen without heavy make-up and tight jeans, tucked into boots. I dedicated a great deal of my time to becoming really, really good at pool. There were always people to hang out with, other people who'd more or less dropped out, like me, or townies on the dole, looking for gigs for their punk bands at the student union. And I phoned home every Sunday without fail, telling my mum that everything was great. John would answer the phone very occasionally, but he'd hand over the phone to a hovering Win pretty quick. 'Hello? You all right? I'll get your mum.'

The duty of keeping in touch would be mine alone for ever, and if I forgot to phone on a Sunday I'd dread phoning to apologise. One time, when I'd let it drift for an entire week, and when Win finally called me, her voice dripping with angry contempt at my neglect and disrespect, I shat on a newspaper on my bedroom floor rather than tell her that she'd woken me up at shameful Sunday noon. Anyway, it would have been hard, telling Win I had something more important to do than talk to her. I feared her. The incident is such a perfect example of infantilisation that it doesn't even qualify as a metaphor.

When Win wasn't managing, with some dark genius, to deliver a silent treatment over the phone she would usually ask me if I'd got a boyfriend yet, very brightly, and I'd always say no. Which was true. Despite all my bravado and the sexy swaggering around the pool table, I was terrified of getting into a situation where I was alone in my room with a man, because two things had happened early on at St Andrews. One was that a couple of guys I'd seen around, and who seemed friendly and fun, had turned up at my door quite late, after I'd gone to bed, and I'd let them in. They were drunk, and we'd chatted at first. Then one of them had asked if I had anything on under my nightie. Of course not. It was my nightie.

The two of them had dragged me out of my bed, out of my room, into the corridor – nightie over my head as I tried to hold it on, cover my body and stop the harsh, tough, institutional carpet from burning as they heaved. In that I was unsuccessful. I had the scrapes of friction burns down one hip and thigh, one breast, one shoulder and one arm to show for it. They giggled hysterically but quietly throughout, making soft, high noises that escaped through their noses. I made no sound. It was in none of our interests for anyone to hear or see. Strangely, they escorted me back to my room when they'd finished, like gentlemen. I told no one about the incident for a long time. Shame, again.

The other thing happened not long after. I was too naive back then to call it what it was, which was rape. There had been a corridor party in the hall of residence. I don't know who organised it. But lots of people had come, including one guy who'd chatted to me and made a suggestive remark. I'd laughed it off. 'Maybe later. If you're lucky.' Much, much later, after the party had long dispersed, after I was in bed, drunk, in the dark, half asleep, he slipped back in through my unlocked door, took off his trousers, got into the bed, silently fucked me, got up, put on his trousers, then left. I felt that I'd deserved this second experience of 'sex' for 'leading him on'. No doubt he did too. Once more, I told no one.

My closest friend at that time was Rebecca Marshall, who lived along my corridor. She was a punk maths genius from Droitwich, and had been a scholarship girl at Roedean. Whatever that meant. When John and Win had driven me up at the start of university – a generally doleful duty they sombrely performed – Rebecca had been pulling her trunk to her room. (Trunks! In real life?! They all had trunks.) My parents had looked at her, bent over and wearing a mac with torn-out newspaper cuttings about Sid Vicious glued all over its back, then looked at me with a 'Look at the sort of people you'll have to mix with' expression on their faces. In fact, however, one of the many great things about Rebecca was that she was every bit as uncertain about early 1980s sexual mores as I was. Her dad was a vicar.

Rebecca had adopted the time-honoured strategy of young women, the one that had prompted hysterical manias among female groups since Rudolph Valentino's day. She'd developed a massive crush on an unavailable man. Crispin was a second-year divinity student from Wolverhampton. She'd met him on the train, he was handsome, he'd charmed her, and she was crazy about him. I thought Crispin was an arse and was astonished to find that he was considered something of a Lothario. He was affectionately nicknamed 'Plunger'. One of the jokes in the previous year's edition of the rag week magazine had been: 'I didn't know why they were called divines until I slept with Crispin.' Or words to that effect.

Crispin seemed to me to be vastly overconfident about his irresistibility to the ladies. But I admired Rebecca's approach in principle, and soon found my own unavailable second-year student to have a massive crush on. Mine was Paul. Both Paul and Crispin were part of that pool-playing bunch of liminal students who hung about at the union. Rebecca and I spent a lot of our time ascertaining what parties they were going to, and contriving also to attend. Paul remained indifferent, even though I didn't know how I could be more obvious. Years later, when we were friends, I confessed all this to Paul, who said he'd had absolutely no inkling whatsoever and would in fact have been more than amenable. (In the mid-1980s I introduced Paul to his wife – Maria, a former St Andrews townie – who had to slip a note in his pocket before he got her message.) Crispin, however, would constantly pay me attention behind Rebecca's back, endlessly asking me out and telling me that he didn't like

Rebecca – how could he? – because I was the only one for him. What can I say? It passed the time. It got me through my second year of university.

The time would have passed anyway, of course. I, however, did not. In order to stay at St Andrews I had to do summer resits. Since another of the conditions under which I was attending was that I would spend all holidays at Clyde Terrace, I went home and studied. Win and John were furious that I'd failed. I told them that university studies were really hard. Which they were not. Anyway. I passed the resits and asked Mum and Dad if I could go to Edinburgh, meet a friend – also Deborah – who was living there, and spend the weekend with her as a little reward to myself. They reluctantly gave me permission to have the weekend away. Which was a bit weird, since I was almost nineteen anyway. But I was still going along with them, so that relations wouldn't sour even further. Doing your best to minimise your own needs in favour of someone else's was one of the burdens of being loved and having a family. The struggle to fulfil the unreasonable demands of others was part and parcel of family relationships.

I went to Edinburgh, we two Deborahs went to the pub, and there I fell into conversation with a man called Callum. He was dressed in biker leathers, tough-guy clothes. But he seemed delightful, just chatty and friendly, keen to talk about his ex-girlfriend. He adored her. But she'd recently dumped him. He was heartbroken. It turned out, as we all walked home, that his flat was just along the road from Deborah's, and he asked us both to come up, meet his flatmates and have a joint or two. Other Deborah said she was tired, and I went up to the flat with Callum. No flatmates. But that was fine. We talked. We smoked a couple of joints. He called me into his room to show me his ex's drawings. He'd mentioned that she was at art college. They were good. They had a delicacy that I felt this man had too.

When he leaned in to kiss me, that was fine. But things started going too fast. As he tried to pull off my jeans, I started to say no. He kept going and soon I was on my back on his bed and struggling hard.

'No! Please!' I said, becoming desperate, and added, like the magazines advised, 'I have my period.'

By this time he had my arms pinned behind my head and my body pinioned under his. He was strong. I couldn't move.

'I wish I'd known. I could have had some of the chapter round as witnesses, got my red wings.'

The total change in his character, the full engagement of biker culture, the calculated nastiness and horror, was like a blow. The blows themselves were like something out of Wile E. Coyote and Road Runner. Gripping both of my hands with one of his, he started to punch my head. I really did see stars – big, pale yellow, cartoon stars, fizzing and disappearing like fireworks. There were moments of unconsciousness, and every time I came round he'd bash me on the head again, until he was done.

As we lay on the bed and I silently sobbed, he said: 'Don't I get a cuddle?' Petrified and revolted, I let him put his arms round me. I waited until he was deeply enough asleep and crept out. I wandered the streets for hours, thinking about going to the police and how unlikely they were to take my word against his. When it was late enough in the morning I went back to Deborah's, pretended that I'd had a nice time and said that something had come up, so I had to get the train back to Motherwell right away. I wished that I had the kind of mother I could tell about such a thing being done to me. But I didn't.

This crime that was committed against me had several weird postscripts. One is that when term started again, other Deborah turned up, telling me that Callum seemed smitten and had given her a letter and a parcel to pass on to me. The parcel contained a silver necklace. The letter contained seemingly heartfelt words about what a marvellous time he'd had meeting me, how much he'd love to see me again and how greatly he hoped I'd get in touch. It was then that I did tell Deborah what had happened, and I still see the deepening twist of shock and confusion – maybe a touch of disbelief too – in her face. I can't talk to her about it any more. Deborah died of breast cancer many years ago, leaving three daughters behind.

Another postscript is that some years later, also in Edinburgh, another friend told me that she'd met a lovely man called Callum, whom she'd agreed to see again the next evening. I knew, with a cold certainty, that it was him. So I told Eileen about the rape too, and begged her not to meet him. She laughed. This guy wasn't a biker. Nothing like one. There were plenty of Callums. But as he walked her home across the Meadows, courteously, after their date, he gestured to a notorious biker pub, told her he used to be a biker and used to drink there. Then she felt the cold certainty too.

'Do you know someone called Deborah Orr?'

'No. I don't think so.'

'Well, I think you do. I think you raped her.'

'No. Not that. It wasn't rape.'

'It was.'

'Tell her I'm sorry. Tell her I've always regretted it. Tell her I've changed.'

Eileen passed all this on to me by phone, and my boyfriend of the time was listening. As Eileen expressed how taken in by him she'd been, what a nice guy he'd seemed, I said that he'd seemed like a nice guy to me too. The boyfriend, who knew all about the rape, didn't like what he'd heard, judging as he did from my side of the conversation, and kicked me hard in the back. Crispin. Rebecca's old crush. He'd been postscript number three.

I learned the old-fashioned lessons from this rape, lessons that place the blame on the victim, lessons designed to obscure from rapists the fact that they're raping someone at all. Lessons that still work, in their job of assisting rapists in fooling themselves and their supporters. I stopped drinking alcohol. I started to dress differently, in a long, voluminous tweed skirt and Edwardian-style high-collared blouses. My hair I swept up in two wings, like something out of the old television series *The Onedin Line*. I bought a camel coat. I started using a hideous, frumpy handbag that Win had pressed on me ages before. I opted for natural-looking make-up. And I decided, most dysfunctionally of all, that what I needed was a boyfriend to protect me and keep me steady. But who? It needed to be someone I knew. Someone who really, really liked me. Someone I could trust. Someone who would share his own vulnerabilities. Someone who understood true intimacy. Maybe someone who'd seemed keen for *ages*.

Eureka! Crispin and I hadn't only spent the last year exchanging banter. There had been soul-baring too. I knew a lot about him. How he had been adopted, like his two adopted siblings, none of whom had any genetic relation to each other. How his adoptive parents had been very churchy, bringing up their three children as Christians. How they'd nurtured his early talent for music. (He was a gifted pianist, wonderful singer and natural performer. He could pick up any instrument and play.) How he'd been in a fairly successful Christian pop group as a teenager, and how that had led him to study at St Mary's College, the St Andrews University school of divinity, founded in 1410. How he'd lost his faith and now wanted only to become a professional musician. How he believed that his 'real parents' had been artistic, theatrical, musical, entertainers, famous, somehow stopped, by cultural convention, from bringing up their son themselves as they had wished to.

This folk tale, this creation myth was dear. It was touching. It made me tender towards him. He was a seemingly confident and brash young student, so sure of himself on the surface . . . He was so vulnerable. Beneath that protective surface he was a bit lost. I felt protective of him too. I felt that there was a job for me to do, in supporting him, in understanding him.

I knew exactly what it was like to have parents who seemed to come from a different world to the one you felt you belonged in. I wasn't adopted. But in some way, like him, I was a changeling, like the changelings in the Scottish folk stories I'd loved so avidly as a child. That I still loved. Crispin's sealskin had been taken and hidden, like mine had, like the Selkies' skins had been stolen from them and hidden, so that they couldn't return to the sea. Could we help each other to find them, and live together in our own true elements? There was a part of me so stuffed with myth and fiction that I couldn't tell it from reality. Even the regularly deposited Mills & Boons I'd find in my parents' room. Somehow, not liking the man to begin with, having a gut feeling that there was something off about him, was a primitive reaction, easily set aside, an instinct that perfect romance overcame. Even, perhaps, a necessary condition of perfect romance.

As is often the way with these things, though, he'd got fed up with playing the faithful suitor over the summer and had started seeing someone else. It was a while before he turned up at the union on a quiet Sunday evening, saw me sitting alone and proposed that we make a night of it. He had, he said, split up with his girlfriend. Of course, we ended up in bed. Pillow talk included the revelation that the ex was in fact in hospital having an abortion. A sensible woman with some sexual confidence might just have seen this as a bit of a red flag. But not I. Instead I consoled him as he explained how he had a horror of abortion because, as a rejected baby, that might have happened to him, had he been born after 1967 and not in 1961.

Also, we'd had actual, consensual, intense, affectionate sex. Which for me was a first, and a highly significant commitment. Almost, from my religious-cult-without-the-religion upbringing and my Mills & Boon ideas about love, a sacrament.

17

Letter to Crispin

Crispin spent much less time on work than even I did. He got kicked out of university in the summer of 1982, having failed to turn up for his exams. He moved to Edinburgh, where I also spent most of my time, heading back to St Andrews on the train for a day each week and going to my tutorials. Somehow I managed completely to ignore for the three years of our relationship what seems laughably plain now – that he continued to plunge merrily throughout. For maybe a year and a half I'd concealed the relationship from my parents, who still insisted that I was responsible for remaining in touch with them, because I'd been the one to leave the family, and that I had to spend all holidays with them.

Christmas 1982 therefore saw me at home, interminably watching telly with John and Win and occasionally still going for a run in the car down Clydeside, which had by then become the Lourdes of garden centres. We'd already had our subdued and puritanical Christmas, just the four of us, a turkey crown and elaborate disappointment with the gifts I'd brought.

One night, at about 2 a.m., in the dead purgatory between Christmas and New Year, I was roused from sleep by my father and told I was needed downstairs. There, sitting on an armchair in the living room, was my tearful mother, holding in her hand a letter I'd written to Crispin, my bag – in which I'd put the letter, stamped, addressed, ready to send – at her feet. They routinely opened letters that were sent to me. I'd asked them not to, but Win had explained that since they were my family I should have no secrets from them, and therefore had no reason to hide anything in any of my correspondence. So they'd opened the letter from Dunn & Bradstreet, who'd been hired to recover the £12 debt I'd run up with the company that lured teenagers into signing up with an offer of cheap albums, then sent their album of the month in the post, charging you if you didn't send it back in time. 'This is an important company. If you don't pay back this money, you'll be financially ruined for the rest of your life. You'll never be able to get a mortgage.'

At that time, 1981 and my first summer as a student, I'd been begging John and Win to let me spend the summer in London with a friend who said I could stay with her parents. 'That's why I need to go to London. To get a job and pay back this money.' I got to go to London and it was wonderful. Well, I thought I was in London. I lived in Teddington and worked at the Wetherall concession at Dickins & Jones in Richmond. Wetherall made reversible capes for English ladies. They were lovely. And also at the pub where I got the chance to become a Hill's Angel.

My parents also opened a letter I got from the criminal court in Edinburgh. I'd finally been caught shoplifting and been charged. I pleaded guilty and was fined £20. I never shoplifted again, though the reaction of Win and John, not the fine, was probably the most effective deterrent.

Opening letters that I was intending to send, though – this was new. Or, more precisely, my parents had never been presented with the opportunity to do so before.

Thus the most terrible inquisition of my life began.

It was obvious to them, Win said, like St Peter for the prosecution on Judgement Day, that I was sleeping with this man. Did I not understand what I had done? Did I not know that I was ruined? No decent man would look at me now, let alone marry me. I was twenty years old. We did not live in 1891, in Thomas Hardy's Wessex. I was not Tess of the D'Urbervilles. (Win had loved Roman Polanski's 1979 film. We'd watched it together, on rented video.) My protests brought nothing but greater anger. Finally, my father spoke.

'This man has lied to you and tricked you. You are no better than a common whore. He does not respect you, or he would not have done this to you. I know this because I know what men are like. Because I am a man. You are a stupid, disgusting little fool and there is nothing more we can do to help you now. You have wrecked your whole life. You are worthless. You must stop seeing this man right away. After that, we'll have to decide what to do next.'

I know this because I know what men are like. Because I am a man.

Oh, God. The self-loathing of it. The sadness. What a pair. What an unfortunate, unlucky pair, so eager to support each other in self-abnegation. So keen to shore up the other in their mutual horror, their culturally fostered mutual horror, of something as simple as sex, of something that should, when they had so much trust and honesty between each other in all other ways, have been a time of physical freedom, a time of release from the rigours and rules that humans place on each other.

Although, it at least explained the near-sexless marriage. My father prized my mother as a woman precisely because she found sex with a man with his, to both of them, foul urges so distasteful. It was a kind of triumph to him, a reckoning, a confirmation, a justification, a reward, that the woman he had chosen was woman enough to find all of it such an awful ordeal. Win, to John, was a feminine ideal. His job was to protect and cherish such a delicate creature, so far from the manly, penisy, ejaculatory world of desire and physicality. Did he know that this was a gender-based repression, designed to strip women of their reproductive power? Not in the least. No more than she did. The two of them were babes in the dark, dank, fungal, scary woods. All their lives. All studenty, I'd urged my mum to read Marilyn French's *The Women's Room*. But she hadn't.

I see it all, of course, from somewhere on the living room ceiling. Both of them in the armchairs of the three-piece suite, my father's high-backed, my mother's lower-backed, like in *Goldilocks*. Me on the settee, switching like a traffic light between tears, attempts at self-justification and fury, aware more than anything else that, unlike a traffic light, I was powerless before the relentless refusal of my parents to allow me to live in the world as the world was, to let me make my mistakes, and maybe even to comfort me when things went awry.

My parents were the gaolers that I loved. The attention that I got from them, whenever they had the chance to pick my bones clean? It was still attention. As a girl I'd had it, even if it was trammelled by their beliefs about the kind of attention a girl should receive. As a woman it had become so rare, so very rare, for the three of us to sit together and talk about me. This, this passionate anger, this repulsion, this condemnation. This feeling of powerlessness under my parents' unflinching belief that I'd let them down by failing to be who they thought I should be? This was what it was to be loved. But it was a long, long time before I had those realisations, consciously. Two-thirds of my life had passed before I allowed myself to recognise that this toxic experience of love was something I'd sought out and repeated, several times, in the hope that I could create a different trajectory, make the mess turn into normal, adult, loving intimacy. Get the bracelet handed back to me. Feel seen. Feel accepted. Be granted permission to be. I was fifty-five when I realised that I had to own my emotional history, and put down on paper the book I'd been writing every day.

Back then, during that terrible family conference, in the depths of the night, in the heart of the family home – there was nothing of that. There was just hunger, a hunger to make my parents see me not as defective but as worthy of their love. How could I have known that this was a road that would never reach that destination?

By listening. God knows, they told me. That night my mother rounded things off by adding, as some kind of double-edged sweetener, 'I love you, Deborah. You are my daughter, my firstborn, and I will always love you. But I'm afraid I don't like you. Not at all.' Fifteen years later, during the fairly brief time when my mother adored her first grandson, when he was a baby, she asked me if I remembered that night.

'Of course,' I told her. 'I'll never forget it.'

And I believed, for a few seconds, that this was the moment I'd craved. The moment when my mother told me that she and John had reached the realisation that they had reason to regret some of the things they had done and said in the past. What she did say, therefore, was a slap in the face that stung all the more.

'I've always believed that it was *meant*. We were *meant* to find that letter.'

I see this now as narcissistic self-justification. Some people can always find ways to justify their boundary-busting, their bad behaviour, their violations of others, their cruelty, their judgement, their condemnation, their rage, their spite, their vengeance. Their vengeance scorches the earth. That way, they destroy any evidence against them. Except that Win didn't destroy the pertinent piece of evidence. She kept the letter to Crispin tucked away in the bureau. The letter to my boyfriend that was 'meant' to be theirs. The second I saw what it was, I tossed it in the bin-bag, heart racing, hands shaking.

I left on the first train after that night of reckoning, for Edinburgh, and a happier start to 1983, at least. With Crispin.

Again, some people might have viewed this farrago as a red flag, notice that maybe a period of distance from the controlling parents from hell should be observed. Not me. I decided that I had to win them round, and enlisted Crispin to help me. It wasn't easy. But it seemed, miraculously perhaps, doable. After a few months of cajoling both sides, I dragged Crispin home to meet my parents. He worked hard at charming and reassuring them. One thing Crispin did know was how to navigate through a complex, soupy, dysfunctional family. But the minute my dad got the two of us alone, he dropped into Victorian melodrama.

'So. When are you going to make an honest woman of my daughter?'

'Well, I don't know. We haven't discussed marriage. We're, er, quite young. Deborah's twenty. I'm twenty-one. It's a bit young to get married. We'll have to see how it goes.'

'Unless you marry our Deborah here, you will have ruined her. She will be alone for the rest of her life now. How would she look after herself?'

'Oh. Well, I don't think that's true. Deborah's, er, quite capable of looking after herself. More than me.' Nervous laugh. 'Er . . . sir.'

John turned away from him, in contempt and disgust so thick that you could cut it into slices and serve it up as the cake at a shotgun wedding. He looked at me instead, so revolted.

'You see, Deborah? This man will never put a ring on your finger. You have thrown yourself away for nothing.'

We made our excuses and left. I did wish that Crispin would at least suggest that we should get engaged, just to make things less of a nightmare. Or that we could get a ring and pretend, for them, that we did intend to marry. To please them. To appease them. Crispin's main gripe, however, was that I hadn't even been a virgin when I first had sex with him, and look at what he was having to put up with.

Somehow, the relationship staggered on. Then I got pregnant and had an NHS abortion on my own, tended to by sneering and disapproving Edinburgh hospital staff who clearly took it upon themselves to provide moral education along with medical services. Crispin had a gig that evening, a triumphant return to St Andrews, to play at one of the university's interminable balls. A few weeks later, as I awaited the arrival of my friend Eileen for the weekend, Crispin vouchsafed that she wasn't the great pal I thought she was.

'Why's that?'

'Because while you were having an abortion, she was fucking me.'

I was poleaxed with shock. 'Why her?'

'Because you didn't have a sister.'

Which rather brought things to a close. Relationships end as they start, but not always quite so viscerally as this one.

There's a postscript to this story too. Crispin got in touch about ten years ago, and enclosed a CD. He'd been told many times over the years, he explained, that I'd become a reasonably successful journalist, working for the nationals. But he'd never believed it (thanks, pal!) until he'd recognised that the face that week on the front of the *Guardian* was indeed mine. Due, he explained, to his great propensity for 'speaking truth to power' – a propensity I was unaware of, never having witnessed him in the vicinity of power – his musical career had not been the global success it clearly ought to have been. Might I punt the CD around any of the people in power in the media that I probably knew.

Crispin also told me that after years of struggle – because it had been hard, very hard – he'd found out who his adoptive parents were. They were, it had turned out, exactly what he had imagined them to be: artistic, theatrical, musical, entertainers, famous. For various reasons, however, he was unable to disclose their names. He had encoded those names in his new stage name, though, written on the CD.

I did listen to the CD, before I threw it and the letter away. It contained versions of the songs he'd written in his late teens and early twenties. Crispin's career didn't falter because he spoke truth to power. It faltered because he couldn't accept that, despite his prodigious talents as a musician and performer, his taste in music was banal, and his own songwriting even more so. I always protected him from that. I always felt sorry for him for that. My secret disloyalty kept me tender towards him. It broke my heart, knowing that the fame and attention he yearned for so much would never come.

I humoured my boyfriend. I trailed off to London and around the studios with him. I agreed with him when he ranted, scarily, that those stupid A&R men had no idea what they were passing up. I was a fucking idiot. I spent several years assiduously stroking a man's fragile narcissism. I got my practice in. I would get better at the job. But I would never get good enough at doing it. One rarely can, unless one is willing to opt for full self-abnegation. Crispin was even jealous of my job at the contract magazine publisher run from a house by a serial sexual harasser of the young female staff. He resented my tiny success because he was the one who was destined for success, not me. It all makes sense, so late.

Not too long after that, as I flicked through a daily tabloid newspaper, I saw a great big portrait of middle-aged Crispin in a great big spread that told his sad story, named his famous mother and condemned her for failing to continue to build a relationship with her long-lost son after a couple of meetings. They mentioned that there was a famous dad as well, and Crispin commented that he'd sat with his adoptive parents as a kid, watching both of his biological parents on the telly in the 1970s. The article said that the father could not be named for legal reasons. I'm not going to name either of them. As he shouldn't have.

But I was seized with curiosity. I remembered the odd stage name, googled it, found my great first love's website and an email address. He got back to me right away, coy, but keen – why wouldn't he be – to let me know who his real dad was. The reason why it was such a big secret. She – she must have been very young when this happened – maintained that the pregnancy had been the result of a rape. He denied it, and had threatened and maintained the threat of libel action if she ever repeated this allegation in public. Crispin did not believe his biological mother's story. He hung her out to dry, in the papers, despite knowing what he knew. For attention. And for money.

Yet it had always been clear that Crispin was not a sympathetic person. He would stand on stage, at every show, in the early days of the AIDS crisis, for example – at a time when there was no cure, when an English chief constable was claiming that AIDS was a punishment from God for sexual deviance, when government information films charmingly portrayed a falling gravestone – and hold up a bottle of glucose drink and quip: 'Lucozade. Aids recovery.' I hated this crass, supposed joke. I never, ever had the courage to tell him what a dick move it was. My tolerance of dick moves in men was LEGION. My guy was a misogynist, a homophobe and completely narcissistic. I knew it all at the time. Or should have. But I ignored it. Craven.

As craven as believing that, despite the racism, sectarianism and homophobia, that despite the abuse he heaped on me for daring to have a sex drive, my dad was not just a good guy but the finest, most splendid man in the world. That's part of my own narcissism. Black-and-white thinking. The ability to edit reality to suit yourself. Maybe I'm still doing it. I'm trying not to. But if you don't try to justify yourself; understand yourself; respect yourself – then who will? Your parents should respect you. Your partner should. But you only get that if you're much less screwed up than I am.

18

Untitled

For many months, I was wretched with the agony of the split with Crispin. My parents could not know. It would be like telling them that, yes, I was indeed Tess, and might as well climb onto that slab forthwith and onward to the scaffold. I'd already been fired from the contract magazine company I'd mainly been working for, after it had become clear to my boss that the endless sexual harassment was never going to get him anywhere. He'd converted a young woman from an escort agency into a girlfriend by then anyway, and was, as he saw it, righteously angry at the various young women who'd previously rejected him. The 1980s really were just another fucking awful decade for young women. For everyone, really.

I'd already finished university by the time the miners' strike began in 1984. I was living in Edinburgh and, like most people from mining families, I was going on the demos, helping with the collections, attending the fundraisers, joining in with the serious fun. And it was extremely serious. A life-and-death struggle. Over in Motherwell, at Ravenscraig, even the unions had decided that there was no alternative but to break the strike and keep the works going. Once you stop steel production, even for a day, it takes a long time to get everything hot enough again. Every stoppage costs a fortune, which is why the works only ever stopped for maintenance for those two weeks each year, why the Fair Fortnight was the time when everyone in Lanarkshire had their yearly break.

But many of the miners didn't understand that, and they picketed the Craig, attracting, in turn, a huge police presence to ensure that the lorries carrying coal got in. (Usually it came by rail, but the railways union was on strike in sympathy.) There were various skirmishes. On one single day in May 1984, 300 people were arrested outside the Craig. Thatcher herself praised the actions of the men of Motherwell for keeping the steelworks going. The compliment did not go down well. The steelworkers hated breaking the strike. But they had to. There had been a hugely damaging national steel strike in 1980. It lasted thirteen weeks and lost the British steel industry a lot of business as well as a lot of money. Steelworkers knew there was little in the way of forgiveness. They wanted to get back on Thatcher's not-so-bad side. They had their own future to think about.

Things in Scotland were already grim. Even John and Win were concerned about the Thatcher government, although they'd voted her in for a second time. They'd been particularly irked by the legislation giving people the right to buy their council house. They felt that all the good places – like Clyde Terrace – would fall into private hands. Families in the position we'd been in when we were back in Shields Drive would be stuck with no choice except the worst of council accommodation.

They were not wildly impressed with the unemployment situation either. They were, in fact, constantly sick with anxiety about the future. John was the only person in the family who still had a proper job that paid a proper wage. Win was doing telesales in Glasgow, selling photocopiers on commission. After her redundancy at Smiths, I'd gone into Glasgow with her and we'd tramped around all the agencies,

Win grasping my hand, until she'd got *something*.

David, after he'd finished school, had got on a Youth Opportunities Programme – a YOP – as a trainee panel beater at a local bus company. He liked the work, but it ended when the state stopped providing its just-above-the-dole wage. It was well understood that all of these job programmes, and also the accelerating numbers of people on incapacity benefit, were a way for the government to doctor accelerating unemployment figures. The famous slogan of Thatcher's 1979 campaign, coined by the Saatchi brothers, was 'Labour isn't working'. It had appeared on posters all over the country, floating beside a photograph of a massive dole queue. But even with all the employment schemes and the state payouts that didn't appear in the seeking-work lists, dole queues just kept getting even bigger. Under Thatcher. The Conservatives weren't working either.

I was on a government scheme too – the Enterprise Allowance Scheme – and got £40 a week to help me start my own business, which consisted mainly of doing posters for local bands, including Crispin's, and working for the contract magazine publishing company. One job, for an outfit who were extreme Scottish Nationalists, who flirted, I think, with the idea of armed struggle, was drawing comic cockroaches for perforated greetings cards they made their money selling in the head shops of Cockburn Street as roach cards for rolling joints. I thought I was doing okay, under the economic circumstances. This odd but honest toil didn't cut any ice with John and Win though. My parents hated the fact that their kids were basically on the dole. They had been brought up to believe that handouts were for 'the lowest of the low', so they were not impressed by what a degree had done for me. I'd explain that building a career took time. They'd snort. 'This is a *career* then, is it?'

University, as far as they were concerned, and just as they had warned, had been a waste of time that had ruined my life and left me with nothing. John constantly pestered me to join the army. He'd wanted to himself, but had been knocked back because of scars on his lungs. As a kid he'd had scarlet fever and, even more seriously, diphtheria – isolation ward for months, tracheotomy, the lot. Both can leave lung scarring. His had been the only case of diphtheria in the borough for donkey's years – it's an illness of poverty and bad sanitation. He'd been in hospital near Thistle Street, near the Duchess Park, for something approaching a year, because they had to both cure his illness and make sure it didn't spread. He never spoke about it. (But no wonder he couldn't write properly.)

I knew about the scarlet fever from Mum, but I didn't know about the diphtheria until both of my parents were dead. I'd noticed the very faint scar on John's throat and thought I was imagining it, or that it wasn't what it looked like. It couldn't possibly be a tracheotomy scar because if it was, I'd know about it. David only knew because a tracheotomy had been performed on telly while they were both watching, and John had said, in sudden recognition: 'I had that!' John didn't like talking about the past, maybe didn't even remember much of it, or want to remember, I think, because he'd experienced a great deal of trauma as a boy.

John was very withholding at that time, and Win took his lead. This was the period when I defecated on my bedroom floor so that Win didn't know her phone call had woken me. They'd visited me once in Edinburgh, after much pleading from me, making a day of an American football exhibition match that John and David had wanted to see. I'd walked around the New Town and the Dean Village with Win and we'd had a good time. The period of calm and ceasefire made the eruptions of anger, disappointment and contempt all the more horrific.

I found it stressful, continuing to defend my decision to go to university, which I was not at all sure at the time had been the right one, attempting to build an adult life of my own and trying to prove that this wouldn't catapult me out of the family as they'd predicted. I decided when my Enterprise Allowance money ran out – you got it for two years – that I should go down south, where the jobs were, just for eighteen months or so. Get some decent experience for my CV and, hopefully, some money. If I'd been told then that I'd never live in Scotland again I'd have assumed that I was conversing with a lunatic.

I climbed onto the overnight coach to London, and onward to a squat. I was an economic migrant with £40 to my name. I'd thought, back then, that arriving in London with nowhere to live, no money and no job was as tough as it could get. I look back now and see that I was lucky, that it would be near impossible now to do what I did then. I found a squat to live in – central, right beside the Thames near Tower Bridge. I fixed up lots of interviews, got a job at a typesetter, then a job with one of the magazines that they typeset, a trade magazine for sales directors. (In top Ronseal style, it was called *Sales Direction*.) There I met Tim, with whom, it should be made clear, I formed the most 'normal' and 'equal' long-term relationship I've ever had. You could get top-up loans as a matter of course back then, alongside mortgages. Within a couple of years of arrival in London I was the proud chatelaine of half a one-bed flat in Brixton. We completed the sale on the morning after the great storm of 1987. All was well. Except that Tim still hadn't met my parents. My mother agreed that I could bring this latest sexual exploiter of her child to visit for the weekend.

Win had decided that since we were clearly, blatantly living in sin, it was silly for her and John to insist on separate rooms. So Tim and I slept chastely in the hideously uncomfortable double sofa bed. I may even have erected a wall of pillows down its middle.

In the morning, when Tim had gone for a wee, Win slipped into the spare room and said arrangements would have to change because John had been up all night, vomiting at the idea of his daughter being in bed with a man under his roof. Tim was astounded by it all, and not a little put off. I got pregnant again shortly after this, and hoped Tim would want us to make a go of it. Instead, when I suggested an abortion, his face collapsed with relief. This time I went private. I didn't need the dour Scots of the NHS to make me feel guilty again. I felt so guilty that I opted for abortion under local anaesthetic.

Every time my parents made a seismic intervention in a relationship, I ended up pregnant. I didn't set out to do so deliberately. But I cannot deny that the pattern was there. Maybe it was a way of forcing change and commitment in my relationships, to please my parents. I don't know. I do know that their disapproval dogged me, in ways I didn't understand or acknowledge. They didn't even know the half of it. But they judged anyway. Tim and I broke up and I was never really able to explain why to John and Win, who thought they knew why their easy daughter couldn't keep a man anyway.

There were two photocopied sheets in the bureau, of a long poem Win had written in comic celebration of her husband and their family life. It's untitled and it runs to ninety-two lines. I'm mentioned in four of them, though not by name. The lines refer to this time in my life, when I was with Tim and twenty-six.

His little girl who he used to love
Went away to London to push and shove
To get a man she did not wed
It nearly sent John right off his head

My parents. The two of them were like a pair of human chastity belts. Tim's parents, one of whom was a retired air-traffic controller, were, by contrast, elated if we'd help them to heave a sick sheep from their early-retirement smallholding into the back of their Volvo to get it to the vet. Which was fine by me, because I could taste farming in my own spit, and never could discern the metallic taste of steel in the same way. Maybe the land and the countryside was a way to be close to my mum. I'd have liked us to be close.

I'd thought that when my dad died, Win might move down south, to live near me. I looked at some flats and houses in the area, talked to her about returning to Essex and her English relatives. But she was just too distressed by the loss of her husband to countenance the idea of a new phase in her life. She found the courage to visit me and her grandchildren in London one more time after John died, then never came again. I'd go up a lot. I never stopped hoping that with Dad gone, with her loyalties less divided, Win might have conceded that I'd grown up in a different time to my parents, that being 'a career girl', having sex before marriage, living with people 'unwed' were not such terrible things.

But that second-last time I saw my mother? That time in New Lanark? By then we still hadn't had the talk, the one I always longed for, that would straighten everything out. By then it was, all of sudden, far, far, far too late. It was the first time Win had been out in the world for more than a year. That week had been the first time since she'd been diagnosed with secondary kidney cancer in the bone a year before that Win had even made it into a wheelchair.

I'd gone up to the hospice where she was being looked after, hired a cab that took a wheelchair, put some lipstick on my mother and a shawl that she'd crocheted, and gone to the place where we'd always been happy. Win was so glad to be outside again, so glad to see the sky and the water and the tea room. I was so glad to see Win sitting up, in a room full of life, instead of the hospital beds that were all I'd seen her in for ages. We had lunch in the pub, and Win ate with exquisite relish. She was happy to be with her daughter, there in New Lanark. It felt uncomplicated. It felt like we loved each other, in the simplest and easiest of ways.

She died three weeks later.

Win had a terrible death, painful, long-drawn-out, institutionalised. She died in June 2013 in the hospice where her husband had died five and a half years before, in November 2007.

She had already been treated for kidney cancer. I'd taken the train up to discharge her from the hospital where she'd had her operation, the same day my own radiotherapy for breast cancer ended, and spent a week looking after her. There was simply no one else who could do it at that time. And I wanted to. I did still want Win to view me as a good daughter.

Three years on from her kidney cancer operation, Win woke up one morning and found that she couldn't use her legs. She crawled downstairs to the phone and rang me. I was still on the phone to her when my brother's friend Walter got to the house, called an ambulance and went with her to Wishaw General Hospital. At first they tried to give her painkillers and send her home. Walter wouldn't allow it, and after tests she was diagnosed with secondary kidney cancer in the bones of her spine and hip.

Win had been complaining of pain in her thigh and hip, saying she'd slipped when she was putting out the rubbish. She'd shown me the bruise, where the sharp concrete edge of the back doorstep had caught her thigh. It was taking ages to stop hurting. She was always mentioning her fall and her sore leg. Win had found the putting-out of her own rubbish to have been one of the great indignities of widowhood, so David and I had dismissed it as the usual guilt-tripping. By this time, anyway, Win had been complaining about her aches and pains for forty years.

'How are you, Mum?'

'Oh, all aches and pains, as usual.'

We'd been having that exchange for such a long time that Win's aches and pains were taken with a pinch of salt. The aches and the pains of tumours growing in your bones are notably agonising. It's the most painful cancer. In the spine, the pain must have been excruciating.

There was a notebook in the living room at Clyde Terrace. It wasn't in the bureau, where such an item would usually be found. It was by Win's chair, left behind when the ambulance came, containing a shaky, handwritten list of the various pre-scription painkillers she'd been taking and the exact times at which she'd taken them. It was heartbreaking, this evidence of how very serious Win's aches and pains had become, of how she had sat alone, counting the minutes until she could take more pain relief, notebook by her side, so that she didn't have to move to look in it or write in it. I had neglected her.

There wasn't a happy ending for me and Win, though. It was lovely, the second-last time I saw her, down at the Falls of Clyde. When I turned up the next day though, the Sunday, Win said she didn't want to go in the taxi again because it was too expensive. I'd paid for it, not her. I think she felt that I was throwing money at her, as if she was a problem. She said instead that she wanted me to push her down to Airdrie town centre in the very rudimentary wheelchair to look around the shops. I explained that the hospice was at the top of a steep hill, that I didn't think I could manage it, that the shops would be closed anyway and that I didn't mind paying for a taxi at all – quite the reverse. I'd love it. She sulked until I gave in and took her down to Airdrie, finding it hard to stop the wheelchair from going too fast on the way down, sweating with the effort of pushing on the way back up. We were both in bad moods when we parted, and I never saw my mother again.

19

The Last Vestiges of John

The most touching thing that I found in my mother's bureau, after she died, was a little purple plastic zip-up bag,
rectangular and transparent. Inside were the last vestiges of
John – tiny things, fragments of his personal life, things he
would have carried with him wherever he went. There were
three objects: John's steel comb, which he'd had for years, his
plastic library card and a short pencil with the name of a golf
equipment company on it.

My mother had also kept in this bag everything she'd
found with John's handwriting on it, which, since he was
studious in his avoidance of writing, essentially meant examples of his lovely, flamboyant signature. John had the best
signature of all of us, almost a drawing, with a looping J
carrying through to the S and a huge O as the central character, before a zig-zag pair of Rs finishing it off. Win had only
saved three examples. It was inscribed on his plastic library
card; on some other shiny strip of officialdom, from which
Win had cut only the signature; and on a tattered oblong of
thick red paper. This document asserted that 'The holder of
this card is an ex-employee of at least one of the following:
Anderson Boyes, Anderson Mavor, Anderson Strathclyde,
Anderson Group, Long-Airdox . . . and is therefore granted
membership of this car club.'

It was the first I had heard of a car club, and I've no idea what the benefit of being in it was or could be. The rest, I understood. The list of names of these various employers was all the same company, always known locally as AB's. Anderson Boyes. It started as a family-run business in 1899 and by the 1970s it employed 4,000 people in five factories across Britain. Dad had worked for this company under every single one of these names, save the last. My Uncle Wullie had worked there too, and Aunt Betty's boy, my cousin Jack, though he was an engineer in the drawing office – ABs had run a very highly regarded apprenticeship programme. Jack was older than us. He finished school at a time when work seemed assured and when joining a good, solid firm to earn as you learned was preferable to university, with its languid superiority to the real world of work and pay.

Those various renamings tracked AB's slow and painful transformation: from behemoth of the post-war boom, on a twenty-seven-acre site, exporting its coal shearers all over the world, to ownership by a company in one of its major markets, South Africa; to outlying subsidiary of a Chicago company, which moved manufacturing production to Yorkshire, and after just six years sold on the Motherwell technical department to a German group called GBT. A small design team remained in Motherwell until 2010, when the last slender link with Motherwell was broken after 112 years.

My dad had survived many rounds of redundancies before his turn came, aged sixty-two. And AB's had survived longer than Ravenscraig did. The Craig's closure was announced in 1990, ten years after the American-Scots industrialist Sir Ian MacGregor had recommended this terminal course to Mrs Thatcher, straight after the steel strike of 1979. It was all about breaking the unions. The iron lady was not a woman of steel.

Before that strike, in 1978, just two years prior to MacGregor's death sentence, a Labour government white paper had promised a £220 million investment in Ravenscraig 3, which would have doubled the plant's steel-making capacity. That was the future Motherwell had believed it could look forward to. The efficiency of the plant and the quality of its product were never called into question.

Nevertheless, more than 4,400 steelworkers lost their jobs in those final two years of winding down alone. At its peak Ravenscraig had employed 13,000 people and it was still breaking steel production records at the time of its closure, as it had always done. To mark the occasion, on 27 June 1992, Motherwell District Council released one green balloon for each person who had ever worked there. So many green balloons. It was simply unbelievable – that this great landscape of steel-making should be condemned to dereliction. But that's what happened. The Craig was gutted for saleable machinery, and then it rotted quietly for a time, as those last monuments to the Lanarkshire Steelworks had rotted before it when I was little.

Papers released in 1989 revealed a letter from the then Scottish secretary, Malcolm Rifkind, to Mrs Thatcher 'to register my concern about the likelihood of very major job losses taking place over a short period and concentrated in a small area where the alternative prospects for employment are limited'. A note in the margin, written by the prime minister, says: 'No action is required.' Thousands of other papers testified to many further attempted interventions, including from other Tory ministers, making sound economic pleas as well as human ones. All to no avail. The social malaise of these closures and their knock-on effect in the local community were, in large part, what turned Glencairn Tower into Heroin Heights. Modernist blocks had their problems. But the biggest one was that they were built, however imperfectly, for working families, not families holed up together all day, with no jobs, no money and precious little security except that of being among people and places that you know. It's all very well for politicians to tell people to get on their bikes. That's not something that everybody has in them. John and Win, for example, could barely be coaxed out of Motherwell, year in year out, even when they had grandchildren to visit. John visited me in London three times in the thirty years of his life that I lived there, on none of the occasions with much grace. One visit, actually, was entirely spent finding parts and fixing the car to go back to Scotland again. Win was a wee bit better, but not much. They both hated being away from their controlled environment.

He may not have strayed much further than Shotts. But I'm glad John was made redundant, glad he had a few more years of retirement than he might have had. Dad enjoyed his retirement very much and became quite boyish, in a good, playful way. Much of his resentment fell away. He stopped being the Fenian-hating, racist homophobe of my childhood, maybe even stopped believing that his daughter was a whore. Although he never, ever said as much. John was a gentler, less angry man when he was not so bone-tired, when the sensory assault of his work, six days a week, fifty weeks a year, for forty years, had finally abated and when the disruptive rhythms of shift-work had stopped. John played a lot of golf and he spent a lot more time with Win, which made Win much happier too. They were a contented couple in those last years, even if they had given up on their kids as a bad job.

The two of them had been frantic at first, especially Win, who believed, with some justification, that they would not be able to survive on their pensions. So they did what they said they never would, and bought Clyde Terrace for the knock-down price that being a tenant for more than thirty years had earned them. It made them feel so much more secure after all the years of fear. Who could begrudge them that? Not me.

There were some papers in Win's purple plastic bag as well, including the order of service for John's funeral at Holytown Crematorium. Win had asked David to give the eulogy and my then husband to read an old, sentimental poem that she liked called 'May Your Memories Comfort You'. Her son-in-law agreed when she asked, but later told me that such doggerel was beneath his dignity. I hadn't been asked to read anything, so I told Win that I really, really wanted to read 'May Your Memories Comfort You', while Will had had his heart set on Dylan Thomas's 'And Death Shall Have No Dominion'. Copies of both poems were in the purple bag, along with the eulogy, three pages of it, transcribed in Win's block capitals. It was a very, very good eulogy, my brother's. John had a big send-off.

There was a poem that Win herself had written in there too, again printed neatly, in black biro in her slightly sloping block capitals, with a wavy line under the title.

JOHN

I MISS HIM MORE WITH EVERY DAY
MY LOSS IS MORE THAN I CAN SAY
I TEND THE GARDEN – SOW THE SEEDS
ATTEND TO ALL MY DAILY NEEDS
A MEAL IS SUCH A SAD AFFAIR
BUT WOULD NOT BE IF – HE WERE THERE.
GOING OUT, AND COMING IN
ALL ALONE, NOT WITH HIM
GOING TO BED – A LONELY MOVE

BY MY SIDE – AN EMPTY GROOVE
WAKING UP – THE VERY WORST
I SOMETIMES FEEL – MY HEART WILL BURST
COUNTRY WALKS AND SHOPPING TOO
WITHOUT HIM – SKIES ARE NEVER BLUE
VIBRANT AND VIGOROUS WITH BOYISH FUN
HUMOUR AND WIT – SECOND TO NONE
I HUG HIS CHAIR – I SPEAK HIS NAME
LIFE WILL NEVER BE THE SAME
OUR LOVE WAS DEEP – BUT HE IS GONE
MY STRENGTH MY SOUL – MY BELOVED
JOHN.

From the day Dad died until the day Mum died, there was no room in Win's life for anything but grief. A good couple of years after he was gone, having given up on the idea of my mother moving down to be near me, I suggested to her that she should try to find a new focus in her life, something that could occupy or even captivate her. It was, of course, the wrong thing to say.

'I've lost my partner! I've lost my husband!' said an animatedly furious Win, red-faced, beating at her chest with her heavily beringed left hand, her chin dimpled all over with indignation as it sometimes was.

'Yup. We all know that.'

Sometimes, I'm angry with myself for not having the patience for it all. Other times, I console myself by saying that you'd need the patience of a saint. Every day for a year I called Win, asked her how she was, listened to her misery and sadness, hoicked the boys up to visit as often as I could. I managed to drag her on holiday with us once, to the Scottish island of Jura. A second attempt, to Mull, she cancelled while we were at Clyde Terrace, all ready to drive her straight to the cottage. I tried to persuade her to get a passport, come to Italy with us. No.

Sometimes, towards the end, she'd say something she'd never said in those three years. 'I thought you'd make your basement into a granny flat.' I would have, if she'd ever said that this was what she wanted. But in truth, Win in the basement was the last thing any of the rest of us needed.

After a couple of years I started to ease it all back. I had so many other problems, with my work, with my marriage, with my children's schooling, with my diagnosis of breast cancer, Win's diagnosis of kidney cancer, with money. A big chunk of the terrace we lived in had fallen off, so there was building work to organise too. All this, for Win, was just stuff I'd brought on myself for moving away. If anything, Win's resentment about my abandonment of her had become all the greater. She was not a person I could share my own troubles with. She would just look blank if I told her any of them, and perhaps offer that 'Things were simpler in my day.'

There was no sharing of grief about John, no recognition that we'd both lost someone important, someone we knew and loved. There was no closure and there was no moving forward, no acknowledgement that things had changed and that nothing kept Win in Motherwell any longer. And there were so many things that Win couldn't do. She didn't know how to change a plug. She wouldn't get the internet, or cable television. She wouldn't use a computer or a smartphone. She had a mobile, 'for emergencies'. But she didn't know how to use it and didn't want to know. The idea was that, in an emergency, it would be switched on and 999 would be dialled.

In those first weeks after John's death, Win had been so shocked that she was completely helpless. I didn't mind, of course, that the funeral arrangements fell to me. But as I sat in the undertaker's office, Win weeping beside me, I was surprised when, after affirming my answers to every question about our wishes, Win intervened when I asked for a closed casket. 'Oh, no. I want it open. I want to see him again.' I didn't. For me he had gone, and all there was left was a corpse.

On the day when we went, the three of us, to view the body, Win didn't want to go into the room alone. Inside were the last corporeal vestiges of John, lying in a wooden box, looking like a ventriloquist's dummy with his stuffed and painted face – spots of rouge, carmine lips – and his too-big suit draped round a body that had been shrunken by the years of slowly devastating, undiagnosed cancer. It was a truly ghastly sight, that final look at my dad.

Win pulled at my sleeve and thrust something at me. 'You put this in his pocket, Deborah. I can't.' It was a card on which Win had written 'Farewell, my darling', and I looked around wildly, intending to pass on this grisly task, in turn, to my brother. He hadn't even made it into the room, the little bolter. I had to touch this thing that used to be Dad, this thing that I'd never even wanted to lay eyes on, and deposit this token from somebody else in his suit. I wish it had not been the last time I touched him.

It had been hard to be alone with John before he died, because Win kept vigil by his bed every day. But I'd managed to slip into the hospice, before catching a later train than I'd told Win, and sit for an hour, my face on his bed, holding his hands, both of us in strange trances, his courtesy of Morpheus, mine a floating miasma of love, tenderness, regret and communion.

'I never knew how much they loved me.' Those words that Win said John had remarked to her, when he saw how much his children cared about his illness and suffering. They are so haunting. It's so sad, and so weird that he didn't know, because my love for my father, in all his magnificences and all his flaws, felt to me like the strength and the depth of oceans. Win wanted John to feel that she provided all the love that he needed, and she succeeded.

I comforted Win as a daughter should comfort a mother. But I had no mother to comfort me in the loss of a father. There was no acknowledgement that Win's grief was or could be shared. My loss was nothing, and I think my brother felt the same way. No one else had ever suffered grief like Win did, and no one was allowed to suggest that they might be able to see into even the clear shallows on the edge, let alone the dark and infinite depths, of that loss. Win suffered alone, unique and special in her misery. She preferred it that way. It kept her wifely identity safer.

I was surprised, after Win died, to find that David had sometimes found her just as irksome as I had, in her relentless need to reign supreme. They had always seemed closer. She actually drove him spare, he confessed. He told me an anecdote that is very Win. It's a funny story. But it's also miserable.

David had gone out alone one early afternoon – a frowned-upon activity in itself – and had eaten a meal in the local pub, which was exactly the same as telling my mother she couldn't cook (which she couldn't, though the smallest hint at this would have invited a hard tap from the tin opener). Our mother, wounded, had querulously asked what he'd eaten, and he'd confessed to lasagne. 'Not as good as Mummy's lasagne, though, eh?' Win had said, to this man in his late thirties. In a crazy moment of rebellion, Dave had responded by busting through the fourth wall. He'd told her that the pub lasagne had been just as good as hers, but different. Dave says that he met my father's eyes, just for a second, as he fired off this annihilating blast of neutrality. What did those eyes of my father's communicate to my brother? 'You've done it now, pal. Why? Why? Why?'

Win then proceeded to direct heavy, passive-aggressive sulks at Dave for days on end, draping the house in an oppressive, musty blanket of suffocating, familiar woundedness. Over lasagne. We're talking Dolmio sauce here, by the way. No béchamel. No side salad. No way. Which is fine, except when you have to pretend that no lasagne in the world could be better. What do those Italians know? Nothing. What did anyone know? Nothing. It was no way to live, for Win or for anyone else. Christ, it was terrible.

Though the compensation is that – in the brief periods when my brother is deigning to speak to me – we both find lasagne a darkly hilarious gastronomic choice.

'Are you thinking what I'm thinking?'

'Let's have the lasagne?'

'Go on then, you fucking animal.'

That sort of thing. What was it all about?

Win was terrified of the world, and her need, her vast need, was for her family both to protect her from others and affirm that no one and nothing was more precious than she was. John took on the role. David and I simply wouldn't. The closest I ever got, when she was alive, to naming the thing that ailed Win was neurosis, or anxiety, or depression. But it was all more complex than that, and more simple. Win was completely dependent on John and John was completely dependent on Win.

One thing that we would have liked to have found in the bureau was Win's will. She hadn't made one. She'd told me she hadn't. 'I want you and David to split it equally between you. There isn't much. Whenever we got any money, John spent it all on that golf.' Which wasn't true.

I'd given her papers to sign, granting us power of attorney

under Scottish law, to save all the hassle of an intestate death. Win said she'd take a look, but she never signed them. They were still in her handbag after she'd gone. She did, however, accuse me of being after her money, and David too. He'd borrowed her bank card to get her some cash and forgotten to give it back. Once, Win would have been suspicious of me, but not of David. As her life ebbed away, my mother saw us as co-conspirators, even telling me that she knew we were lying to the medical authorities, saying she was ill when she wasn't, just to get her out of the way. I wondered about dementia, and the hospice organised a brain scan. It was fine.

'There's nothing wrong with my brain! Nothing at all!' Win said in told-you-so triumph. How can you explain to your dying mother that her brain might be fine but her mind was disordered, in a way that brought suffering to everyone. The psychological coping mechanisms my mother and father had developed during their lives were subtle, yet extreme. Their co-dependence was impenetrable. In the absence of my dad, Win became paranoid in her suffering and loneliness.

In families with narcissistic aspects – and most families do have some – there's usually one child who is the golden child, the child who reflects all the positive characteristics the parent wants to see; and one child who is the scapegoat child, the child who absorbs all the things that the parent doesn't like about themselves, or wouldn't, if they could see themselves in the child at all. Any other siblings are lucky – they tend to be neither one thing nor the other. In a larger family, other siblings dissipate the intensity of the contract between the two siblings at either end of the spectrum. My brother and I didn't have that. It was just the two of us.

It's painfully easy for me to see why my brother would have found more favour with my mother. There was, perhaps more than anything else, the accident of his sex and gender.

He was male and he was boyish, then manly. David was a handsome, healthy, confident kid who became a very attractive young man – smart, funny, talented, popular, extroverted and good company. His social life was intense. He got on with everyone. He was a part of the social fabric of the town in a way that I never was. He was a positive male archetype.

Me, though? I'd been a pretty little child. But after I learned to read, I couldn't stop reading. Which meant, because I'd sneakily read when the rest of the house was asleep, that I was tired all the time. I looked pale and wan. And the things I wanted to talk about – *Jane Eyre*, *Wuthering Heights*, *Oliver Twist*, plants, trees, woods, walks, the dog, folk stories, gardens and latterly, of course, macramé – were hardly the stuff of fascination to my peers. I was shy anyway, and increasingly anxious as the bullying and the excluding escalated. I was a worry to my mother in a way that David was not.

I was, as my mother would say, not unkindly, 'a bit old-fashioned'. I could persuade other children to step into my world of fantasy and wonder for a while, especially when we were all younger. But even those who were initially as enthralled as I myself was would get bored or feel bossed about. All that just got worse as I grew older but resolutely stayed well out of the way of puberty. Even that was not without its challenges.

Although Win encouraged me to remain uninterested in boys and in bra-wearing, she did want me to look feminine and pretty. For a girl, that was very important. But this made me feel anxious too. I was forever messing about with my hair and the curling tongs, upset about my 'cow's lick', which meant I couldn't have a sleek fringe, longing for a 'Purdey' like Joanna Lumley in *The New Avengers* and, it seemed to me, all other girls. *The New Avengers* would mean that I was fourteen or fifteen at this time. Plus, I also kept forgetting about the blasted curling tongs, and left shiny brown grooves of melted nylon in my bedroom carpet.

Win thought I was too young for make-up, but should start wearing clear, pink-tinted nail varnish, of which she bought me a bottle. There were two difficulties. One was that I was good at doing my left hand with my right, but not so good at doing my right hand with my left. The other was that a little bottle of varnish was so useful! I could, as just one example, paint a pattern on the large, *very* triangular pebble that I'd found, varnish it and suspend it in a macramé sling. I proudly gave the – in retrospect – hideous result to Win, who seemed delighted. (I did hear her telling John later that it would leave her with bruises on her chest, but we all humour our kids in their endeavours and Win certainly did that for me.)

The big problem was that the varnish ran out far too soon, leaving me with none. So I borrowed Win's more sophisticated pink pearlised varnish, which I soon discovered was even harder to put on than the clear stuff. There hadn't been much left, but I pretty much finished it. I should have confessed at the time, but I didn't. I just guiltily hid the empty bottle in my macramé bag. I knew she'd be angry. I knew I'd be in trouble and I hated being in trouble.

Win found that the nail varnish was missing a couple of hours later. I knew because she started shouting. 'Where's my nail varnish? Deborah! You've taken my nail varnish, haven't you? Don't go in my bedroom! Don't touch my things!' Win seemed so furious that, in panic and fear, I denied all knowledge of the crime. Which was silly. Who else could it have been? This made Win all the more angry. 'You're a liar! You're a coward! You're a sneak! Get out of my sight!'

I grabbed my bag, ran out of the house and to my friend

Valerie's place, in a hysterical state of weeping and juddering. Through great, heaving sobs I told Valerie and Mrs Lewis what had happened. Except I didn't. I stuck to my story. I had no idea what had happened to Win's varnish. Her ferocious attack, her dreadful character assassination had been unfair. They were so sympathetic, and Mrs Lewis, I could tell, was very troubled by it all. GOOD.

After I'd dragged myself, snivelling, around their flat for a couple of hours, I lifted my bag and the empty nail varnish bottle plopped out, right in front of the two of them. Mother and daughter exchanged an astounded look. 'So. There's the missing bottle of nail varnish,' Mrs Lewis said in a stern and disappointed tone. 'I think you'd better go home now, hadn't you? You've got some explaining to do. You need to apologise to your mum.'

Win took my confession very well. She could see what a state I'd got myself into, and that the trauma of the day had been punishment enough for me. Win was more than capable of real empathy, in a way that full-blown narcissists – people who would receive a psychiatric diagnosis of narcissistic personality disorder – never are. Narcissists can experience sympathy, can intellectually understand when a person is suffering when it suits them, even respond and comfort in a way that seems exemplary, but is acted. They don't actually know what another person feels like. They don't care. They fake it to make it, as the Alcoholics Anonymous slogan goes. Win's narcissism was all focused on having a daughter who reflected well on her, by embodying her notion of feminine mystique. It wasn't all-pervasive. It wasn't who she was.

The oddest thing is that, trivial as this incident was, it remains something I find really hard to admit. I've done some shitty, weak, thoughtless and even immoral things in my time. I've inflicted unintentional cruelties on others, and occasionally intentional ones. But the shame about the bottle of pink pearlised nail varnish still throbs darkly in my psyche like a Gollum, like a craven, greedy, manipulative, self-serving creature who would sink to the depths of hell rather than look in the mirror. I wanted to be a good girl who didn't get into trouble. But I was a bad girl who did.

The whole point of the story is that it is, or should be, trivial. Win said as much at the time. 'It's just an old bottle of nail varnish. We shouldn't hurt each other like this over a silly old bottle of nail varnish.'

Yet, pink nail varnish, back then? It was the essence of femininity. My mother wanted me to be a feminine woman, but she also feared the competition. She wanted to be in control of the process whereby her daughter became a woman. I had to do it the way she said, without helping myself to her own private props and accessories. It took me a long time to see that both Win and John wanted me to stay at home because they wanted to ensure that I stayed a virgin, that my personal value to them as a daughter was trumped, easily, by the universal value they both believed without question was all that a woman possessed – her sexual and reproductive purpose, which only one man, by taking complete responsibility for me for the rest of my life, could earn. They never forgave me for defying them on this, and I think that the more I proved them wrong – by supposedly 'having it all' – the more determined they became never to admit or give any sign that maybe, deep down, they knew they'd behaved badly. I behaved badly in turn, and that was where the focus always had to stay. Somehow, though, when they were alive, I could never fully see it. So when I was told I was unlovable by someone else who ought to love me, I would always remember how hard even my family found it, my mum, my dad, my brother. And I would believe the person who told me that I was the problem.

I wear nail varnish in many colours now. But never pink.

There's no baddie in this story, not really. The baddie is patriarchy. The baddie is narcissism. The baddie is trauma. The baddie is human fear, passed down in its doleful paralysis from generation to generation. I think of my parents when they were children, hearing the planes flying overhead, hearing the bombs exploding into the important, strategic cities, London and Glasgow, that they lived so near to. I think of their older brothers and sisters coming home – none of my aunts or uncles died in combat – all so reticent about what they'd seen and done, all quietly getting on with being brave, celebrating the spirit of the Blitz, building a country fit for heroes. I marvel at all the fear that generation was obliged to suppress. John and Win were weirder than most. But I think that, both the youngest, they may have been golden children. Growing up is harder for the golden children than for the rest of us . . .

And who could have known? Who could have seen that a row over nail varnish would stay with a person for ever? Who understands, as they bring up their children, or teach other people's children at school, or even tease and bully their peers? Only the evil people – the full-blown narcissists, the psychopaths, the Machiavels, those people psychology calls the dark triad – do any of this on purpose. You don't even have to come across one of those to sustain the damage that makes you vulnerable to them in the future.

That thing that snags in your mind for ever makes you feel for ever defective, unsalvageable. It can be anything. For me, that nail varnish storm, more than any other single thing, has meant that when someone tells me that I'm essentially defective, it always sounds like a truth about myself that I want to hide and they can see. It awards people too much power over me, people who do not have my best interests at heart.

But that's all stuff that lies deep down. There are also huge reserves of common sense, guts, determination. I always want to redeem myself, be perfect – and though that can be a burden too, it's also a gift. There is – and there always was – an understanding that it shouldn't have been so hard to just ask my mum if I could borrow her 30p nail varnish, because she wanted me to start looking after my nails, and that it shouldn't have been such a giant drama when she saw that I'd borrowed it without asking. There was already so much hidden animosity and distrust between us. Too much. I was still a child at that age, more so than most fifteen-year-olds. It was the relationship that was defective and, it turned out, unsalvageable, not me, not her. Part of me knew it, but the most vulnerable part of me never did and maybe never will. This, more than anything else, propelled me away from Motherwell. I'm glad I struck out into the big wide world. Finally, in my late fifties, I'm learning its lessons.

20

The Cupboard

There was nothing in the bureau that would have given a clue for a second to the fact that Win and John's daughter had moved away from Motherwell, had gone to live in St Andrews, then in Edinburgh, then in London; had travelled all over Europe, the Middle East, seen the Americas, Australia, Africa. Nothing at all. Not a trace.

There was far, far too much of it to fit in the bureau. It was all in a cupboard. I'd had absolutely no idea. There had been interest there after all, and pride, all neatly piled here in these secret stacks and box files. Magazines I'd worked on or edited, even little pieces I'd written for the company in the house in Edinburgh when I was in my early twenties. Things I'd completely forgotten about. A copy of the very boring sales training newsletter I'd edited while I worked at *Sales Direction*. Copies of *Sales Direction*! Copies of *The Viewer*, the magazine that I'd assistant-edited in the couple of years running up to television deregulation in the mid-1980s. A couple of old issues of *City Limits Magazine*, where I'd been deputy editor. It was basically an archive.

There were clippings of the pieces I'd written for the *Independent* or the *Guardian*, copies of the whole newspaper when a piece had been flagged on the front page. How many times had they mentioned that they'd read one of these?

Maybe three times? Maybe four? One or two of those when Win was furious.

'I read that piece you wrote about being bullied at school,' she said tensely over the phone. 'I kept wondering when I'd get a mention, the way I went up to that school, the way I fought for you. But nothing.'

'I'm sorry, Mum. But it wasn't about that. It was about what it felt like to be a child being bullied. There wasn't room to bring in other themes. I didn't do it on purpose.'

Or:

'I read the piece you wrote about Motherwell. You made it sound terrible. Everybody thinks so.'

'Everybody? The *Indy* sells two copies in Motherwell, on a good day.' Win and John must have been half of the newspaper's Motherwell customers.

I'd thought that my work embarrassed them.

But in this cupboard there were also copies of the *Weekend Guardian*, the colour supplement I'd edited in my early to mid-thirties. When I'd first told them about the job, Win had said:

'Well, I don't really understand what you do. I see a lot of people's names in here, people who have written the articles and taken the photographs. But I don't see yours. I like this bit, The Questionnaire. But look. It's got someone else's name on it. It's got "Rosanna Greenstreet" on it. And her photo. She's pretty, isn't she? What do you have to do with this, then?'

'Well, that sort of looks after itself. Rosanna sends out these questionnaires to people in the public eye, they send them back to her, and she edits a topical one and sends it to us every week. If I don't like one, though, I can ask her to do a different one.'

'Do you do that a lot?'

'Well, I haven't done it yet . . .'

'So, you're the office manager?'

'Sort of. I guess. It's more *creative* than that though . . .'

The issues of the magazine that they'd kept were the ones that did have my name on, the ones where I'd written the pieces.

Here was my interview with Michael Crichton, as the film of his novel, *Jurassic Park*, was about to be released. The crime writer Michael Dibdin was supposed to be doing it, but his flight had been delayed and he was still circling about Los Angeles when interview time came. It couldn't be postponed, so I'd done it over the phone. I got Crichton, who was charming, to describe his office, for colour. I didn't say I was in the room with him. But I didn't say I wasn't either. Bit naughty. But needs must.

Here was my interview with Tom Hanks, 4,000 words squeezed out of a thirty-minute chat in a hotel room, four hours before deadline. I'd done it myself, because, really, it was too big an ask of anyone else. Unprofessional.

Here was my interview with Jarvis Cocker, done by me because, despite a fair amount of evidence to the contrary, I felt a connection to the lyrics of 'Common People' that seemed like mine alone.

Here was a long piece written from Kabul, just after the war, just after 9/11. Here was a piece from Mozambique, as AIDS was killing its mothers and babies.

Here was my *Weekend Guardian* cover story about the demolition of Ravenscraig. I wasn't able to stop it. No one in Motherwell, Britain or the world was able to stop it. But at least I could mark it, give the Craig the send-off it deserved. A lot of what I know about John's working life comes from talking to him when I was doing that piece – that week, when I went to Motherwell and sat in the library of my childhood, researching the history of coal and steel in my town, talking to our parachuted-in English gentleman of an MP, Jeremy Bray, collecting memories.

We all went on the day, 28 July 1996. We stood near the gates of the complex, behind the cordon, Mum, Dad, David and me, along with Murdo MacLeod, the brilliant photographer from the Isle of Lewis who did a lot of work for the magazine at that time. The crowd was sparse. There was still a lot of bitterness. It took six seconds for that huge blue gasometer and those four massive, elegant cooling towers to come down. The gasometer, collapsed on that contaminated ground, looked like a flattened tin can. Our cover image. The end.

It was hard for us to know what to do with ourselves, the whole thing was so quick, so decisive and so shocking. It was really, really gone. So we went to the pub, The Cleekim Inn, Murdo carrying his vast amount of heavy equipment. It didn't take long for us to attract the attention of the locals.

'Is there fillum in that camra?' one scary-looking guy asked Murdo.

'No,' he replied, looking worried.

'Have ye goat fillum in yon big bag?'

'No.'

'Whit? Aw that gear and ye cannae take a pucture?'

'No.'

'Okay. Look. Huve ye's ever seen a dug play pool?'

'No.'

'Moan then. Moan roon ra back.'

So, cautiously, Murdo more or less attempting to swallow his expensive equipment, we moaned roon ra back, where our new friend asked us for some change to put in the pool table. He racked up the balls, broke, and we all sat and watched while a black and white collie – quite like long-dead

Tina – leaped up, grabbed each ball in her mouth, one by one, in a pinpoint-accurate sideswipe, then sent each one down a pocket with a satisfying clunk. Murdo had long since raised his camera.

'Aye, pal. Ye cin take a pucture noo, eh?'

Pot the dog. It was perfect. Providence had conspired to give the Craig a happy ending, of a kind. For the men of The Cleekim Inn – selfish, narcissistic fuckers as they'd always been – life in Motherwell had changed less than it had for most.

Epilogue

There's no special view now, of heaven or of hell. No stunning, dystopian panorama. No world unto itself. Mainly, there's grass. After the Ravenscraig site was decommissioned, its buildings flattened and shovelled away, its earth decontaminated, there was just a big hole, in the town, in the shire, in so many people's lives. A road runs over the site now, the land that for so long was a place only steelworkers could step onto, the land that everybody accommodated, every day, without even knowing that that's what they did.

Places that seemed far away, it turned out, were near, if you didn't need to go round at least one Monaco to get to them. Out on that road, finally, you could see the shape of the town itself, see that it was just a long, thin crescent, curved around the works, clinging to them for dear life, like a baby monkey clings to its mother's back. The Dalziel works is still there. It hangs on, the last producer of the last of Motherwell steel. If you pass by it at night, you see rabbits hopping about. Rabbits at the Dalziel works! John and Win, defensively, used to say that the area was better in many ways without the plant, cleaner, fresher. Nature thrived all the more. You could breathe more easily. Until you didn't breathe at all.

I once heard Motherwell, in a property-buying show, called 'a dormitory town for Glasgow'. The description made me wince. I haven't been back since David and I broke up our parents' home, since we riffled through the bureau. I'm one of those people now. One of those people who've been through it on the train. That's what people often say when I tell them where I'm from. 'Ah. I've been through it on the train.' Or: 'Oh, yes. You have a football team.' We do. It's fan-owned. Even our Premier League team doesn't attract the big investors, and maybe that's just as well. Ra Well.

It's a long time since Win died now, relatively speaking – a bit more than seven years. She died when I was fifty years old. I was devastated by her loss, because she was my mother, because she had died in such pain, physical and mental, and because my dream of a decent mother–daughter bond died with her. But her death also gave me freedom at last – freedom to say that I didn't want to be like her, didn't want to be married, didn't want to live through my husband, didn't want to force my kids into being my subservient companions, didn't want to retreat, stay home, stop moving forward. I even got rid of the bureau. I had to jettison a lot of stuff after my own family's home went the way of the family itself, and was divided up to provide 'natural justice' for my ex-husband. I sold the bureau to Howard, a dealer in Bermondsey, for £40, in a rarely regretted transaction.

Win would never have done that. Win's life had stopped by the time she was fifty, more or less. She often said it was 'too late' to start this or that, or go here or there.

I will go back to Motherwell, though. I miss it. I still walk the countryside of my childhood, so often, in my thoughts, still feel a thrill when I see a wood anemone, some ransoms, a sloe tree, the plants I discovered on that land and looked up in my Ladybird books. I had a decade of crisis, one parent or another ill or dying, my children in emotional pain and crisis, my body the site of a war against the multiplying rogue cells that wanted to kill their host. I couldn't go over it. I couldn't go under it. I had to go through it. As the children's classic says.

When it was all finally over, when Win, John and my husband were all gone, I was diagnosed with complex post-traumatic stress disorder. The symptoms – dissociation, panic attacks, convulsive shakes, obsessive rumination, terrible, terrible feelings of entrapment – don't manifest themselves until it's all over and you've stopped repressing your emotions, in your efforts to be who other people insist you should be, in your efforts simply to get through the days.

My symptoms are slowly subsiding. One of the ways to soothe yourself, the experts say, is to spend a lot of time in nature. When I think of Motherwell now I think of the marshland, the river, the meadows, the hills, the fields, the gardens, the trees, the flowers, the soft beauty of the valley. This Motherwell survives, and it helped me to survive. And eventually to take charge, to take complete control, of my own family, in my own words.